Getting Grants

Getting Grants

CRAIG W. SMITH
and ERIC W. SKJEI

HARPER COLOPHON BOOKS
Harper & Row, Publishers
New York, Cambridge, Hagerstown, Philadelphia, San Francisco
London, Mexico City, São Paulo, Sydney

A hardcover edition of this book is published by Harper & Row, Publishers.

 For information address Harper & Row, Publishers, Inc., 10 East 53rd Street, New York, N.Y. 10022. Published simultaneously in Canada by Fitzhenry & Whiteside Limited, Toronto.

First HARPER COLOPHON edition published 1981.

ISBN: 0-06-090834-3

85 10 9 8 7 6 5 4 3

ACKNOWLEDGMENTS

With heartfelt gratitude to

Nancy Bellard
Kenneth Boulding
Tom Chester
Allen Ginsberg
Frances Hailman
Loretta Hempstead
John Hessler
Ann Klepper
Caroline McGilvray
Porter McKeever
Judy Michalowski
Web Otis
Shelley Pierce
Hank Rasé
Laurie Shields
Bill Somerville
Tish Sommers
Kirke Wilson

Contents

Preface xiii

Introduction 1

I. THE GRANTS ECONOMY TO THE RESCUE 7

Grants Infiltrating Everywhere 8
What Is the Meaning of All This? 10
The Amazing Silence of Universities 12
Taking a Very Broad View 14
The First Sector is Great, But . . . 16
The Second Sector Tries Out Four Techniques 17
The Third Sector Emerges 19
Pumping Money: The Structure of the Grants Economy 23
How's the Blood Pressure? 26
Can We Make It Work? 28

II. GRANTSPEOPLE 30

The Most Important Nonprofession of All 31
The Typical Grantsperson: One Hassle After Another 33

The Ideal Grantspeople: One Success Leveraged on Another 36
Big Bird Is Fundable: Joan Cooney Transforms Public Television 36
John Hessler and Ed Roberts Help Make America Fit for the Handicapped 41
Tish Sommers and the Old Gals' Network Take on CETA 48
Hank Rasé Creates a Golden Opportunity 53
What It Takes to Be a Success 63
The Grantsperson as Entrepreneur 64
The Flexibility of the Grantsperson 67

III. FINDING YOUR WAY INTO THE BRIARPATCH 70

Beggars and Thieves 72
Your Funder Is Your Friend 73
From Genus to Species: A Funder Taxonomy 74
Corporations 75
Profile of a Corporate Grantmaker: The Abex Group, Inc. 79
Researching Corporate Funders: Tools and Resources 83
Private Foundations 85
Profile of a Private Foundation: The Rosenberg Foundation 87
Researching Philanthropic Foundations: Tools and Resources 95
Community Foundations 100
Profile of a Community Foundation: The San Mateo Foundation 103
Researching Community Foundations: Tools and Resources 109
Government Funders 110
Profile of a Government Funder: Appropriate Technology 116
Researching Government Funders: Tools and Resources 121
State and Local Government Funders 131
Mistakes to Avoid in Approaching the Funder 134
Avoiding the Category Trap 134
Inside Technical Assistance 137
New Approaches in TA 141
Further Resources 143

IV. BECOMING MORE BELIEVABLE: HOW TO USE THIRD PARTIES TO SUPPORT YOUR PROJECT 147

Four Kinds of Believability 149
How to Find a Sponsor 153
Shopping Around: What to Look for in a Sponsor 154
Seven Reasons Why a Sponsor Needs You 154
Alternatives to Finding a Sponsor 156
Consumer Protection: What to Watch Out for in a Sponsor 157
Beyond Credibility 160
How You Can Relate to the SDS 164

V. PACKAGING: THE GRANTSEEKER AS A PROPOSAL DESIGNER 169

The Fivefold Function of the Proposal 170
Structure: Why, What, and How 172
The Why Section: The Pitch 173
The What Section: The Goal 178
The How Section: The Plan 181
Evaluation Design 185
Embellishments: The Title Page, The Abstract, and The Future Funding Plan 188
Once the Funding Decision Has Been Made 191
Sample Formats 191
Further Reading 214

VI. CURRENT TRENDS AND FUTURE POSSIBILITIES 215

General Trends 216
Funding for the Arts 218
Funding for Education 221
Funding for Social Rehabilitation 224
Funding for Science and Technology Research 226
Funding for Religious Groups 229
Funding for Health Care 231
Funding for Urban and Rural Development 233

Funding for Economic Development 235
Funding for Other Areas of Urban Development 236
Funding for Rural Issues 236
Funding for International Issues 239
From Trends to Resources 242

VII. GRANTSPEAK: LEARNING THE LANGUAGE OF GRANTS 244

Appendix A: Foundation Center Libraries 265
Appendix B: Regional Foundation Associations 274

Index 279

One of the greatest needs of
our day is to find out how to
get the money to the crackpots
with the creative ideas.

—Kenneth E. Boulding

Preface

I have read this volume with great interest. It is a "how to" book which will be useful to large numbers of people in what might be called the "grants market," both those who are potential recipients and those who are potential donors. It should indeed expand the grants market and make it function better.

It is also, however, more than a simple "how to" book. Without losing or confusing the basic "how to" information, it also manages to squeeze in a surprising amount of "what for?" It looks at the larger implications of the grants institution and the grants market of society and sees it as an increasingly important supplement not only to ordinary markets in which things are exchanged, but also to the bureaucratic budget system in which the activities of organizations are directed from above, information is transmitted through the hierarchy, and the activity of members of the organization is determined. There are many similarities between grants and budgets. Both involve a transfer of money from one account to another with the object of changing human activity. The evils as well as the power of bureaucracy arise because the activity is tightly specified, along with the results. In a budget organization money is transferred from the top of an organization to a department with objectives which are defined explicitly and often in great detail by the top executives. In the case of a grants system, however, the objectives are in part created and specified by the recipient, who then has to try to find somebody who favors these objectives and is prepared to make a grant for them, whether private or public. Paradoxically enough, therefore, one of the purposes of the grants economy is to provide a partial simulation of the market in the middle bureaucratic organization, and a substitute for pure bureaucracy and budgets. This is the allocational significance of grants, that is, the way in which they change human activity and product.

I commend this book, therefore, not only to the practitioners of the art of making and receiving grants but also to the theoreticians, who will find much that is instructive in the down-to-earth quality, what might be called "reflective practicality," of this volume.

Kenneth E. Boulding
University of Colorado

Getting Grants

Introduction

Every year the search for new ways to solve human problems is leading thousands of people to grants. Whether they were originally trained as teachers, artists, scientists, or nurses, they are discovering another vocation: They are becoming grantspeople. Because they are mystified by the world of grants, which seems complex and bewildering, they waste valuable time and energy until they learn its ways. But when they do, they find that it can work as a powerful catalyst for social change. And it can even transform their lives.

Grants are not ripoffs or handouts, nor are they quite like donations or contracts. The grants culture is a specialized, little understood, but essential part of the American economy. Its primary function is to stimulate social research and development into areas that a business or civil service mentality might either overlook or consider too risky to explore.

As one grantsperson put it, "Grants march in where the Big Boys fear to tread." By fueling America's experiments in social change, grants can compensate for the wear and tear caused by the pursuit of profit or the inertia of bureaucracy. Grantspeople identify new social needs and help find new ways to meet those needs. The phrase that once rotated around the barrels of Kaiser cement trucks—"Find a Need and Fill It"—is more likely to be seen today on the T-shirt of a young filmmaker working out a way to use public broadcasting to get Chicano kids to learn basic skills. Entrepreneurism is being reborn in the world of public service.

The challenges that these entrepreneurs will face in the 1980s and 1990s will be those posed by our Era of Limits. Instead of clearing out the wilderness and building railroads, entrepreneurs will be bringing their inventiveness to bear on meeting national needs as inexpensively as possible. Despite the fact that new grant programs are still proliferating, the boom years of the 1960s and early 1970s, when grants were easy to get, have ended.

Over the next few years our social institutions are in for rough times. Faced with crises provoked by the conflicting forces of inflation, unemployment, and human rights, they might decide to choose the safest, tried-and-true course, and to preoccupy themselves with their own security, eventually to ossify. But this tendency could be slowed, blocked, or reversed if grantspeople learn to activate the latent power of experimentation and renewal that the grants economy represents.

Now that taxpayers have revolted against the "Golden Fleece" of extraneous grant projects, success in the grants world depends on the effective design of grant projects, that is, proposal writing that helps funders make their dollars go as far as possible. Despite new competition, grantmakers still complain that they get very few good proposals. Despite the money crunch, millions of dollars still go unclaimed.

We invite you to join the trend toward imaginative, successful grant projects. You don't have to be altruistic, but you do have to come up with an idea for a grant project and then convince a funder that it is in the public interest. Consider the following examples.

POETS PERK UP KIDS

A West Coast school district had a hard time getting its third graders to concentrate on the basic skills—and the local artists were starving—until grants for $250,000 from the U.S. Office of Education and local private foundations created the Poetry Playhouse. Poets and actors were brought into the classroom to act out poems, show the children how to do the same themselves, and teach the teachers how to incorporate all the resulting enthusiasm into lesson plans. Now the program is built into the curriculum. Other districts have adopted the idea, and an educational station is begging for broadcast rights.

DUNG TO GAS

A small energy research company based in Colorado, Bio-Gas, Inc., recently received a $300,000 grant from two major utility companies to build and operate a plant that turns sheep manure into methane for residential heating and cooking. If successful, the project will show us how to harness enough gas from all the nation's livestock to provide for nearly 200,000 households.

OUT OF THE CLOSET AND INTO THE GRANT

A few years ago, gay advocacy groups couldn't get started on the search for funds. When they applied to the IRS for tax-exempt certification, a candid bureaucrat wrote back, "We don't give the 501(c)(3) status to unapprehended felons." After a lot of political pressure the exemption came through. But their proposals were rejected anyway. United Way said, "You must be joking." No one would believe them when they claimed that gays are discriminated against. But they will soon have hard evidence—HEW awarded $500,000 to a group called CHEER (the Center for Homosexual Education, Evaluation, and Research), attached to San Francisco State University, to collect and study cases of discrimination against gays.

QUICK REMEDY

It was the end of the worst winter in years. The Arabs were raising oil prices and the coal miners had gone on strike. The miners' gripe was not money but working conditions. As a case in point, black lung disease wasn't being effectively treated. Congress responded by offering $60 million to any agency that could offer the best solution. A Colorado firm, Medical Data Systems, parlayed its knowledge of rural health care into a great idea: Mobil vans would test suspected cases and transmit results to central computers. Physicians would fly in as needed to treat cases, using rural hospitals. No new bureaucracy or complex administration was required. It was so successful that MDS grew from a staff of thirty to thousands almost overnight, and they were soon negotiating with the Arabs to fly their health system into the desert.

HOMESTEADING THE URBAN RANGE

Out of the craters of the burned-out South Bronx has arisen a grant-supported phoenix: The People's Development Corporation, a tough group of ghetto dwellers who are determined to make their neighborhoods livable again. With the help of $1 million in federal grants so far, they are salvaging ruined apartment buildings. Under a system called "sweat equity," each member donates at least ten hours of work per week to whatever needs doing—hammering, plastering, painting. In return, a member is guaranteed an apartment in the renovated building. President Carter endorsed the project as a way of renewing neighborhoods and recommended that the concept be applied to other blighted cities.

NEW BUSINESS FROM WOOD SCRAPS

In the forests of the Northwest, loggers used to throw away the chunky remnants of native hardwoods—oak, maple, madrone, alder, and mahogany. That was before a small group of ecologists got $145,000 in CETA money to show how marketable products, such as chairs, tables, tool handles, mirror frames, toys, grain mills, and seed sifters, could be made from such scraps. After eighteen months on the grant, some have gone into business on their own, and a Forestry Network has been set up to tell other people how to salvage wood scraps.

TRANSCENDENTAL MEDITATION BEHIND BARS

In the field of corrections, the word on everybody's lips is "recidivism," a fancy way of talking about the revolving door that finds the same prisoners returning to jail again and again. In some states the recidivist rate approaches 50 percent. It is understandable, therefore, that the California Department of Corrections was willing to take a chance with a Transcendental Meditation proposal to use a $24,000 grant to try out its program at San Quentin and Folsom Prisons. The Transcendental Meditation workers report that their program has kept all but three of fifty-eight ex-prisoners out of jail for two years. They also claim they are not surprised, since they have already used other grants to show the effectiveness of their method with other "stress populations": alcoholics, drug addicts, the mentally ill, and overburdened health workers. The TM organization is using the test results to prove that their approach should be written into the rehabilitation budgets of our social institutions, since it could be a less-expensive, more-effective method than other methods of therapy now being used.

DOLLARS FOR DOCUMENTARIES

Unless they were willing to spend their days making soap commercials and their nights on their real work, filmmakers who wanted to deal with serious social issues have had few real options. But now, grantmakers are beginning to see the light. Among topics funded recently by the Film

Fund, set up to support public interest cinema, were these: the life of a Latina woman in the Southwest, political conflicts over rural water rights, and the relationship between agribusiness and American eating habits. Last year the Fund gave $126,000 to nonprofit filmmaking ventures, some of which have been successful enough to take the for-profit plunge by selling shares in their films to private investors.

CUTTING THE COSTS OF DYING

The Public Health Service of HEW was upset over the alarming jump in operating costs for nursing homes (from $1.8 billion to $11 billion in just a decade!), which were using up nearly half of all Medicare funds. One grantseeker presented the PHS with an outline for an education and training program that could keep many of the dying at home, cared for by paraprofessionals supported by CETA funds. The project would humanize the environment of death and dying, create trained hospice workers, and reduce Medicare allotments. The Public Health Service made the grant and is now considering shifting some of its nursing home subsidies into training funds to support home care—preparing for the time when those CETA funds run out.

Who knows what grant ideas will come forth next? If you have an idea, a vision of change, the next move is yours. But we can help you make it. Before you begin, you need to know more about the grants culture—who the funders are, what they look for in a grant project, what the stages of the grant search are, and what obstacles you have to surmount. In short, you need to be told what you need to know before you knock on any funder's door.

Our book is not a laundry list of grant programs, most of which change frequently. Nor is it a canned formula for writing The Proposal. Those books have been written; frankly they are not of much help. Before you can use the vast amount of technical information available about grants, you have to know how the world of grants works. Then you can decide whether you want to be a part of it and how to go about it. Before becoming a grantsperson, you need a broad view of the terrain you will soon inhabit. So, rather than focus immediately on where to go and what to do, we precede that practical advice with a description of the principles and processes of the unique world of grants, one that lies close to the heart of the American economic system, yet one that has room to accommodate the most breathtakingly radical visions of the future that can be conceived. The advice we give is based upon successful experience in winning grants as well as thorough study of ideologies, the possibilities, and the problems of the grants culture.

After reading this book, you will know what you have to do to get a grant. You will have learned how to organize and manage the proposal writing process. You will have a new perspective on the skills and attitudes that you will need in your grants search. You will understand more about the role and function of the grants system in American culture. You will have gained a preview of the process that you will be experiencing, one that is risky and frustrating but which can also be highly rewarding. You will know how to enlist the assistance of the prospective funder during your grants search, and you will learn how to organize a support network around your project.

We cannot promise that you will get funded, but reading this book should reduce the time you spend going around in circles. Not only are we trying to orient you toward getting a grant efficiently, we are also trying to help you get a grant in the right way, so that once your project begins to operate, you can do just what you planned to do, what needs to be done, and what you do better than anyone else.

Despite popular belief, "grantsmanship" is not really about getting the dollars. It is knowing how to work *with* the grain of the grants culture, so that you fit within its logic and come out smiling at the end of the search. Once you learn this art, money comes easily.

I

The Grants Economy to the Rescue

In the past few years the sum total of the grants economy has grown almost geometrically: from below $29 billion in 1968 to $122 billion in 1977, a more than 400 percent increase. Grants are defined here as voluntary transfers of money to public or private nonprofit organizations—and sometimes individuals—by government, private foundations, and corporations.[1] This growth rate far outdistances by proportion the concurrent rise of the business

[1]Just what the term *grant* ought to encompass is controversial. For a broader definition, see Kenneth E. Boulding, *The Economy of Love and Fear: A Preface to Grants Economics,* Wadsworth Publications, Belmont, Calif., 1973.

These figures include governmental contracts (except defense contracts) as well as grants. To compile the 1968 approximate figures we added three figures: $18 billion in grants from the federal government to state and local governments, about $10 billion in direct federal funding of private nonprofit agencies, and about $2 billion in combined private foundation and corporate contributions to nonprofit organizations. By 1978 those categories had expanded to around $80 billion, $36 billion and $6 billion, respectively. These figures are drawn collaboratively from the Advisory Commission on Intergovernmental Relation's pamphlet "The Intergovernmental Grants System," Government Printing Office, 1978, p. 8; Ralph Nelson, "Private Giving in the American Economy, 1960–1972," Filer Commission Research Papers, pp. 115–134; *Giving in America, Towards a Stronger Voluntary Sector,* Report to the Commission on Private Philanthropy and Public Needs, Department of the Treasury, Washington, D.C., 1975; "Giving in America—1976 Annual Report," American Association of Fund Raising Counsel, New York, 1976.

sector,[2] and it has more than kept pace with the rise of governmental bureaucracies.[3] Grants have been the fastest-growing economic sector of our generation.

During this period the number of grantors and granting programs have also risen phenomenally. In the 1930s there were only a few hundred foundations; today there are over 30,000. Before LBJ's Great Society there was no governmental granting system to speak of; today there is a briar-patch of thousands of units of government at local to national levels giving out federal dollars through over 1,400 federal funding programs.

Despite some fluctuation, the overall growth pattern of the grants economy until now has been steady regardless of whether we happen to enter phases of fast growth of our GNP, when foundation and corporate grants increase, or periods of recession, when government grants tend to increase. Through 1979, governmental granting has grown in both Republican and Democratic administrations. The system of private philanthropy shows a similar pattern. Private foundations have shown a continual though not dramatic rate of increase. Donations given directly by corporate grantors have greatly increased in size from 1972 to 1977.[4] The expansion of the grants economy has been a hidden reality of contemporary life.

GRANTS INFILTRATING EVERYWHERE

Grants have not only grown in size but also in scope. For example, there used to be two main directions of private foundation giving: philanthropy aimed at helping out the indigent and subsidies of the cultural pursuits of the leisure class. Not so long ago,

[2]The growth of the GNP during most of this same period has been at the annual rate of about 6 percent (Nelson, op. cit., pp. 115–134).

[3]While writing an eye-opening book about scandalous practices among high level consultants to government, a group of Nader-oriented lawyers chronicled the phenomenal rise of the "contracting and grants sector," which they compared to the relatively slow rise of the bureaucratic sector of government during the same period. See Daniel Guttman and Barry Wilner, *The Shadow Government,* Random House, New York, 1976.

[4]For specific trends of corporate philanthropy see *Annual Survey of Corporate Contributions,* 1977; The Conference Board, 845 Third Avenue, New York, N.Y. 10022.

the philanthropic world seemed preoccupied with bringing the ballerina's leg a full 180 degrees off the floor. Today private foundation grants support activities that cover nearly all aspects of life and benefit all economic levels, especially the middle class.[5] Name a subject and there will probably be foundation support to define it, explore it, create options to it, or expand it.

The range of governmental grant support has expanded similarly. Federal funding used to be limited to the area of welfare. Today the federal government gives grants to support just about anything that can be arguably defended as being "in the public interest," a term that seems to have included everything at one time or another.

The expansion in the categories of funding has been accompanied by an increase in the range of functions performed by grants. In the 1960s, Great Society grants were the naïve instrument for attempting to transfer wealth from the rich to the poor. Today the range of uses of grants has been expanded to the point that they are a vehicle for accomplishing any sort of national goal: getting people off welfare, stimulating new industry, revitalizing the culture, curing cancer, controlling inflation, curtailing unemployment, preserving the environment, desegregating schools, getting people out of state institutions and into society, computerizing libraries, postponing senility, developing new energy sources, creating new art forms, enforcing civil rights laws, consolidating public services, reviving ghost towns, tracking down runaway fathers, building lighter weight railroad cars, and providing vocational counseling for transsexuals.

The kinds of organizations that receive federal grants have also radically expanded. Their dependence on grants seems to increase from year to year despite the unstable, short-term character of grants. These include organizations in those fields that were once supported only by volunteers and donations or other kinds of

[5]The question of "who benefits?" from grants has been explored in a scholarly study that looked at the effects of different forms of grants. The study concluded that even grants that were intended as redistributive gestures to the poor often ended up benefiting the middle class and even wealthy classes, hence the title: *Redistribution to the Rich and the Poor; The Grants Economics of Income Redistribution,* Kenneth E. Boulding and Martin Pfaff, eds., Wadsworth, Belmont, Calif., 1971. This theme was also present in Guttman and Wilner, op. cit., passim.

income. For example, in 1957 state and local budgets included only 8 percent from the federal government. By 1976 this percentage had grown to 20 percent, making federal dollars their largest source of revenue, in many cases more than even sales or property tax income.[6]

The same creeping dependence on grants can be seen in school districts, hospitals, universities (even private ones), advocacy groups like handicapped, women's organizations, public media, housing, transportation, schools for all age levels, museums, libraries, parks and recreation facilities, research institutes, arts centers, YMCAs and YWCAs, activist organizations, health care facilities and churches. Even the Girl Scouts of America no longer rely on cookie sales alone—they have professional proposal writers on staff.

Both the federal government and foundations have encouraged this infiltration of grants into every area of our land by increasing the assistance they give to grantseekers. It used to be that to get a federal grant you had to have enough clout to relate with bureaucrats in Washington or socialites in New York. Today there are government officials in thousands and thousands of towns, cities, county and state governments who do nothing but help people get federal dollars. Grant getting is no longer confined to big cities. A computer with information on most federal grants is now accessible to every county in the country.[7] Foundations have also hired staffs and greatly increased the amount of public information available regionally in libraries from Spokane to Little Rock. The grants economy has become as ubiquitous as apple pie.

WHAT IS THE MEANING OF ALL THIS?

Before we rush right out to try to get a piece of that pie, we should investigate what we are getting into. What does it mean to play a part in this system? Why has the grants economy grown so? How do we make sense out of the apparently haphazard, all-encompassing, ever-expanding nature of it? The issue is not at all

[6]Advisory Commission on Intergovernmental Relations, *Significant Features of Fiscal Federalism,* 1976 ed., Vol. 1 (M-106), Washington, D.C., p. 34.

[7]See Chapter 4.

clear. If you look to the American public, all you encounter is confusion over whether it is a cancerous growth or some new sign of vitality.

Take the feminist versus "profamily" matter. When the two forces met head on in the International Women's Year Conference in Houston in 1977, everyone thought the main issue was competing views on the role of women in society, but the real bone of contention was the appropriate use and extent of government grants. The conservative forces were shocked that the liberal women got a grant, that is, public money, to put on the conference in the first place. Said Anita Bryant, "Well, look at that Houston Convention last year. The government gave the feminists $5 million and Phyllis Schlaffly not one penny. It was a closed shop."[8] Furthermore, the profamily faction has consistently complained that it will cost too much in grant dollars to finance the changes in our social institutions that passage of the Equal Rights Amendment would mandate, citing the current costs of compliance with equal rights for the handicapped as an example.

But the argument went even further. Some profamily conservatives were concerned that the new grant support following ERA passage would make it financially preferable to females to live outside the family, making domestic life a less attractive option. They feared that grants would usher in a new era of institutional care of dependents (children, the elderly, the infirm) which could erode and destroy the family unit completely.

California's not-so-domestic governor, Jerry Brown, brings this argument even closer to the subject of grants. He feels that by taking over one social function after another the state displaces home-based care by providing services traditionally offered by the "mutual support system" of the family and the voluntary sector. As people become more and more dependent on the state, the family forfeits responsibility to take care of its own.

Those who defended the grants system, on the other hand, claimed that women have a legitimate right to federal grants as a precondition for correcting their discriminated position. Some of them demanded massive grant programs for comprehensive day care, for rape victims, for battered women, for job development for

[8] *Playboy,* May 1978.

divorced and widowed women, and for counseling for all other groups of victimized women. To be sure, the feminists wanted more than just to air their views. They wanted control of the means to bring about change. Funding alone would increase the options available to women, making it possible perhaps for the first time in history for women to be as independent as men. Cancerous? These people feel it is the legitimate and proper role of government agencies in a postindustrial society to support any group's aspirations for self-reliance. Alongside our budget support for defense, the cost of such support is paltry.

THE AMAZING SILENCE OF UNIVERSITIES

You might expect that universities, long held to be bastions of critical thought, would be getting to the bottom of an important social phenomenon like this. Maybe they can tell us what is going on?

Not a chance. All the information available on campus is usually concentrated on the second shelf of the metal bookcase in the Grants and Contracts Office in the administration building. And those books are just lists of sources, sources that change every year. On the campus itself there is hardly a course on the topic anywhere.

How about the economists? Some of them, especially the younger ones, have a social consciousness. Don't you suppose they would select grants as their dissertation topic? Not according to our survey. Economics is still dominated by people who assume it to be the study of for-profit transactions. The business of America's 250,000 public and private nonprofit organizations doesn't generate much interest. Those economics graduate students who feel too confined by the study of the market usually prefer to defend the nostalgic Marxist-Socialist viewpoint with its unquestioned assumption that state bureaucracies are better at solving social problems than businesses. Economists have not yet discovered grants as an interesting midpoint between public and private solutions to national problems.

Shaking our heads at overly theoretical economists, we might go across the street to talk to the Business Administration professors who, according to their brochures, give practical "how-to" courses that prepare students for "nitty gritty" economic realities. Are there such practical courses on grantsmanship for MBA students? Not a one.

And the kind-hearted professors of the Social Welfare and Social Work departments? Surely, they must find grants useful to prepare students to go out and serve the public. But no. They assume that Master of Social Welfare students will enter secure civil service careers rather than take the maverick route of grants. A growing number will be surprised after they get their degrees. When they apply for a job, the interviewer might well ask them, "Can you write proposals and administer grants?" These poor, would-be social workers may be job hunting for quite a while.

Do Public Affairs or Public Administration fill the gap? Those departments also assume that "public service" means getting a job in government, and that once you get classified as GS-12 you won't need to know how to hustle grant bucks. But that was before the tax revolt slashed revenues from property tax rolls and forced local government staff members to hunt down "other sources" (i.e., granting agencies) to make up the difference.

How about City and Regional Planning? The planners learn how to assess the needs and solve the problems of man and nature but not much about getting the funds to finance their rational visions of society. Political science, likewise, tends to assume that politics is a matter of voting behavior and the theories of power and whatnot—ignoring the fact that control of grants by elected officials has become a primary expression of their power.

Sociology seems to cross social science disciplines. Maybe sociologists might look at grant projects as case studies in social change. But there is hardly a monograph on grants in any sociology journal. And the English department? Literature, yes. Composition, yes. Creative writing, yes. Technical writing, maybe. Proposal writing? Never.

Finally, you might expect at least partial treatment of the subject in any number of specialized fields like Women's or Ethnic Studies; International Affairs; Religion; Urban and Rural Development; Educational, Hospital, or Arts Administration; Biology; Ecology, and so on. After all, the students in these departments may graduate with fresh critical ideas that could never be examined, demonstrated, and put into practice except through the use of grants. However, even the most astute of them will be ill-prepared when they sit down to write their first proposal. Without knowing how the funding system works, they may have to choose between teaching jobs (where ideas remain in the realm of thought) or the hard-nosed world of business (where ideas are often stifled by the demands of the marketplace).

Why don't universities teach about grants? "We always study ourselves last," the old story goes. Universities might be too close to the subject to be objective about it, since they have become increasingly dependent on research grants to keep pace with inflation. In fact, the federal share of income in higher education now amounts to 60 percent, which is six times its portion in the early years of this century.[9] Most university administrations jealously guard their grants and contracts secrets. It is not a field noted for information sharing. Another explanation may be that academia just has not caught up. Grantsmanship is generally learned in practice and is changing constantly.

A more philosophical explanation may be that granting falls between the cracks of the categories that shape the curriculum. If you do not have an accepted category, you do not exist in the eyes of the categorizers. Such is the case with grants, which are academic nonentities: not quite political, not quite economic, not quite social, not quite personal, and not quite respectable. You can't even understand how grants work through interdisciplinary efforts because the topic lies underneath rather than in between what is now going on in academia. Higher education focuses on specific kinds of improvements rather than on the economic process that aims at bringing about improvements, that is, granting.

TAKING A VERY BROAD VIEW

With the pearly gates of American academia closed to the issue, we may have to look elsewhere for a framework broad enough and free enough from the lines that crisscross universities to understand the subject of grants. Such an expansive view is possessed

[9] *Giving in America,* op. cit., p. 35.

by Kenneth E. Boulding, a self-proclaimed "sit-and-think" type who ponders basic questions about reality from his tiny office at the University of Colorado's Institute of Behavioral Science. He has been at it quite awhile. He began his academic training as a pure economist studying in the Oxford of 1928 with Lord Keynes, the founder of modern economics, amending the classical discipline to include a theory of the interaction between the market and the modern state.

Over 50 years, 25 books, and 500 published articles later, Boulding's views have evolved beyond economics' limited parameters toward what he calls "general systems theory." These days he considers himself a scientist. Evidently, others agree, since in 1979 he became President of the 140,000-member American Association for the Advancement of Science, the largest academic professional association in the world. From this vantage point, the theme recurs in his writing that a key to an understanding of the problems of man lies within understanding "the theory of the grant."[10]

Boulding has been so preoccupied with the topic that in 1967 he and his friends coined the term *grants economics* and got together with colleagues from around the world to form the informal Association for the Study of Grants Economics. The association has since delivered 325 papers on the topic at various academic conventions. Many of these papers have already been, or will soon be, converted into a dozen or so books on the topic.[11]

The Association has been almost ignored by U.S. economists,

[10]According to Boulding, the well-being of any society or organization depends largely on the strength of its "integrative system," the propensity for the values of love, loyalty, and mutual identity to pervade relationships rather than the competing values of "threat" or "exchange." So, the key is to understand its integrative aspects. That is where grants come in: "The theory of the grant seems to me to be the central concept of the integrative system," he says, in "An Economist Looks at the Theory of Sociology," Sociology, Winter 1967. "Grant" in this sense is defined much more broadly than is intended in this book. As the authors here use it, "grant" refers only to a form of "explicit grants," which are just a small part of the total "grants economics" referred to by Boulding, which includes the sum of all the various sorts of "one-way transfers" of goods and services (whenever *A* gives to *B* without *B* giving back something of equal value in return) going on in the economy. See also Boulding's *Economy of Love and Fear: A Preface to Grants Economics,* Wadsworth Publications, Belmont, Calif., 1973.

[11]The grants economics series began with Wadsworth Press (Belmont, Calif.) and has been taken over by Praeger (Special Studies, New York).

who have been too busy examining the bark of trees through a microscope called "econometrics" to have much interest in the contours of the forest that Boulding and his colleagues were delineating.

What makes the work of these economists pertinent to any grant seeker is that they have shown that the grants economy is not just some bizarre tack-on, some appendage to the large-scale activity of business and government. But it is an extension of government's attempt to solve some of the problems that are inherent to capitalism in its mature stages. The view that is revealed from our reading of this body of grants economics literature is that there are three interdependent sectors in the economy. If the world of business enterprise is the first sector, government is the second and grants are the third. The second sector grew up to solve the weaknesses of the first, and the third emerged to complement the first two. To make this point, a historical digression is necessary.

THE FIRST SECTOR IS GREAT, BUT . . .

America, founded by a bunch of individualists, was from the beginning clearly a country that would take free enterprise about as far as it could go. Also we were pretty good at the unregulated practice of buying and selling on the open market. It proved to be, particularly in our early years, an effective way of organizing society. It broke down stuffy class barriers, promoted civil rights, and tapped the inventiveness of the people so that an abundance of unheard-of technological innovations, like airplanes and computers, came gushing forth. There seemed to be no end to the array of ideas that could be converted into services or products for the market.

So the net effect was to create a kind of national optimism. And another wonderful feature of the market was that it was self-corrective: If a service or product couldn't cut the mustard, it was given an F by the consuming public, who refused to buy it. (Remember the Edsel?) It seemed to involve a lot of tough decisions made without resorting to an authorizing hierarchy. Adam Smith explained that an invisible hand seemed to guide economic life, so that society as a whole benefited by decisions motivated purely by self-interest.

The market was efficient and worked well as long as the pursuit of profit was expressed in ways that benefited the whole populace. But as time went on, the self-interest of businesspeople and the public interest drifted further and further apart. Businesses began to use their privileged place on the market to squeeze out newer arrivals. Tycoons teamed up with their cronies to drive out the competition; monopolies emerged. Alarmed by these events, the public looked around for some way to correct the vices of a market economy gone awry. The invisible hand, the guiding principle of free enterprise, soon became a fist.

THE SECOND SECTOR TRIES OUT FOUR TECHNIQUES

Government appeared to be the appropriate corrective instrument. But as it tried out one method after another to do so, one more vigorous than the next, each time it created a new level of bureaucracy. Four forms emerged.

1. Regulation

Government regulates industry—policing it so that it does not deceive the public or bully the little guys. Government soon found that this approach, although unavoidable, has real limits. It is all too passive; it puts government in the role of simply reacting when things go wrong. By making government into a watchdog, it creates a built-in adversary relationship to businesspeople, contributing to their greedy image. It is negative and uninspired, which may be why regulatory agencies have sometimes been guilty of corruption and collusion with the agencies they regulate.

2. Tweaking

Government "tweaks" industry so that business enterprises get channeled into areas that are in the public interest. Government has at times gotten artful in this area, the bureaucrats acting like bonsai masters guiding the development of shrubs. Tweaking refers to altering the tax system, imposing penalties for vices here, giving deductions there, tampering with wage and price controls, setting policies that build incentives and remove barriers to the kind of market enterprises that fit into governmental policies. This approach avoids the mushrooming of bureaucracies like the regulatory agencies. It has been found until recently to be effective in containing public problems such as inflation and unemployment. But in the last decade there are signs that this approach does not allow government to take an active enough role to encourage industry to develop along new lines. So it has been necessary to develop a more initiatory approach to problem solving.

3. Welfare

Government redistributes wealth—a more active approach transferring wealth from one group to another. We have found that one by-product of capitalist society is a widening gap between the powerful and the powerless. With the unemployment of urban minority youth approaching 50 percent in some areas, this disparity threatens the overall stability of society. Particularly after the urban riots of the 1960s, government has looked for ways to transfer not just money but also skills to the disadvantaged. Public subsidy of the poor did not exactly contradict the practices of free enterprise, as many supposed, since it had the advantage of increasing the market for consumer goods, encouraging new industrial productivity. One problem with redistribution, as it turned out, is that the recipients of welfare unwittingly become dependent on their benefactors. The other problem is that the processing of welfare recipients is time-consuming and degrading.

4. Enhancing Production

A more acceptable corrective strategy better suited to the pro-growth ideology of free enterprise is for government to take an active role in *stimulating* industry to move along new lines. This is the rationale for much of our public investment in research and development. Normally, industry puts up its own front money to develop products and services for the market. But it is easier to find private backing for *Superman* than for a line of medical products that could cure cancer. In the last twenty years, government has been more and more willing to spend the money necessary to test out new ideas, demonstrating their potential application until private industries have been willing to step in and finish government's work at a profit. This is how government creates new markets that would not have existed without such stimulation. In this way the health, defense, computer, space, agricultural, solar, and some other energy industries were developed.

Largely out of an effort to accomplish these four ways of steering the First Sector, the modern bureaucratic state was created. But soon the bureaucracies began to show signs of problems of their own. The public agencies often became cumbersome and unwieldy. Decisions were made without good input from the lower ranks, so error accumulated. The bureaus often were as complacent as private monopolies, perhaps even more so, since (at least until the defaulting of Cleveland in 1979) government agencies could count on surviving from one year to another.

THE THIRD SECTOR EMERGES

More importantly, the government bureaucracies began to find themselves ill equipped to respond to their complex problems—particularly those involving the reallocation of wealth and the stimulation of new kinds of industry through research and development. Increasingly government began to sidestep the civil service pathways and contract out (or "grant out") these functions to nongovernmental organizations that had the expertise or community support necessary to get the job done cheaply and quickly. Furthermore, these organizations provided to government something that the bureaucracies never had—that is, the power to *initiate,* to put into practice ideas and methods that were beyond the reach of the cultural and ideological influences that dominate civil service. With its grants and contracts, government unwittingly created and bolstered a Third Sector of hundreds of thousands of new private nonprofit organizations and thousands more "special projects" stuck awkwardly on the organization charts of long-established governmental and traditional nonprofit organizations.

The term "Third Sector" deserves some discussion. It is not a governmental idea, but one introduced by philanthropist John D. Rockefeller the Third, known as JDR III, who passionately extolled its virtues before his death in 1978. It is significant that the idea was introduced by a JDR and even more significant that it was offered by the third generation of JDRs. The Rockefeller family went through the same dynamic over three generations that America is going through in a more general and less obvious way.

The first JDR was the ideal entrepreneur of the First Sector. He generated more wealth than just about anyone of his generation. His son, JDR II, was the hero of the Second Sector, a driving force behind that superinstitution of government, the United Nations. JDR III was no rebel against the money of his grandfather nor the public service inclinations of his father. Those were his own legacy and his working base. But he was unimpressed with the ability of business or government when it came to what really mattered. The difference, he maintained, is that "Business is supported by its profits, government by taxes, the Third Sector by voluntary contributions. At the heart of it is individual initiative and a sense of caring."[12]

As the heartless quality of government became more apparent, the inspirational private nonprofit sector became a usable national resource and in some cases a more appropriate recipient of public money than government itself. Perhaps this is why new tax and budgeting policies of the federal government in the 1960s and 1970s brought billions into the new sector. The grant recipients were not quite private but not public either. They found themselves lodged insecurely in society's cracks, full of energy, low in profile. The Third Sector inhabitants gradually found labels that gave them a place. They became "adjuncts" to the hospitals, "support services" to the public schools, "research institutes" to the universities, "action programs" to the local governments, "associations" to the professions. Tenuous though it may still be, the Third Sector emerged with a style of its own—a style formed by its own economic underpinnings, by grants. Nowhere else has this sector emerged in such force as in contemporary America.

While the character of this grants sector may remain questionable in the eyes of the businessmen and bureaucrats of the First and Second sectors, it developed some interesting and perhaps

[12]From a speech to the Nation Conference of Corporate Chief Executive Officers, Tulsa, 1977.

appropriate qualities. In fact, policymakers soon found that grants are free of many of the built-in limitations of both business and government and are capable of combining the best features of both of the other sectors. Here's why.

1. Grants are short-term, using soft money as opposed to hard, which means that they can be put to more *ad hoc,* flexible uses, establishing projects that are needed at the moment. They aren't usually intended for continuing what was done before, which is the focus of funds used within government. The short-term nature of grants means that they must prove their own worth, since refunding usually depends on the demonstrated success of the first grant. It also means that grants can finance high-risk explorations into public problems; if the grant project fails, the public does not suffer a huge loss.

It is this feature of the Third Sector that particularly appeals to John Gardner, who has become its leading spokesman.[13] As a former HEW Secretary he speaks from experience when he says that "in the Third Sector a hundred ideas can be born and die every month without the slightest ripple. In government the introduction of just ten new ideas a year can provoke a major crisis and the attempt to eliminate ten old ideas that have proven not to work can bring down the whole system."[14]

2. Unlike the bureaucracies, grants are competitive. Since the grantor can choose between many prospective grantees, the old boys might well be squeezed out by the new gals, if they have a fresh idea and a good proposal. The competitiveness of grants is a quality-control factor that is unique in the world of government bureaucracies and is becoming more and more scarce in business.

3. There are thousands of granting programs. Unlike the employer-employee relationship, the funder doesn't really have the upper hand in the grantor-grantee partnership since the grantee frequently has the power to narrow down his or her choice to the

[13]Gardner is Chairperson of a Third Sector Committee, sponsored by Aspen Institute of Humanistic Studies (2021 Mass. Ave. N.W., Suite 400, Washington D.C., 20036) after JDR III's death. The Committee is establishing a framework that will influence the activities of a new organization spearheaded by Gardner's to be called Third Sector, Inc. or Independent Sector, Inc. that will conduct educational and technical assistance programs for the sector.

[14]From a speech to the Council on Foundation Convention, Seattle, 1979.

right grantor. Furthermore, the grantee doesn't have to consider a single grantor a benign or terrible father figure since he may work with several grantors at once, lessening his dependence on any one source of income. While both business and government are becoming centralized and hierarchical, grants are decentralized. Most project directors of a grant program can call the shots.

4. Grants favor experimentation. They are created to increase knowledge that is in the public interest. That means that grants often explore new approaches that seem to be far ahead of the methods or ideas being applied conventionally. The kind of research and development possible through grants is much more far-reaching than is possible in government laboratories, for example, which must cope with the lethargic influence of civil service routines. Grants can extend as far as the most isolated garage inventory or the most radical social advocacy group to tap their creativity and convert their energy into forms that can be offered as solutions to public problems.

5. Grants can bypass credentials. In either government or business, it is usually necessary to move up through the ranks before achieving positions of real power. By the time you arrive there, you have been so indoctrinated by in-house standards or those of the academic professions that you are not likely to exercise your power in a fresh way. In the granting system, however, it is possible for a well-designed concept to substitute for experience.

6. Grants do not overemphasize the profit motive. While they encourage enterprise and self-interest on the part of grantees, they don't offer the lure of monopoly power. There is no personal ownership of grants, which are usually controlled by public and private nonprofit corporations without stockholders. All a project director can expect is a reasonably good salary, perhaps an inside track on some valuable information, and a chance to do what he or she really wants to do.

How can these potential qualities of grants conceivably get businesses and government out of the problems they face? Well-conceived grants can reinforce governmental efforts to redistribute wealth and/or stimulate new and appropriate industrial productivity.

Examples: If the government is having a difficult time getting welfare recipients to work, it can give a grant to a self-help project conducted by a group of ex-welfare mothers who have found a way to help them to develop their own jobs. If governmental in-house labs don't have what it takes to develop a solar energy industry, government can give grants to solar-oriented researchers and activists who have the energy and skills necessary to get the job done. If industry can't employ 6 percent of the labor force, government can involve the unemployed in grant-funded training and apprenticeship projects to make them employable. If regulatory bureaucracies are ineffective, the government can give grants to study what is wrong with them and how to reorganize or even dismantle them. If there are too many government agencies fulfilling the same function, a grants project may be able to consolidate them. If the practices of a hospital are too expensive, a grant could be used to broaden the functions of nurses to reduce labor costs. Yes, grants—that is, public money—can be used to figure out how to save public money.

PUMPING MONEY: THE STRUCTURE OF THE GRANTS ECONOMY

Our discussion so far has demonstrated that the grants economy has its own logic, its raison d'être. But what does this Third Sector look like? How does it work? It can be understood more concretely using the analogy of a circulatory system, one that pumps fresh blood through veins into a heart and then out again through arteries to replenish the tired blood in depleted areas of the organism. Similarly, as depicted in the chart on the following page, the grants economy goes about the business of revitalizing American society.

Following the elements shown in the chart, the grants economy works like this: Each year our money flows into a huge pool, the *U.S. Treasury* (A), from two main ducts, one filled with a share of the income of *Individual Taxpayers* (B) and another comprising a share of the income made each year by *Profitmaking Corporations* (C). The flow from these two sources into the Treasury is regulated by the *IRS* (D) which acts according to policies set by the U.S. Congress. Much of the money circulates or gets lost within the central pump, but a good deal of it flows out through veins back to the

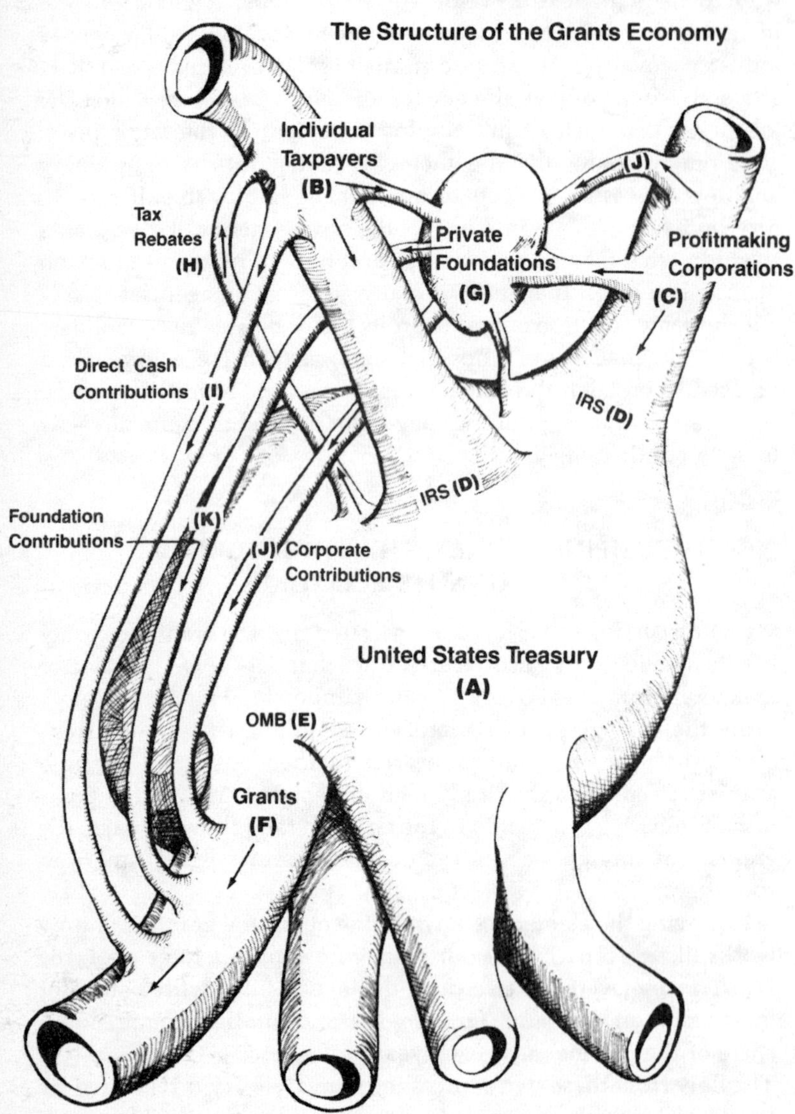
HEART CHART
The Structure of the Grants Economy
Individual
Taxpayers
(B)
Tax
Rebates
(H)
Private
Foundations
(G)
(J)
Profitmaking
Corporations
(C)
Direct Cash
Contributions (I)
IRS (D)
IRS (D)
Foundation
Contributions
(K)
(J) Corporate
Contributions
United States Treasury
(A)
OMB (E)
Grants
(F)

whole organism, the country. It flows out through several streams, according to the dictates of the U.S. budget which is administered by the Office of Management and the Budget, *OMB* (E). One vein channels money to defense, another to welfare, one to pensions, etc., and another goes to *Grants* (F), which as used here also includes contracts. These streams then send money to depleted areas of the organism which require revitalization.

This simple apparatus (A through F) is what we might call the primary structure of the grants economy, since it describes how approximately 80 percent of the money gets collected and dispensed. But the "circulatory system" is actually more complicated than a mere pump. There is a "secondary structure" (G through K) which allows money from both of the two major sources (B and C) to be diverted directly into the *Grants* stream (F) without having to first pass into the *Treasury* (A). This is the system of private contributions, which is actually encouraged by government through a complex series of tax deductions for charitable contributions. Since the IRS as such a pivotal force is creating this system, the private contributions apparatus cannot be considered to be independent from the government granting processes. Rather, it is a kind of back-up system which could be called upon to solve social problems if the primary mechanism (A through F) breaks down, clogs up, or dries out.

As if to compensate for its coercive methods of extracting tribute, the IRS allows wealthy individuals to have their say over how and to whom their contributions are made. They may do so by setting up their own *Private Foundations* (G), or by establishing them in their wills. The government does not allow these to operate whimsically, however, since these foundations must give a small share of their investment income back to the *IRS* (D), which uses it to cover the costs of policing them. To add even more complexity to this structure, the IRS also returns money to less wealthy individuals in the form of *Tax Rebates* (H). Further, the government also allows individuals to make *Direct Cash Contributions* (I) into the grants stream, without setting up their own foundations. This form of direct contributions primarily benefits religious groups.

Profitmaking Corporations (C) also have ways of avoiding payments to the IRS by becoming grantors themselves. Many businessmen feel that they are more efficient and effective at solving social problems than government. The government is willing to give them a chance to exercise their skills as donors and it gives tax deductions for grants made by corporations of up to 5 percent of their annual profits.

Those corporations which take up their option to be philanthropic have three optional ways of doing so: They can set up their own *Corporate Contributions Program* (J). Or they can establish a *Private Foundation* (G) or contribute to one that is already set up. The trustees of the foundation have some discretion over the flow of *Foundation Contributions* (K) out of this pool and into the *Grants* stream (F). Seen this way, the foundation is a mini-government except for the fact that it does not have the power of forcing contributions through taxation. As a third alternative, corporations can also donate to United Way–type organizations (sometimes called United Funds), which allocate money in a way similar to the foundations.

HOW'S THE BLOOD PRESSURE?

The apparatus that we have just described emerged to correct the pathologies of the whole social organism by "pumping money" into needy areas. But what are the pathologies of grants themselves? What about Senator Proxmire's Golden Fleece awards and all those other well-publicized scandals in the grants world? Is this circulatory system healthy? Or on the verge of a heart attack? Does the cash go all the way to where the problems are or does it get clogged in the middle? Any hardened arteries? Do the organism's ills actually get cured in this way or is it afflicted with a cancer so malignant that all this granting is merely cover-up, a postponement of its inevitable demise?

According to Boulding, the cure provided by grants definitely has its own negative symptoms. There are at least four of them:

1. Poor Feedback (or Edsel's Law)

One problem specifies that once the grant is allocated, the grantors are frequently unconcerned about whether a mistake has been made. Grantors are susceptible to Edsel's law, which Boulding describes in this way: If Ford produces an Edsel for the marketplace, it soon finds out if it has made a mistake, but if the Ford Foundation or HEW produces Edsels in the grants economy, it takes a long time to find out that a mistake has been made and still longer to have this information affect the decisions of those who have made this mistake. The Ford Motor Co. isn't likely to forget its Edsel very quickly, but there is no guarantee at all that the Ford Foundation won't go ahead and fund another "Edsel" of a grant project next year. A fundamental problem of grants is that grantors don't usually have a good memory of what worked, so it is hard for them to know the consequences of their decisions.

2. A Tendency to Foster Dependence (The Sacrifice Trap)

Another problem is that grants can increase dependency rather than the independence of the recipient of the grant or the population it serves. It is very difficult to design a grant project so that the money is used to overcome further need for money. Grants are susceptible to what Boulding calls the Sacrifice Trap, in which the funder keeps giving to the disadvantaged, not because the grants are helping them but because the funder doesn't dare cut off the flow of dollars. One reason is that if they stopped giving, it would imply that they had given in vain previously.

3. A Tendency to Monopoly (The Old-Boys' Network Syndrome)

Since the grantor-grantee relationship is short-term and therefore precarious and unstable, it is hard for the grantor to know whom to trust. Amid the complexity of all the options open to a grantor, it is understandable that most funders prefer to go with those who already have a proven track record, since they can be trusted not to violate the cultural norms of the granting agency. Partly for this reason, the funds are monopolized year after year by the same organizations.

4. A Tendency toward Misuse

Since grants are to a great degree beyond the grantor's control once they are given out, the funds are often diverted toward uses that the funder did not intend. Special project funds earmarked to pay the extra costs entailed in fulfilling the goals of a program frequently get converted into operating funds that end up helping to solve an organizational crisis, to cover up mismanagement, to soften the effect of inflation, or simply to fatten the pocketbook of the grantee.

CAN WE MAKE IT WORK?

Some studies maintain that these problems of the grants economy are so great that taken as a whole it must be judged a failure.[15] Yet for those of us who have ideas that we want funded, the real question is: Can we make it work? Can we get a grant, do what we want to do, and not be bogged down by these problems? Do we want to be a part of this Third Sector?

To answer that question, we have to look to the people who are already using grants and see if the kind of person who has emerged out of the grants economy can bring out the potential for personal freedom and social change that grants seem to offer.

Our search for the ideal creature of the Third Sector, the grants hero, is not so farfetched. After all, the classical economists postulated that the smooth functioning of the First Sector requires the emergence of a personality type called *homo economicus.* Economicus is a species that is "unconcerned about anything except the pursuit of profit. He buys as cheaply and sells as expensively as possible. If his business enterprises fail, he will eliminate the source of error through diligence and attention."[16]

Although homo economicus may be fantastic as a business person, he would not be the best grantsperson. Economicus might use the grant as a substitute for business, as a new scheme to boost profits and pick up some easy money. Economicus's point of view might be too narrow and security-oriented to fulfill the broad goals of many grant projects.

[15]See *Redistribution to the Rich and the Poor, The Grants Economics of Income Distribution,* Kenneth Boulding and Martin Pfaff, eds., Wadsworth, Belmont, Calif., 1972. Several of the studies demonstrate that the real beneficiaries of many grant projects are those who know best how to manipulate the system.

[16]Ludwig von Mises, *Epistemological Problems of Economics,* Van Nostrand Reinhold, New York, 1960, p. 197.

Nor would our grants hero have the same qualities as the ideal government worker of the Second Sector, a person who could be called *homo bureaucraticus.* Such a creature may function well within the procedural decorum of government bureaucracy, but when he or she gets a grant, would surely adhere too formally to the rules and regulations. When some civil service types enter the grant world, we can imagine their using grants merely as a way of extending the cold hand of social planning or as a new form of welfare. Bureaucraticus may not have enough initiative to make grants work.

Is there an altogether new mentality, a Third Sector approach? Does *homo grantus* exist? To answer that question, we must turn to the group of people, grantspeople, from whom this new species must emerge. It's time to find out what it's like to be a wheeler-dealer of the grants world.

II

Grantspeople

If grantseeking ends up being a cynical process of milking the funder for all you can get, or a selfless matter of reforming our social institutions, the responsible parties for the whole thing are the grantspeople. The world of grants is created in their image, reflecting their confusion and inspiration. Most people assume that the kingpins of the funding system are the funders with the dollars. That's not true: The only people capable of mobilizing dollars and thereby grinding out the latent power in the granting system are those enmeshed in proposal writing. Even the mechanical procedures involved with giving out money will bend to these deft artists living in the cracks between public and private institutions.

This chapter defines and locates grantspeople as a hidden class. It describes the typical hassles of the bewildered novice, the incredible success of the experts, and underscores the importance of their having both an entrepreneurial spirit and a broad perspective as the basic recipe for success.

THE MOST IMPORTANT NONPROFESSION OF ALL

Grantspeople are those who pull together proposals for grant projects—or oversee the activities of others who do. They are the ones responsible for making sure that deadlines for submission are met. Sometimes they create the idea itself, see that it gets funded, and then direct the implementation of one of a series of funded projects. At other times they are the hired hands who simply write up someone else's ideas and have no part in it after the proposal is sent off. Sometimes they are free-agent, community-organizer types, who single-handedly bring together several nonprofit agencies to work on a problem. Other times, they are the grants coordinators of large institutions, who work with staffs of writers and clerks that can number into the hundreds. They may be profit-making consultants who are motivated by their own financial gain alone. Sometimes, though not often, they are actually on the staffs of the proactive brand of funding agencies that generate their own in-house proposals and then find a grantee to bring them to life.

Whether they are "big shots" or "small potatoes," managers, or active practitioners, naïve or cynical, their work is to return again and again to a cycle of proposal preparation that averages maybe six weeks to two months from beginning to end, but can be as short as one day or as long as nine months. The process may recur continually, each time quicker, until the grantsperson is able to generate, say, three proposals a week; or it can be sporadic. The heavy work season has traditionally been the late winter and the spring. But with the recent reorganization of federal bureaucracies and more frequent meetings by foundation trustees, submission dates are now being staggered throughout the year.

Oddly, grantspeople can be at the top or the bottom of the organization chart, or in rare cases, free agents who are independent of any group. In any case, they usually have a function different from those they work with. Unlike their peers, who usually work with givens—a set income, a set decision-making structure, a set market for services, the grantsperson is often an organization's "agent of new possibilities," someone in charge of obtaining altogether new sources of money, launching new projects that often reset the organization's course. Such grantspeople are sometimes considered aliens by their own peers, since they always have one foot outside the organization's world. This insider/outsider function explains why grantspeople often have more power and independence than others higher up the ladder. Successful grantspeople usually have complete access to decision makers and policy setters.

It is hard to estimate the size of this group, since they aren't registered. There are no degrees in grantsmanship that can be offered. Grantspeople have not formed themselves into a professional association, although they do have one academic journal[1] and a few trade magazines.[2] Even if they do nothing but fret about grants, they prefer to be called by conventional career categories: scientists, artists, intergovernmental affairs specialists, nurses, administrators, planners, VISTA volunteers, board members, hospital directors, church secretaries, musicians, school teachers, management consultants, or even fundraisers.

Another reason that they stay in the closet is that nobody ever intends to become a grantsperson—because the grant-getting process is usually considered to be a rather unfortunate means to a laudable end. People become rhapsodic over the various ideas that grants finance, rather than interested in the grants process itself. Most of us focus on what we are working toward rather than what we have to do to get there. If you are a university president, you would rather give speeches than discuss government guidelines with grantseeking department heads. If you are an artist, you prefer to apply your design skills to your favorite medium rather than to a grant proposal. If you are a social worker, you would rather be out "helping people in need" than hassling about the next grant. If you want to be a scientist, you, like this poor biologist, resent the time spent doing federal paperwork rather than experiments in the laboratory:

> I have ceased being an active researcher. Oh yes, I hang around the lab a little, but almost my entire effort goes into the process of getting and renewing my grants.[3]

[1]*Grants Magazine, Journal of Sponsored Research,* Virginia White, ed., Plenum Publishing Corporation, 227 West Seventeenth St., New York, N.Y. 10011.

[2]Trade Magazines: *Foundation News,* 1828 L Street, N.W., Washington, D.C. 20036; *Grantsmanship Center News,* 1015 West Olympic Blvd., Los Angeles, Calif. 90015. There are other publications that pertain to specific subject areas.

[3]A medical school chairman (*The State of Academic Science: The Role of the University in the Nation's Research Effort,* Change Magazine Press, New Rochelle, New York, 1978, p. 193)

If you get a job as a grantwriter for a public television station, chances are your real motive is to maneuver yourself into a choice job producing documentaries about the important issues.

This tendency of the grantsperson not to recognize or accept his own field and appreciate its own integrity explains the passivity and bewilderment of the average grantsperson, who, arriving there by accident, feels like a leaf in the wind, caught up in forces beyond his control. Consider these victims of the grants game.

THE TYPICAL GRANTSPERSON: ONE HASSLE AFTER ANOTHER

Like most other grantspeople, you felt like you jumped into deep water without knowing how to swim when you learned that you had to write a proposal.

As a leader in the feminist community of Atlanta, you are instigating the development of a rape crisis center. You thought you could arrange it with donations or the financial support of the YWCA. But the Y is broke and everyone says there is federal money for battered women. You have already seen several planners from the state level of the Law Enforcement Assistance Administration, and all you got was confused and angry by their incomprehensible language and the strange way they talked about "client populations" and "impact." They gave you some forms to fill out. You stare down at the first one. How could you possibly tell them, in the 2 × 6 inch squares, what you feel about the way rape victims are treated? How can you put your beliefs in their language without compromising yourself? What do they mean by "measurable objective"? Who will read the proposal anyway?

You are an English major just out of Boston University. At the last minute you decide not to go to graduate school. So you move back to Seattle to get a firmer grip on your life. The only job you can find is as a grants writer for a school district, paid hourly, no fringe benefits. Various minority teachers in the district get sent to you. You are supposed to interview them and then write up their projects. But there is more to it, you find, than just writing down their ideas. You cannot get yourself to begin writing the proposal until you are possessed by the problem they present. Despite the fact that you are white, you find yourself sounding like a militant American Indian one week, demanding redress of past inequities against the Lumi Reservation. Next week you are a blind person arguing for an audio-based library system to increase the educational self-sufficiency of the "hearing-impaired" community. Then, before the week is out, you are a black teacher concerned about the widening white-minority gap in the basic skills. Your black studies project using individualized instruction and criterion-referenced testing with a built-in "career ladder" is just the answer. The next week you feel sick and cannot bring yourself to go back to work. You decide to give graduate school a try after all.

You are the Director of Grants and Contracts at a midwestern state university. The legislature is tightening its fiscal control, refusing to provide an inflation adjustment for next year's budget. The president decrees that each academic department must cut its budget by 10 percent. One by one, the department chairpersons come filing into your office to plead with you—and occasionally even demand—that you get them more research grants to keep them from having to fire faculty members and cut back existing programs. You know, but they do not, that since the National Institutes of Health unfavorably audited several universities last year, there is likely to be less rather than more research funding available. You suspect that the cutback might be a good opportunity to dispense with incompetent researchers and do-nothing administrators. It annoys you to have to cover up the mismanagement that created this crisis. "They don't want research but just to appease the faculty," you fume. You plead your case to the president, who is unsympathetic: "Get those grant proposals out, Jones," he says ominously.

The sign on the door says Housing Consultant, but you are known in the business as a "packager"—someone who puts together public housing projects and offers them to the Department of Housing and Urban Development. The legislation allows you a cut for your services: $27,500 for each closure. You thought this year was going to be a blockbuster. Nixon had held up billions for years. Carter has just released them for housing assistance to low-income elderly and handicapped persons.

But things have not worked out so well. The package that you put together includes a lawyer, an accountant, an architect, a contractor, a politically appropriate "sponsor," support from "the community," and of course HUD itself, through its regional office. The problem is that as you try to tie up one end of the package, parts keep falling out the other end. The lawyer steals your information and offers it to a competitor. The church freaks out at the amount of front money it must commit. The Department of Housing and Urban Development comes down hard on the sponsor for not knowing how to administer a housing project. And the HUD funding is held up, which forces you into cash-flow problems that your banker refuses to understand. The stronger the smell of the $27,500, the further away it gets. You get fed up. After your second gin and tonic your new lawyer asks you what you really think about public housing. You smirk, "Those pork barrel projects, are you kidding? They're the biggest scam going in government."

Inflation. The cost of liability insurance. Soaring medical equipment expenses. The unionization of even the professional workers. The hospital director comes to tell you that you are the only hope to get the General Hospital out of this mess. She has an inside tip from the Health System Agency about lots of funds available for preventive care and thinks that might be the answer. So go get those grants. "Sure," you say, "preventive, hmmph." You know that the real problem is that doctors are incredibly defensive and arrogant and are alienating the nurses and orderlies, who respond with high absenteeism and turnover rates. That's the real problem. Even if we got preventive care grants, General Hospital wouldn't know what to do with them. All we know is drugs and surgery. The hospital staff either does not understand or is threatened by all this "holistic" nonsense. The whole thing makes you feel so tense you quit early and go practice your yoga.

Feel sorry for these hassled grantspeople? Poor babes struggling to stay afloat. When the sharks chomped at their heels, no wonder they didn't like it. Chances are none of them will remain in their jobs more than, say, two years, unless they manage to harden into insensitivity in order to endure.

THE IDEAL GRANTSPEOPLE: ONE SUCCESS LEVERAGED ON ANOTHER

These case studies may be typical, but they are not the whole story. Other grantspeople approach the same work with a different attitude. Instead of relating to their role resentfully, they turn the tables on the whole matter. By taking responsibility for the grantseeking role, they can sometimes single-handedly transform an organization and the world around it and at the same time become more powerful people. Four success stories—in public television, the handicapped, employment and training, and solar energy—will show you what we mean.

Big Bird Is Fundable: Joan Cooney Transforms Public Television

The meal was over. As the guests around the dinner table sat sipping their coffee, it was clear they were not satisfied. One of them was a young man named Lloyd Morrisett, Vice-President of the Carnegie Corporation, the foundation at the forefront of educational research and experimentation. He mentioned observing his three-year-old daughter watching TV as though hypnotized. Perhaps there was a way to use TV to bring out a child's potential. All sorts of research papers stacking up on his desk concluded that half of a child's intellectual development took place before the age of five. And yet so little was being done to stimulate learning in the early years. Certainly, TV never appeals to a child's intelligence.

Director of a New York antipoverty program, Timothy Cooney, picked up the idea. An early childhood TV program might help prevent some of the complex problems of the inner city, which become so ingrained by the time kids grow up. His wife, Joan Ganz Cooney, was listening. She had just completed an hour-long film on the problem of urban poverty for WNDT, the New York educational station, and was eager to take the next step—to do something about it. How about a TV show for preschoolers aimed particularly at the inner city ghetto?

So emerged the idea for *Sesame Street,* the most popular long-running show on television (with 9 million loyal viewers out of a national preschool population of 12 million). It is also TV's most awarded show (twelve Emmys, one Peabody, and just about everything else).

Sesame Street was quickly picked up in adapted form by twenty-six countries—even Rumania wanted it. It put public television on the map in America, attracting mass audiences for the first time. It demonstrated that top-flight entertainment and the best of education are not intrinsically opposed but can go hand in hand—a discovery that produced a wave of other shows (e.g., *Zoom, Mr. Rogers*) attempting to do the same thing. Until *Star Wars,* it was the dominant media influence over a whole generation of kids. Educationally, the show worked: Tests found that the more kids watch it, the more they learn—even ghetto kids who were the "target audience." Although some liberal parents criticized the show as an influence that makes children passive, Margaret Mead took the side of the masses, commenting that "*Sesame Street* is the most responsible program that has ever been developed for children . . . They realize that this is a show for them."[4]

The most expensive television show of its kind, *Sesame Street* cost $8 million before any broadcasting took place at all. But neither Joan Cooney nor her friends had to put up any front money or go to the bank for loans. It all happened through the artful solicitation of grants and, once they were received, through knowing how to use one to get another. After the first decade of programming, the show passed through its dependence on grants to become self-sufficient. Joan Cooney is still president of her organization, the Children's Television Workshop (CTW); dinner guest Morrisett has become chairman of its board. Children's Television Workshop is solvent and is still sending creative waves throughout the television industry.

This is how it happened.

The first step was a "feasibility study," which is known to insiders in the funding business as a grant to help you develop a proposal for another grant. Through Morrisett, Carnegie gave funding to Cooney's employers at WNDT, who gave her release time to find out what preschool kids were watching and whether

[4]*Sesame Street: 1,000 Hours of Perpetual Television Experiment,* Children's Television Workshop Publications, New York, 1976, p. 18.

educational TV programs might appeal to them. She discovered that children had a high media literacy and were surprisingly responsive to innovations in the television format and treatment. For example, in 1968 *Laugh-In* was such a breakthrough because it adapted the technology of thirty- and sixty-second commercials to create a rapid, unconnected series of visual moments charged with humor and satire. Cooney found that preschoolers were able to stay with the program even though the content was over their heads. She concluded that if the commercial format could be adapted to entertainment, it could also serve educational ends. "The program would be an educational *Laugh-In* for children," she said.

Her study also found that preschoolers in the inner city almost always have their TV sets on at home and that they watch it more than any other age group.

Inspired by her emerging concept, Cooney and her team put together a proposal for major funding creating Children's Television Workshop, an independent, grantseeking, nonprofit corporation. The Carnegie people, impressed with the idea, agreed to put up a few hundred thousand. And they even went across town to get the Ford Foundation to match it. But both grants still were not nearly enough. An expensive two-year development period was necessary to bring in top-flight television professionals, early childhood specialists, and researchers. And they needed funds to launch a national door-to-door campaign just to get inner city mothers to turn on the educational stations, since public television in those days was associated with stuffy professorial types analyzing news clippings from the world press.

The CTW team knew that foundations could only pay initial start-up costs. Washington was the only possible source of ongoing funding. Yet the Office of Education of the Health, Education, and Welfare Department (HEW) had not yet considered linking education with television, perhaps because it had defined its role more narrowly as serving public schools rather than children per se.

Like generations of entrepreneurs before her, Joan Cooney was undaunted: She would simply have to open up those funds. The CTW team learned that the Office of Education had funds for closing the gap between high and low achievers before it widens irrevocably in the late school years. The Office of Education figured that it would take $3 billion to accomplish this by sending 12 million preschoolers to school—but Cooney pointed out that *Sesame Street* could reach most of them for a mere $7 million, or one cent per show per child.

The Office of Education officials were so impressed with CTW's cost-benefit arguments that they agreed to fund the development costs out of their Research and Development budget—and even threw in an extra million for good measure. Furthermore, they "set aside" an allotment in future budgets to go for television projects of the same order.

But then, unlike millions of other grantspeople before her, Cooney did not breathe a sigh of relief and say, "The feds came through. We're funded. Thank God that's over." She took a more cautious approach, eventually even returning that extra million. She knew that government support would soon mean government control unless she "diversified the funding base" of her organization. In other words, she had to get funds from other granting agencies.

The Children's Television Workshop soon put together separate packages for separate funders, remaining independent of all of them. Packaging was not new to Cooney. Her production work required the same skill. Each hour-long segment of *Sesame Street* became a package of separate minute-long sequences loosely bound by a theme—such as the letter *D.* The same sequences could be removed and recombined with other sequences around a new theme in another program. Each program could stand alone or be joined with others in a progressive series. Being a television producer turned out to be ideal training for a grantsperson. She put together proposals that could stand on their own or work together if all were funded.

Cooney knew that it is much easier to get funding to pay for the generation of new projects than to cover the operating expenses of ongoing activities. And, sure enough, when *Sesame Street* became a household word it was hard to ask for its continued funding as a "research" project as the Office of Education insisted. One way around that problem was to keep innovating the program so that it was a "perpetual experiment," with constant breakthroughs in content (such as bilingual sequences, or ecology programming).

But the OE wasn't entirely satisfied and balked at giving CTW millions each year because it kept them from funding other new demonstration projects. However, by this time a community of millions of supporters had gathered around the program, which CTW encouraged to put pressure on Congress, which in turn put pressure on the Office of Education. The lobbying worked. By 1974, the Office of Education had created a special line item in its budget for *Sesame Street,* thus bringing it out of the government grants process and into the more reliable contracts system. *Sesame Street* had legitimated itself as an institutionalized service to the public.

With *Sesame Street* secure, it must have been tempting for Cooney to consider going back to her craft, television production, rather than continue to run around putting proposals together. But instead she hired a top-notch executive producer and stepped back into a position as the behind-the-scenes president of CTW so that she could continue to manage the unfolding of her organization, which was based not on just one program but on a concept that was still in its infancy. By stepping out of her career in production, she was actually accepting her new career as a grantsperson, the agent of a process that involved continually getting and spending grants. That move was the secret of her success.

President Cooney proceeded immediately to focus on developing "spinoffs" from her main show by requesting start-up money for new projects. New HEW grants were solicited to begin *Electric Company,* a reading program intended for *Sesame Street* graduates that was broadcast not only in homes but also in classrooms. The series is now used around the world as a means of teaching English to both children and adults. Children's Television Workshop also created field offices, staffed by full-time coordinators paid by VISTA grants. Grants from Mobil Oil paid for the first free issues of *Sesame Street Magazine,* now fully self-supporting by subscription and newsstand sales. Other corporate grants have gone for new educational explorations that have resulted in programs on health, ecology, and science. Each grant contributed to CTW's reputation as a pathbreaker in both entertainment and education. That reputation in turn helped them to get other grants.

But new unrestricted sources of income had to be generated to pay for the mounting overhead. In the first year of CTW operations, nongrant funds amounted to 5 percent of income. Nine years later it had climbed to 50 percent, and that figure is still rising.

The first move toward autonomy was to license manufacturing companies to produce and distribute toys, books, records, and games that responded to the appeal of the *Sesame Street* host characters and muppets (part marionettes, part puppets). Another was to create a publishing company to produce a range of educational materials for teachers and parents who wished to reinforce the curriculum of the show. A third approach was to transfer *Sesame Street* abroad.

The need for CTW to replace grants with market-based enterprises has grown faster than even these income-producing ventures—a fact that prompted the company to create profit-making subsidiaries, which recycle money back into CTW operating funds. The major impetus for these enterprises came from a whopping Ford Foundation termination grant of $7 million. Rather than refund CTW year after year, the Ford Foundation is helping to boost CTW into self-sufficiency by helping it to purchase a Hawaiian cable TV franchise and two radio stations, which are intended to provide investment income in future years.

Finally, CTW's own programming has gone commercial. Realizing that it had assembled a child-oriented production capability unparalleled in the television industry, it is now offering adult-oriented programs to the major commercial networks. Why not? After all, those first *Sesame Street* audiences have now grown up. And so has CTW.

John Hessler and Ed Roberts Help Make America Fit for the Handicapped

Quadriplegics going to college? It just didn't seem possible, especially because of the barriers imposed by their physical limitations and need for constant medical attention. Staying alive was enough of a problem, to say nothing of moving around, attending classes, studying—doing all the things that any student needs to do. But the combination of the powered wheelchair, new antibiotics, and the experimental atmosphere of Berkeley in the early 1960s offered new options.

One of the ironic problems of the grants culture is that efforts to "help out" the unfortunate, while they have succeeded in many respects, have also been the source of unconscious paternalism, which has isolated the recipients of philanthropy and made them forever dependent on philanthropists, charities, and welfare. The severely handicapped have been a primary target of this dependency syndrome, which not only pervades general attitudes but is also built into funding processes as well.

Until very recently, the notion of "rehabilitating" a disabled person hadn't been pursued: Both the handicapped themselves and the providers of services to them tacitly accepted the assumption that there was just no way to assimilate them into the American mainstream. No one asked how this could be done, nor did anyone wonder to what extent the concept of "normal" could or should be reshaped to fit the needs of the handicapped. If you were blind, deaf, or paralyzed, you were a member of a highly segregated minority and that was that.

What efforts there were to make the handicapped autonomous focused almost entirely on vocational rehabilitation. Anyone who grew up disabled soon learned about state Vocational Rehabilitation departments, which have been the main vehicles used by the government to help the handicapped leave institutions for paid employment.

The Vocational Rehabilitation system worked but only in the narrowest sense. It ignored the fact that any disabled person needs all sorts of special products, skills, and other kinds of support—in short an entire environment adjusted to his or her needs—to be able to really function in a world dominated by the able-bodied. It did not deal with the attitudes that the disabled and the able-bodied both hold about physical handicaps.

Some of the first seeds of change were planted in Berkeley by Dr. Henry Bruyn, Medical Director of the University of California's Cowell Memorial Hospital. Bruyn took a bold step in 1962 when he began an experimental residency program for two quadriplegic students, Edward Roberts and John Hessler. His intention was to find out whether or not the severely disabled could function like normal students if given the necessary backup support.

Although he could not possibly have foreseen it at the time, Bruyn's program set in motion a process of change in the image of disabled people across the country and the world. It also began a period of reorientation of attitudes that is beginning to break down the barriers that physically and psychologically isolate the handicapped.

Bruyn's first two residents, Roberts and Hessler, soon came to exemplify the evolution of this new consciousness. By 1967, Roberts, having received his M.A. in political science from the University of California, would go on to become a doctoral candidate in the same department. Hessler would receive his B.A. in the same year, then go abroad to live in France for a year, returning in 1969 to complete his master's degree in French. The new possibility of greater autonomy and mobility for the severely disabled would lead first to the expansion of the University of California program, then to the founding of a separate, community-based program that would quickly attract national attention. Inspired by the example of their Berkeley peers, other disabled individuals across the country would begin to form communities, autonomous coalitions of quadriplegics, paraplegics, the deaf, the blind, and other physically disadvantaged groups, who would all join in the search for new avenues to self-reliance.

Today, Edward Roberts heads California's Department of Rehabilitation, overseeing a $100 million budget. John Hessler, assistant director of the same department, is busy learning what the grants process looks like from the other end, from the perspective of the funder, as he works to establish other centers up and down the state.

Hessler and Roberts lived at Cowell from 1962 to 1966, dependent on a variety of state and federal grants to pay for the cost of their room, their attendants' salaries, and the medical care needed to keep a severely disabled person healthy. During this period, they came to know the grant regulations they lived under so well that more than once they found themselves coaching new state and county representatives assigned to the program.

By the time they were approaching graduation, and, like any other incipient graduate, wondering what they were going to do next, the Cowell residency program was slowly beginning to expand. In 1967, it received $50,000 from HEW's Rehabilitation Services Administration (RSA). A small community of the disabled was forming. The seeds of healthy competitiveness were sprouting out of a new sense of peer pressure. When one disabled person could demonstrate even a small step toward self-sufficiency, others were inspired to work just a little harder themselves to become self-reliant.

At the same time that the community of the disabled was forming, the federal funding system that would fuel its growth was also beginning to emerge, influenced partly by the creative waves coming from Berkeley. In 1968, as part of an Office of Education program known as Upward Bound, Congress passed legislation intended to benefit disadvantaged students of all kinds. When the Office of Education came to writing guidelines for this program, it turned to Roberts.

Hessler became a part of the new directions too. Aware that Office of Education funds were available, he convinced University of California representatives to give credit to students willing to help him develop a proposal for the Office of Education. The university agreed; the proposal was proposed; and Hessler's application was approved for its full request of $81,000, with not one budget item deleted or lowered, not even a request, unusual for the time, for a specially equipped van to transport disabled students.

The Physically Disabled Students Program (PDSP) at the University of California was formally inaugurated in 1970, with Hessler as its first Executive Director. Operating with an advisory committee of disabled students, it served seventeen severely disabled students in its first year, providing funds for attendant salaries, housing costs, transportation, and advisory services. Of the initial seven disabled-student programs funded nationwide under Office of Education auspices, the program at the University of California quickly received recognition as the pacesetter, because, according to Hessler, "it was the first program of, by, and for the disabled. We refused to let the walkies do it for us." The first signs of a national community of the physically disabled were beginning to emerge.

By the end of its first year, the program was an unequivocal success. Disabled participants were becoming more active, and therefore healthier. In its second year PDSP was refunded for $90,000. With only 10 percent more funding than it had received in its first year of operation, it was now servicing seventy-five persons, four times as many as in its first year. Many new participants were quadriplegics, but the program had expanded to include paraplegics, the blind, and others with less severe disabilities.

Something was happening that had not happened before: a coalition that cut across handicapped lines. Previously, the different types of handicapped people had tended to avoid each other, a tendency that was reinforced by separate funding systems. By and large, the various groups had tacitly rejected the notion that they shared a common identity and relationship to the world at large. Now they were discovering how much their experiences overlapped and how important it was to begin to work together for the years ahead.

As the coalition began to encompass more and more kinds of people, a potential crisis emerged, which was adroitly transformed into an opportunity for further innovation. Fully half of the new PDSP participants were not University of California students, and the program's guidelines clearly limited its benefits to enrolled students. Afraid that HEW might cut the program back, or even declare some of its past expenditures ineligible, Hessler considered the problem and came up with what turned out to be a profoundly important idea.

The concept of "independent living" became a rallying point. Hessler knew that the university setting would not allow the kind of action-oriented program that the concept of "independent living" implied, especially since his plan envisioned broad-based support from noncampus elements of the Berkeley community. Campus organizations were by charter limited to study groups, and Hessler and his group had already moved, through its own dynamics, away from study and demonstration into practice.

So, sensing that the time was ripe, he composed and sent off a three-page concept paper—essentially a miniproposal—to other key members of the disabled community in Berkeley, outlining what needed to be done to make the Center for Independent Living (CIL) a reality and how to do it. The letter stirred an excited response: Within days the first meetings to discuss the idea were being held. To avoid perpetuating an all-too prevalent deference to his leadership role, Hessler appointed a peer as leader of the fledgling organization, provided the ten original core CIL members with office space, a phone, and mailing privileges, and then pushed them out on their own. (He remained on the CIL board until 1974 and then gave up that link also.)

As Hessler describes those years now, he emphasizes that the central concept underlying the establishment of both PDSP and CIL was self-reliance: "We saw an opportunity to create our own jobs," he says. "There were a lot of professionals working with disabled programs who were making a very respectable living, and we saw no reason why we couldn't do the job as well as, if not better than, they could."

The first grant search of the Center for Independent Living was a resounding success. Applying to HEW on its own, it received a $54,000 training grant. The organization has faltered once or twice since then but has never looked back.

An unmistakable élan characterized the early years of CIL, a sense of urgency and diversity that could at times be shocking to an unconditioned outsider: dozens of people in powered wheelchairs rolling through the halls of the CIL headquarters, a former used car dealership on Berkeley's infamous Telegraph Avenue; conferences on the evening news; impromptu meetings with other segments of the handicapped world, with the blind and the deaf; and a tangible, growing conviction that the hour of the handicapped had arrived, one of the last of the many waves of revolutionary fervor and consciousness raising that Berkeley was ever to witness. The first wave of what was to become a solid, highly diverse, articulate *community* of, by, and for the handicapped, an altogether new cultural phenomenon, was mounting.

The annual budget of the Center for Independent Living, which still comes predominantly from federal funds, now exceeds $1 million annually. In a move toward fiscal self-sufficiency, CIL now sells and repairs powered wheelchairs, has designed an improved wheelchair prototype, and has even considered the possibility that it might one day develop its own manufacturing and distribution setup.

Hessler acknowledges the remarkable success that PDSP and CIL have enjoyed over the last decade, but he cautions that these years were not without mistakes and hard-won lessons. In 1973, for example, CIL momentarily lost touch with its dream—opportunities to secure large grants were being missed; CIL leadership was growing tired. An intense board meeting ended in a change of executive directors. The program was soon back on the right track, however.

One of the most valuable lessons learned, says Hessler, is that "it can take just as much effort to go after $200 as $20,000." He cites this example: One PDSP fund-raising strategy was to organize a campus referendum—students voted on whether or not to allocate 25 cents every three months ("a quarter per quarter," as Hessler describes it) out of registration fees for the disabled student program. The lobbying effort needed to get the University of California's student government to put the referendum on the ballot took about 40 hours, and another ten to fifteen hours went into staffing a public information booth and printing and distributing leaflets during the week before the election.

The measure passed with a 19:1 margin, bringing an annual grant to the PDSP budget that in 1978 reached $60,000. By contrast, Hessler points to a protracted struggle that he became involved in to secure HUD Community Development funds. Nearly 300 hours went into this effort. The Physically Disabled Students Program netted a grand total of $200. "After that," says Hessler, "I never went for anything less than $50,000."

The disabled community in Berkeley also pioneered in effective, and on occasion highly dramatic, use of media coverage. When Governor Reagan tried to cut attendant care funds in half in 1970, the state capitol was immediately besieged by disabled protesters. During television coverage of one sit-in, the cameras turned to Hessler, who gravely declared that he intended to commit suicide if the cuts were upheld. A local judge saw this footage and blocked Reagan's order, calling the crisis a matter of life and death.

The Center for Independent Living was one of the first handicapped organizations to successfully lobby to get a city, Berkeley, to commit General Sharing funds to a street-decurbing program, a practice that has been followed since all over the country.

The prowess of CIL as a grantgetter has not been due to the paternalism that caused the independent living movement to arise. It has always demanded equal, impartial consideration. For example, it has let it be known that it won't hesitate to appeal rejections: If it is refused grants, the turndown must be for unimpeachable reasons or CIL will fight the decision. After one rejection from a funder, CIL challenged the decision, taking advantage of a virtually unheard-of grievance procedure. Pursuing the grievance became an opportunity to educate the funder to CIL's purpose and approach. The decision wasn't reversed, but the interaction had the effect of actually creating a new alliance that came in handy during later successful grant pursuits.

Independent living for the handicapped is no longer a dream of a single organization, it is now a national movement. One state after another has altered the practices of its vocational rehabilitation system along the lines of the advocacy approach taken by CIL, beginning with the selection of disabled individuals to head agencies in different parts of the country.

Tish Sommers and the Old Gals' Network Take on CETA

No grant program has been more controversial, larger, or more directly tied to public policy than CETA, that cute-sounding ("cita" means a romantic rendezvous in Spanish; Sita is a seductress in Hindu mythology) acronym with the bureaucratic definition of Comprehensive Employment and Training Act. It is the "jobs bill" of the Department of Labor, the nation's effort to eliminate the problems of unemployment that started creeping up on us with disturbing regularity during the 1970s. It is not intended as a "make-work" project: CETA has the more challenging goal of helping the nation's unemployed, underemployed, and unemployable become free of further governmental support. If allocations are made according to 1979 projections, by 1984 about $80 billion will have been spent in this effort.

That sum is a lot of money. Spending at that level is hard to defend to taxpayers who have to foot the bill through their own unsubsidized labor. Yet everyone agrees that somehow we need to alter the economy and the unemployed so that jobs and people are matched up. But how to do it? The reality of how CETA was designed is that policy setters had to make quick decisions based on available information and the pressures of interest groups, groups like unions, local governmental associations, nonprofit groups, planners, economists, and lots more, all part of the informal employment and training network in this country. Through jockeying and juggling, Congress finally worked out its jobs bill with qualifying amendments declaring how and when the money would be spent. Buried in this bill were hidden assumptions about the meaning of terms like "job" or "career," about the best way of classifying them, about what the terms "disadvantaged," "underemployed" and "unemployed" mean, and about what it means to get someone ready to earn a living. It may seem minor, but how those terms are defined can determine who gets the money and who does not.

In the process of drafting the legislation, it is possible for highly pressured policymakers to miss the point. Common sense ideas can escape them. They might not realize how they could fulfill their mission as quickly, cheaply, and effectively as possible. They may choose the wrong categories or define them inappropriately. Maybe there are powerless, hidden populations who desperately need financial support but who fall through the cracks between categories. How do these disenfranchised populations get a piece of CETA's pie?

Tish Sommers knows the answer. Working with a small group in her Oakland apartment, she identified one such hidden population: 7 million older women. Even though their needs fit the intention of CETA legislation, the funder's guidelines excluded them. Calling upon the enormous political skills of women's organizations and nonprofit groups staffed by women volunteers, she and her team combined a savvy publicity campaign and state-level and national lobbying activities with a persevering grants strategy that opened up CETA funds to this new population. They also introduced ideas into the employment and training system that sent shock waves through it: the notion that volunteer labor and job training are closely connected, the concept that millions of "nontraditional" jobs can and should be created instead of only focusing on training the unemployed for the few available traditional jobs; the view that household skills could be transformed into income-earning skills, and the understanding that the best way to become employed is to learn to like yourself. The old boys who once hung around CETA may never get over the onslaught of the old gals.

Tish Sommers was divorced at age fifty-seven in 1973. She was not alone. She was only one of millions of such women, most of them shocked at the sudden loss of the emotional and financial support of a breadwinner. As well as divorced and separated women, this group also includes widows and the wives of unemployed men. Sizable as it is, this population has been ignored by the welfare system. Without dependent children, they do not qualify for federal support. They have no unemployment benefits, no social security. Without updated job skills, there is usually no work for them except the most menial kind of wage labor. Their numbers increased significantly in the late 1960s and 1970s, due to the phenomenal rise of divorce following passage of "no-fault" divorce laws. As a group these women have hardly been vociferous about their problems. Even the feminist groups, led by younger women, have failed to recognize their special needs.

But the winds suddenly changed in 1974. There was tremendous interest, largely stirred by CETA and the dwindling job market, in the whole subject of work. The Grey Panthers were telling Americans about aging. The women's movement was moving away from discussion and toward solving the problems of specific groups. The field of "career development" was in vogue. Sommers, a past board member of the National Organization of Women (NOW) and the founder of a job training program, got together with some friends who were in a similar situation and in the true fashion of consciousness raising, created a study group called the "We Should Live So Long Collective."

An outcome of their discussions was an organization, Jobs for Older Women. The next step, of course, was to look for money. There were two ways to go—hustle grants for the aged or for employment. Since CETA did not yet recognize these women as an eligible group, the new organization attempted to pry loose some of the funds of the Older Americans Act, administered at the county level. And of course they encountered the inevitable Catch 22: The bureaucrats told them that "aged" money could not be used for employment. But they fought and won, capturing $9,000 in their first year, along with a warning that the grant would not be renewed. They hired a staff member and put her to work coordinating volunteers that were already swarming around the small office donated by a local Presbyterian church.

Surveying other funding options, Sommers soon realized that her group did not qualify for any funding program. With their grant running out in only a few months, they had to act quickly or all would be lost. They decided to go for broke: forcing funds loose from the state legislature and budget-minded Governor Brown. Declared Sommers, "When you're working on a grass-roots level, you either conform or fight, and we always fight."

Forcing funds loose meant drafting legislation that had teeth in it: legislation that would set new policy and earmark funds to implement it. It meant a full-scale media campaign, crisscrossing the state to excite grass-roots support, and persistent lobbying in Sacramento.

But they needed a unifying concept. The term "Displaced Homemakers" was coined. As awkward as it sounded it seemed to fit, since it emphasized the critical point that most of these women had been dumped from their jobs in the home and therefore deserved public assistance. The category created new momentum. Soon the term decorated the title of a bill introduced by a state senator laying out what the women wanted: a major demonstration project with training money, stipends, health care, and the usual overhead funding. It also popped up in newspaper headlines and was discussed on talk shows. "Displaced homemaker" was on its way to becoming a household word.

Climbing into an old VW, Sommers and her crew took to the road. Supported by contributions of "$100 here and $50 there," they hit all the small California communities, from Escondido to Eureka, talking to Chambers of Commerce, local NOW chapters, YMCAs, church groups, and whoever else would listen to their appeal to write Sacramento and demand passage of SB825.

Blitzed in the final days with letters, mailgrams, carloads of elderly women knocking at the doors of legislative committees, the Assembly passed the bill almost unanimously. The Senate vote was unanimous. Characteristically, Governor Brown waited until an hour and a half before his deadline before signing the bill into law. The bill created a new nonprofit Alliance for Displaced Homemakers Center and gave it $200,000 to run a model training program for two years.

The real political success, however, was the creation of a base for a national movement. Sommers continued to work for a while at the training center. Then teaming up with a shrewd politician, collaborator, and friend, Laurie Shields, she found it more to her liking to leave the staff and concentrate her efforts on pushing the movement across the country. Having secured one year's continuation funding from the state for the Center, she realized that legislative changes at the national level were needed before lasting inroads could be made.

Sommers and Shields decided on the same tactic that had worked before: creating a local groundswell, in the states, before approaching the center of political power. They visited nearly every state (except Alaska and Hawaii) on a conference tour, getting strong support from Commissions on the Status of Women and more traditional women's groups, such as the League of Women Voters. Within months, twenty-eight states had introduced bills modeled after the California example. About fifteen passed, but not all set up training centers because funding was so tight.

It was time for a frontal attack on CETA. Sommers and Shields knew they fit perfectly the intention of the legislation that created that program. They decided to change the law in their favor.

The next step was to enlist support from national organizations with real power in Washington: The American Association on Aging, the National Council on Aging, NOW, and others. Momentum was building. In response to an appearance on the Phil Donahue show, 2,000 letters of support poured in. Soon Sommers and Shields were invited to give testimony at hearings held in both the House and the Senate. They also enlisted support from the Women's Bureau, a little-known division of the Department of Labor that had not previously played any advocacy role. President Carter himself responded to these developments by authorizing displaced homemakers as eligible recipients in all CETA titles. In 1978, the Department of Labor had declared that it would earmark $5 million out of next year's budget for displaced homemaker programs. But Sommers, Shields, and their friends still were not satisfied. They wanted 2 percent set aside out of each year's mammoth CETA budget for their cause. An amendment to that effect was introduced in the Senate, and despite the antispending sentiment of the inflation-weary Congress, the rule passed. As of that day, the displaced homemaker had a place in the economic scheme of things.

As for Tish Sommers' latest activities, a foundation has offered her a grant. She accepted the offer and went to work on a series of national conferences that would raise issues about the next steps to be taken in the Displaced Homemakers movement.

Hank Rasé Creates a Golden Opportunity

"Welcome to Golden, the Town Where the West Remains," reads the archway between false fronts on the main street of this arid, rugged town, which prides itself on its seclusion from the hustle-bustle of Denver. The place seems right out of an old-time movie—lots of folks hanging around drinking Golden's own Coors beer.

Such tranquility is deceptive. Who could guess that the U.S. Department of Energy (DOE) is pouring millions upon millions of dollars into this area, making it into a very modern center of energy developments that may soon shake the world?

If you drive along the twenty-mile country road between Boulder and Golden, you may come across scruffy youths holding placards, singing protest songs, and sitting on the railroad tracks. They are attempting to block the next trainload of plutonium (used to make triggers for nuclear bombs) headed for an installation called Rocky Flats. You see, recently organized DOE has within its mission the development of sophisticated nuclear weaponry for the Department of Defense, and Rocky Flats plays a central role in DOE's strategy. This importation of plutonium has beome the latest issue for Colorado's broad-based environmentalists' movement, whose members consider the indestructible substance to be uneconomical, dangerous, unrecyclable—in sum, evil.

If these protesters are vehemently antinuclear, they are just as avidly prosolar. That is why it might surprise you that by traveling only a few miles down the road to the other side of Golden, you will find Rocky Flats' benign counterpart, also funded by DOE, called the Solar Energy Research Institute (SERI). No protesters here. This is where they come to apply for jobs, since SERI has been scheduled to expand from its present start-up staff of 360 to a possible 6,000 over the next few years. Its budget, set at $65 million in 1978, is expected to rise proportionally.

But even those figures do not really show its significance. Solar Energy Research Institute has the awesome responsibility of bringing together all the nation's resources to "promote the widespread use" of solar energy. That means using methods that range from laboratory science to tinkering with various ways "to remove barriers and build incentives" to create a powerful solar industry in this country and the world. Today solar technologies are still trendy toys that intrigue the American public. It is up to SERI to convert these playthings into technologies that are competitive enough to appeal to energy consumers now dependent on dwindling reserves of oil, gas, and coal, and who see no future alternative but nuclear power. SERI must create an attractive third alternative.

The Solar Energy Research Institute is and will remain the largest collection of solar specialists under one roof, all committed to the notion that the "soft path" is indeed possible. The Department of Energy is willing to gamble on this long shot. But, of course, they are playing it both ways.

The Institute will be lodged in undistinguished temporary quarters until a dramatic new facility is constructed on a mesa directly above them. One of the makeshift offices is occupied by Hank Rasé (Ra-ZAY), right-hand man to SERI president, Paul Rappaport. These days Rasé has a lot to do with guiding the full-speed growth of the Institute. On any given day, his work could involve helping to work out a deal with Saudi Arabia to build solar cities in the desert—sort of a reverse of the oil crisis, with the Arabs acknowledging their dependence on our expertise. "The Saudis will put up $100 million and lots of sun and SERI will come through with the technology. It's a flow-through arrangement with DOE," says Rasé. Or he might be involved in painstaking negotiations over next year's requested budget from DOE, which still has not given the Institute the freedom it wants. Or it could mean a phone call to an environmentalist who wants more attention paid to biomass in Oregon rather than windmills in Arizona. On another day he may deal with a businesswoman who insists that an insulation product is ready for the market even though SERI says it should be put through more tests.

Hank Rasé is clearly at the center of things. This young planner with a smooth voice and a desk piled with neatly stacked papers has been with the operation from the start. In 1975 Governor Richard Lamm convinced him to leave his job as an educational planner to launch an uncertain career with the dubious title of Director of Proposal Preparation. That meant that he was to be the link between all the groups that were already trying to get SERI for Colorado. After a series of delays, the Colorado legislature had finally allocated $75,000 in a "seed grant" to pay Rasé's salary, clerical supplies, and research support by student interns. He was to meet twice a week with a committee selected by Lamm that was already at work doing background for the SERI proposal.

It is odd, in a way, that the State of Colorado should be so involved. Usually, state governments do not consider it their role to be making such an overt effort at stimulating grants or contracts for new industry. The last time Colorado had mounted a similar attempt to obtain federal money was when they tried unsuccessfully to get a contract for a proton accelerator, a loss which now delights the state that is saddled with the Rocky Flats problem. The solar issue could not have come at a better time for Lamm, however. Although a Democrat, he was accused of being anti-growth (he vetoed the Colorado Olympics). "Not true," he insisted—he was merely against the wrong kind of growth. Bringing SERI to Colorado was a chance to attract a clean industry, at a time when oil shale developments were tearing up the state's Western Slope. The Institute would attract a lot of well-salaried professionals as well as entrepreneurial spinoff industries that would manufacture solar equipment on a world scale. It would also win the favor of the environmentalists.

At about the same time, a young environmentalist, Gary Hart, became Colorado's U.S. Senator. The team of two, one working locally and the other nationally, created the right momentum to generate a "competitive" proposal.

When Congress made its annual lump-sum allocations for federally sponsored research in 1974, it included a provision calling for the establishment of a solar research institute that would consolidate and expand all current solar Research and Development activities, which were at that time disbursed throughout National Aeronautics and Space Administration and National Science Foundation laboratories. The provision came one year after the oil crisis that slapped America in the face with the reality that our source of oil was precarious and limited. It started the country thinking about exploring other energy avenues. Naturally, the nation's Research and Development system was the place to uncover new possibilities. Rather than continue to sponsor research through the government laboratory system, which was considered too sluggish for the high-speed need to develop solar applications, the government chose to award SERI to a single contractor, after a competitive bidding process.[5] Sputnik had created a huge system of space Research and Development that took us to the moon. Couldn't the oil crisis be turned to our advantage by motivating us to achieve the impossible dream of tapping the power of the sun?

As soon as the oil crisis hit, various powerful members of Congress (the late Senator Humphrey, Senator Kennedy, and Senator Church, among others) created what became known as the "solar coalition." Congress's Office of Technology Assessment came through with a study to show that a solar industry in this country would indeed be possible if it were supported with the right combination of incentive and research. Soon an additional billion dollars was in the energy budget with solar research high on the list of promises.

Naturally, these new developments created quite a stir among the states, which were all imagining themselves going down in history as the place that learned to harness the sun and offered that knowledge to the world. For example, New Mexico's legislature put up nearly a million dollars to pay for a very-high-profile proposal, including elaborate portfolios, presentation, site visits, brochures, and other promotional efforts.

Lamm and Hart took a more cautious approach. They selected a committee that brought together every sector in Colorado that had something to say about solar energy: representatives of major universities and research institutes, the state's principal industrial laboratories, independent researchers, and manufacturers. Even the oil companies, some of whom had recently shifted their headquarters from Houston to Denver, supported the project. Those firms had responded to the oil crisis by diversifying into energy

[5]Such "sole source" contracting is only one of many kinds of contracting processes used by the federal government. For a good overview of prevailing methods, with an emphasis on contracts to universities, see Bruce Smith and Joseph Karlesky, *The State of Academic Science: The Universities in the Nation's Research Effort,* Vol. I and II, Change Magazine Press, New Rochelle, New York, 1977.

conglomerates. So they strengthened their investments in coal, oil shale, and even did a little solar research on their own. That is why they found energy-abundant Colorado a very good place to be and why they weren't exactly threatened by the prospect of SERI's being located in Colorado. "It was very easy to create a consensus around the solar issue," Rasé said on reflection. "I guess it's because the sun is considered the mother of us all."

But it was up to Rasé to integrate all this good feeling into agreements. And he learned that it wasn't always easy to keep the consensus together. His first job was to travel around the state interviewing various groups to get their support for the proposal. The committee had adopted the strategy that their biggest asset was to build the broadest possible base of support in Colorado. He found that "solar" was everything good to everybody until it got down to the specifics of "what to" and "how to."

Factions with impassioned, contrary views appeared: The university types favored the academic research model in which science could be conducted free of the pressures and controls of government (and the public). Others favored the industrial laboratory model with its close links between research and the development of products ready for manufacture and sale. The environmentalists favored the "low-tech" approach to solar energy, concentrating on disposed grass-roots applications—greenhouses, an emphasis on indigenous materials, and an attempt to fit into local climates and work-force compositions that change from region to region. On the other hand, some favored the "high-tech" applications, insisting that their approach was more cost-effective and "realistic." And then there were the disputes among the researchers themselves, who favored either "passive" or "active" approaches to solar use. Some preferred investing in one particular kind of solar energy over another, like solar ponds rather than mechanical collectors.

Out of those controversies, Rasé learned that there was no such thing as "solar energy" at all but a lot of diverse threads tangled together and heading in different directions. Different parts of the state threatened to come out with their own separate proposals, which Rasé knew would undercut the united effort that he needed. Folks from Durango, Pueblo, and Colorado Springs wanted SERI located in their home towns.

After winning over all local sectors, from high rise to grass roots, the next task was to choose the right "manager-operator," the organization that would actually sponsor the grant. The natural place for any good Coloradan to turn was to one of the two main, state-supported universities, which already had extensive research facilities and, in the case of Colorado State University, quite a track record in the solar field. After reviewing the universities' case, Rasé and committee went back to study the legislation calling for SERI. They noted that it emphasized research that would lend itself easily to "commercialization," a term new to the Research and Development field with a meaning that is still not quite clear. It had something to do with extending beyond the conventional framework of just researching something, demonstrating it, writing an article, and then calling it quits. The government wanted SERI to go beyond the passive investigative role to actually transform energy use in the United States through establishing contact with industry, banks, the media, state governments, and even by employing community organizing methods. University researchers in their ivory towers, protected by tenure and their propensity for theorizing, tended to be too isolated to create links to new markets. Paradoxically, their isolation has not resulted in their sponsorship of high-risk, exploratory research of the sort that SERI wanted to generate. Furthermore, universities still tend to be oriented toward separated academic disciplines rather than along interdisciplinary lines, as required by SERI. Besides considering these issues, the committee was also concerned that a Colorado-based sponsor might seem too parochial to DOE, which wanted a truly national facility. They finally rejected university sponsorship and turned out of the state to look for a more "industrial" model.

Industrial laboratories, however, were not really suitable either. The Research and Development supported by private corporations tended to be a little too close to the development of market products for comfort. Industries by and large tend to focus on short-term solutions with immediate applications, rather than the kind of long-range exploratory work planned by SERI.

After rejecting both university and industrial models, the committee was left with one more alternative model: the private research laboratories, an ideal alternative, since such institutes are already nonprofit, interdisciplinary, and familiar with projects that span the physical and social sciences. Rasé and his team sent out feelers to the few institutes that seemed to have the skill required to manage the project.

They soon found out that most of the big institutes, like Battelle, had large investments in nuclear research but not in solar research. Battelle had power in Washington, but its nuclear orientation did not endear it to the ecologically inclined members of the committee. It was just that the big institutes did not know much about solar energy. Solar research introduced a shift in emphasis away from complex, high-scale, expensive technologies, like those developed for the aerospace industry. The people who do that kind of research naturally tend to focus on large-scale solar technologies. Rasé and the committee knew that if SERI lost the support of the environmentalist movement, their proposal was doomed to failure. By going with a big research firm that might be able to strengthen their credibility with the Research and Development Old Guard, they risked losing their environmentalist support.

So they kept searching. And of all places, Kansas City came up with the best bet: a relatively small outfit called the Midwest Research Institute (MRI) that already held over a million dollars in contracts for solar research. What was more important, it had avoided investing simultaneously in large-scale technology or nuclear energy. The Institute was so enthusiastic about the SERI project it promised to divest all its other work in the solar area if it got the SERI contract.

Rasé's work, however, was hardly over—the matter of beating out the competition still remained. As the deadline neared, the SERI issue became one of the hottest in Washington. It seemed that everybody who was anybody on the Hill was getting into the act. Part of the problem was that a study by ERDA (the Energy Research and Development Administration, which was later consolidated into DOE) of how SERI should be put together requested various states to respond by telling ERDA what they thought of the whole project. However, instead of writing back about the project's design, many states took a highly territorial stance, taking this opportunity to claim that their region would be the perfect site for such a facility. The late Hubert Humphrey of Minnesota got into the battle as well as Tip O'Neal of Massachusetts. New

Mexico, Florida, and California also joined in.

Soon there were two main groups of competitors: the "sun belt," extolling the advantages of their abundance of sun, and the "frost belt," which answered the "we-got-sun" argument by claiming that most of the research would be simulated in laboratories anyway and there were plenty of solar applications that fit the north too. Colorado, which is neither North nor South, took a middle way in that particular controversy, claiming the validity of both sides, which later turned out to be to its advantage. In fact, everything Rasé and the committee did to mobilize support was effectively low-profile and low-key. Instead of sending delegations to Washington, the Colorado committee surveyed the people they knew in the administration and in the various Research and Development agencies. Then they regularly called these contacts to "inform them about the progress of our application" and to suggest that they might "check how things are going at that end." Senator Hart quietly went to work getting support from states that were not submitting an application. When President Ford vacationed in Vail, he met with an informal committee delegation to "receive information" about Colorado's proposal. They used the same approach with ERDA: "We were careful not to overplay our hand," says Rasé. "Instead of coming on strong, we just admitted we didn't have all the answers and kept asking for their input." At the same time the Colorado team kept letting everybody know how broad a base was developing in the state.

Rather than focus on winning Washington over, they took pains to get Washington to come to Colorado. The key visit was from the top solar-geothermal expert at ERDA, who spent three days in tightly scheduled meetings with researchers and all other groups that could demonstrate support for the project; he was impressed by the fact that the right atmosphere existed in Colorado. Perhaps more than anything else, that did the trick.

But Rasé and his team knew they couldn't rely on a soft sell alone. They made sure that ERDA knew that everything in the Colorado-MRI proposal was conceived according to the intention of the request for proposals: The site of Golden was just what the guidelines required—close to an international airport, with close proximity to a major graduate school, and next to an entertainment and cultural center.

The next step was to choose a director for the project. Again parochialism was to be avoided. They needed a Ph.D., a recognized researcher in the solar field, and a proven administrator. That narrows the field down pretty far, of course, which explains why Paul Rappaport, former director of RCA Laboratory and a path-breaking solar researcher in the area of photovoltaics (turning light into electricity) was not only selected for Colorado's proposal, but was also written into several competing applications submitted from other state committees that knew he was unquestionably the man for the job.

The award was made and Colorado was selected, but the political furor was not over. Some of the losers, particularly those with powerful Congressional delegations, grumbled. They complained that since solar energy lends itself to diverse regional applications, there should be separate regional centers. Colorado responded by pointing to the legislative call for a "consolidation of efforts." A compromise was worked out creating four distinct regional centers that would focus on the development of commercial applications, on "removing barriers and building incentives" to complement SERI's development of products. The sites for these centers were chosen with politics as well as geography in mind: Minnesota got one. Massachusetts got another. Another one was sited in Georgia, which may have been influenced by the fact that by this time President Carter was playing a role in SERI's development. The Western Center was placed in Oregon.

The Department of Energy is complementing this national network by developing all sorts of programs to help stimulate other activity in the gray area of "commercialization." They include planned grant programs to stimulate public participation and increased confidence in solar energy, changes in building codes, the creation of loan incentives for banks, the development of new land-use policies, changes in the price structures of utilities, help for states that wish to enact "solar rights legislation" at the state level, and provisions for tax credits and "market pools" for the purchase of solar equipment.

Today SERI's position as the leader in its field is established worldwide. An international branch is underway. With an eye toward its long-range goal of halting the spread of nuclear installations, SERI has already developed bilateral agreements with Japan,

Spain, Mexico, the Soviet Union, Iran, and Saudi Arabia. If the Institute is successful, more countries may join in multilateral agreements. SERI may also bring the solar movement to the Less Developed Countries (LDCs) in a manner being worked out with the collaboration of the Agency for International Development, which already operates an LDC grant program in appropriate technology.

It all seems to have worked out just fine. Rasé and staff must be euphoric, right? Not quite. Even with a multibillion dollar agency backing you up, there are still pitfalls along the trail toward the establishment of this new industry.

The Solar Energy Research Institute may become too fat. The Department of Energy has chosen to put all its solar eggs in one basket for the sake of efficiency. But the drawback is that, without any competition, SERI could develop the complacency of any monopoly and the sluggishness of any bureaucracy. Rasé feels that the urgency of its mission, shared by all the staff, will counter that tendency.

Another potential problem may develop around the fact that SERI has not yet worked out how it will assure equal access to the valuable information it will be developing. Such knowledge could be skimmed off by people close to the project. The SERI staff has to learn how to stimulate new industry while at the same time not playing favorites with particular industrialists, which is not always easy to do. A related problem is how to determine when a product is ready for the market, and conversely, when a market has been prepared for a product. The link between public research and private commerce is still elusive.

An even greater problem, however, is the struggle to span the wide gap between DOE and the environmentalists. "For one thing, we are not really as independent of our funder as we'd like to be," said Rasé. "Our researchers recently submitted a proposal to DOE on the development of ocean thermal energy conversion. They hacked it to pieces—it came back completely changed. We're really still a Kelly Girl service to DOE." The Institute has to negotiate each year's budget with forty different DOE managers, so it must tread lightly now in order to become independent in the long run. In the next few years, if Rasé and the SERI staff play their cards right, they may win enough trust at DOE to be written into the line items in each year's budget and gain the prerogative to implement or even develop the nation's solar policy. But this process could take a while and it's risky. Many of the boys at DOE are not exactly serious about the solar program. Another area of independence sought by Rasé is the right to set priorities for its own grants and contracts program. Although SERI will increasingly contract out a lot of its research functions, it doesn't yet have the ability to determine what it will contract for or even the processes it will use to do it.

Rasé is less concerned about dependence on DOE than about possible trouble from the environmentalist groups, who are SERI's real constituency. "There are many who think we are going too slow, who think we should be the advocates that we just can't be," he says.

Can SERI strengthen its hand with DOE and the grass-roots groups, at the same time keeping both groups on its side? Chances are that Rasé himself—and the other skilled professionals who compose the institute's leadership—will be able to do it. Keeping the groups together, Rasé argues, is "not my doing but arises from the nature of solar itself." Discussing this point, a touch of passion enters Rasé's voice. "Solar energy doesn't have divisions built into it. It lends itself to a coalition that can bridge all gaps. I think that when our nation chooses an energy, it will take advantage of that rather than push one that doesn't have the necessary coalition." And then he added, looking out his office at a distant train moving slowly toward Rocky Flats, "We've seen with the nuclear issue that dissidents can stop a technology in its tracks."

WHAT IT TAKES TO BE A SUCCESS

The grantspersons in each case study were successful in the sense that they not only got grants but they used them effectively. They are indeed examples of *homo grantus,* creatures of the grant world, referred to in Chapter I. They were effective for two reasons: They were entrepreneurial and highly flexible.

The Grantsperson as Entrepreneur

It may seem odd that the successful grantsperson profiled here seems so entrepreneurial. Many people assume that grants are procured by unproductive types or Do-Gooders who are not self-sufficient enough to make it on their own. Yet the opposite is true of our successful grantsperson who has to be a real hustler. In fact, in today's world the entrepreneur is peripheral to the world of business enterprise, whereas he or she is right at the center of grant-getting activity.

Consider the meaning of "entrepreneur." The definitive theorist of enterpreneurism is still Joseph Schumpeter, the brilliant economist who wrote in the early years of this century. Schumpeter maintained:

> That function of the entrepreneur is to revolutionize the pattern of production by exploiting an invention, or more generally, an untried possibility for producing a new commodity, or producing an old one in a new way, or opening up a new source of supply or materials or a new outlet for products, by reorganizing industry.[6]

The entrepreneur's function lies outside the routine tasks that everyone understands, accepts, and takes comfort from. Somehow he has the capacity to see possibilities that are latent in their present form. Entrepreneurs are not necessarily the conceivers of new discoveries, like the prototypical mad scientist, the enraptured artist, or garage geniuses who are far ahead of their times. "Their function does not essentially consist in either inventing anything or otherwise creating the conditions which the enterprise exploits. It consists of getting things done."[7] They are more than likely the ones who link such discoveries to the factors of production (i.e., know-how, energy, and materials) so as to bring to general usage a whole new revolutionary way of doing something.

Entrepreneur comes from the Latin root *inter + prehendere,* or "to seize between." The job of the entrepreneur is to link the creative, idea-generating sector with the business-as-usual sector of our society. "Seize" is a critical part of the concept, since it underscores

[6]Joseph Schumpeter, *Capitalism, Socialism and Democracy,* Harper & Row, New York, 1942, p. 131.

[7]Ibid., p. 132.

the fact that the entrepreneur's work is not passive. There are tendencies for the two sectors to go off in different directions and never meet. Entrepreneurs must be incredibly active—even aggressive—as they carry an idea into popular use. They encounter resistance, since they inevitably have a "disequilibrating impact on the existing products and methods . . . And of course the environment always resists their activity."[8]

To Schumpeter the existence of a class of entrepreneurs is the key to the vitality of any particular society. If entrepreneurs are doing their job, the economy and culture as a whole will flourish. If conditions do not permit their activity, the economy will stagnate. Schumpeter sees the history of industrial societies in this light. Entrepreneurs brought into being such things as the railroad, electrical power, steam, steel, the automobile, and, of course, modern transportation, communications, and computers.

Schumpeter's stress on the importance of individual risk taking may seem obvious. Yet among present-day social theorists it is not widely recognized. Schumpeter rejected liberal and neo-Marxist notions that capitalism grows through a mechanical chain of events, that state planning or tinkering with wage and price controls can produce a health economy. His emphasis on the entrepreneur is humanistic; he believes that the individual creative actor is hardly a mere pawn of historical forces but someone with the wherewithall to influence history drastically. Schumpeter focuses on the importance of intelligence and willpower, which are potentially inexhaustible, as the key to a country's continued growth, rather than the exhaustible elements of labor, capital, and materials.

It is one thing to underscore the social value of entrepreneurs; it is another to ask why they should want to do what they do. What motivates this productive activity? For one thing, their personalities are predisposed to it. They must be capable of accepting the high-risk, open-ended atmosphere that pervades their normal activity and have enough intuition to "take their best shot" at the right decisions, without always being guided by adequate information. They must make a habit of living in constant uncertainty.

It is also true that these psychological traits are brought out by

[8]Ibid.

the conduct of entrepreneurial activity itself. It is assumed that in business enterprises rewards are proportional to risks—the higher the risks the higher the rewards. It may be that entrepreneurs are simply those who see the high rewards and are ambitious and tenacious enough to do what they have to, to become whom they must become, to reap them.

In the business world, monopoly power is, of course, the incentive. If the entrepreneur can be the first on the market, he has a lead on competitors and can develop the means to keep them out.

That is the dismal twist of Schumpeter's theories: The very success of entrepreneurs can set in motion a series of forces that will eventually eliminate the risktaker's role. Once the entrepreneur's place in society is gone, productivity stagnates. Society focuses on the redistribution of wealth (recutting the pie) rather than increasing production (expanding the pie). In such a postentrepreneurial state, technological progress becomes the business of trained specialists who turn out what has already been planned in predictable ways. The monopolies steadily eliminate small-time operators through increasingly efficient methods of mass-producing standardized items. "Things that once had to be visualized in a flash of genius will be produced by system."[9]

Are entrepreneurs dead? No. Our case studies suggest that Schumpeter's sense of history was off: They are being reborn as *homo grantus,* and far from playing a peripheral role, are now at the center of America's efforts to reawaken our productive capacity and, perhaps more important, our culture's confidence in itself. We have seen that it is the function of grants to demonstrate alternatives to our crisis-plagued private and public sectors. If we are going to learn how to convert military into peacetime industries, narrow the gap between rich and poor, shift energy use toward renewable and safe fuels, promote the self-reliance of the disadvantaged, and prevent chronic ill health, the grantsperson will help to show us the way.

What's in it for the grantsperson? To be sure, a Joan Cooney cannot enjoy the monopoly power of a Henry Ford. The grants entrepreneur operates on property that is part private and part

[9]Ibid.

public and never quite her own. The grantsperson has no real patent rights. The proposal itself is public property and, if federally funded, available to all through the Freedom of Information Act. Your success is measured by the degree to which your "model" is imitated by others—rather than by your capacity to keep others out. You can't even use grant funds to pay yourself for developing the proposal. All you can count on financially is a salary at the end of the line if you beat the odds and succeed in getting funded. And you probably won't keep your salary for too long—maybe five years at the most.

The real reward is power, both personal and social. A well-conceived grant project is at the center of the action, and the person who brought in the money can usually call the shots. Once you get a grant, you learn how to get the next one. You find yourself developing new skills and a new sense of freedom from the constraints you once assumed you would have to endure. The grantsperson is motivated by the possibility of doing what he or she really wants to do while getting paid for it. It is a matter of integrating the elements of your life that were kept separate before. If our case studies are any indication, once you begin to establish projects they begin to take on their own momentum. At that point money is not the dominant concern. Whether this motivation is enough to draw more social entrepreneurs into the granting process remains to be seen.

The Flexibility of the Grantsperson

Beyond the appetite for high-risk, high-intensity involvement, the other distinguishing characteristic of the four successful examples is their lack of specialization. Joan Cooney moved flexibly between television, early childhood education, and administration. John Hessler broadened the notion of rehabilitation to include everything from psychological consciousness-raising to restructuring the urban environment. Tish Sommers combined a winning blend of publicity, grass-roots politics, lobbying, and an understanding of the aged and women's movements with knowledge of how bureaucracy works. Hank Rasé was able to sustain a broad enough view to win the support of the anarchistic, antiestablishment environmentalist movement while at the same time successfully negotiating with the nation's spokespeople for large-scale technology. In fact, they find it necessary to live quietly in the area between public and private—giving allegiance to neither but knowing how to manipulate both.

On the public side, grantspeople are not rebels against bureaucracy. They may circumvent it by appealing to the public (through lobbying), but those alternatives are only chosen when the direct approach fails. These grantspeople are capable of giving back to bureaucracy its own language or artfully appealing to the spirit behind the rules and regulations when the literal interpretation fails to work. Or they might adopt the tactics of the muckraker, using the letter of the law as leverage to expose illegal informal practices of the bureaucrats. Grievance procedures, affirmative action strictures, civil rights laws, public information, and networks of contacts are all resources to which the grantsperson has access. To the grantsperson it is really not a sneaky, dishonest activity to manipulate bureaucracy in this way. By getting support for his project, he is doing something that government wants done but cannot do itself. So, the grantsperson is actually complementing government rather than just slipping his pinky into the federal till.

Beside feeling at home in the governmental briarpatch, the successful grantsperson is no stranger to business. He is comfortable with the language of "cost/benefit," "social investment," and "risk capital." Unlike most governmental planners our grantspeople understand when, how, and why to compete. Successful grant-seekers know how to help industry improve its public image, how to build links between grant projects and business developments, how to present a program to a businessman that is not only tax-deductible but will actually help strengthen the free enterprise system.

In addition to this ability to encompass both public and private sectors, our exemplary grantspeople are flexible in another sense. They are able to relate both to the beginning and ending of a project as well as to its harrowing in-between phases. Most people either generate ideas or put them into practice. In conventional society, the visionary and the manager are rarely the same. However, since grantspeople have such a strong commitment to their idea, they are capable of preserving its intention as it passes through the hands of funder, sponsor, staff, and client. *Homo gran-*

tus must alternate between acting as an advocate and as a mediator, sometimes defending the project against the uninformed and at other times interpreting differing points of view dispassionately so that the concept becomes broad enough for others to discover as their own.

The final challenge to grantspeople is to give up control over his own inspirations so that others may become grantspersons too.

The successful grantsperson has the right combination of entrepreneurism and breadth of perspective to make a grants program work. By lining up his own personal interest with the public interest expressed by any grants program, he or she is capable of being outrageously successful not only as a "change agent," but also as a powerful person who is in an ideal position to learn how the world works.

III

Finding Your Way into the Briarpatch

At the heart of the grants culture is a wide and colorful array of funding species—everything from affable eccentrics motivated by vanity and whim, who, if they like what you propose, may pull a crumpled check out of a pocket, fill it in, and send you on your way (e.g., we know of a young hospital staff member who assembled a simple preliminary proposal for a hospice for the terminally ill and sent it off to a number of local philanthropic groups. Without further effort—no phone calls, no follow-up letters, no conferences, no inspection of her credentials or intentions—one sent her a check for $38,000 in the return mail), to dogged plodding government officials buried in labyrinthine mazes of authorization sheets, disbursement vouchers, review cards, and reporting forms. As your experience in the grants world grows, you will encounter a broader and broader spectrum of these creatures, and you will probably tell yourself—with a rueful grimace and a shake of the head—that you just can't generalize about funders . . . that they come in all shapes and sizes, and that you can never know what you are likely to run into next.

Well, you can generalize, and you should. Despite the diversity, which certainly does exist and which we try to organize for you in this chapter, there are common values and perspectives that nearly every funder shares. To be sure, there are fringes in the funding world, as there are in any social group, where the predominant values are either ignored or distorted in pathetic or amusing ways. But by far the largest part of the funder population follows generally logical and predictable patterns of behavior in responding to grant applications. Knowing what these are and why they exist can make your hunt that much quicker, more direct, and rewarding.

Understanding what the funder is like may strike you as irrelevant and boring, especially if you are like most novice grantspeople who want to leap right out onto the trail of the nearest grant and track it to its lair as quickly as possible. Once the irresistible scent of money comes wafting over the landscape, it is nearly impossible for most people to calm their hunting instincts, tighten their belts, and settle back patiently to try to understand what they are stalking, even though they would admit at this point that they don't really have much of an idea just what kind of an animal it is that they should be looking for. They don't understand that the shotgun approach—where you just blast away at anything that moves on the funding landscape in the hope that you will knock something down—doesn't work here.

By this point, having read the first chapters of this book you are already far better equipped for the grants chase than 99 percent of the other grantseekers around. You know something about the existence, the nature, and the purpose of the grants economy itself. You know how the grantsperson can realize the possibilities of grants, and you know something about the challenges that you must respond to in order to succeed in the grants world. You also have been able to shape your concept into an idea that resonates to the funder's perspectives. Now you realize that you are beginning to get inside the grants culture, to see grants from a point of view that is sophisticated enough to encompass not only your needs and wishes, but also those of the funder, the clients of your service, and of others working in your field. Your hunt for the funder has transcended the process of simply bagging the game; like the native American of a century ago, you are beginning to realize how reverence for the spirit of the prey can make both you and it stronger as it sacrifices its existence for you.

But you also have a lot to learn.

Stand on the edge of the grant preserve and listen quietly for a moment. Hear that crashing in the underbrush all around, those mutterings and groans? That is not, as you might at first think, the cry of the wounded grant animal; it is all those other hapless applicants, poachers who stole impatiently into the funding world without adequate preparation and who are now finding, much to their shock and sorrow, that what may look from a distance like a well-manicured and spacious park, with broad paths and carefully tended grounds, can, on closer inspection, turn into a dense and impenetrable jungle, thick with swamps and snags. Any minute now, you'll see granthunters stumble back out into the light, scratched, bleeding, and frustrated.

What are the reasons for all this wasted motion? Why do so many grantseekers loathe and fear the chase?

Because nearly all of them hunt in bad faith, seduced by the pathological mentality of the Beggar or the Thief. Most would deny this, indignantly, but it is still true. Underlying their pose of righteous altruism is the sneaky feeling that they are getting away with something, that the funder is really in charge, and that they are lucky to be getting any support at all. They don't actually feel that they *deserve* a grant.

BEGGARS AND THIEVES

When beggars look for a grant, they do so like supplicants, approaching a powerful father figure and humbly requesting him to bestow gifts and donations, to take pity on them. Unable to see the implicit exchange, unaware of the larger implications of the grants economy, they cannot believe that the funder needs them as much as they need him. So they ask for charity, and once funded, they annually whine for the renewal of the favor. Beggars confuse the grants economy with the welfare system, which reinforces dependency and teaches the recipient to be helpless. Beggars rarely become self-sufficient.

As John May, the founder of the San Francisco Foundation, put it:

> [Supplicant is] . . . a word which is very common in this business . . . And this is something I think people in my trade have to steer away from like the plague . . . the idea that people are supplicants, or that we're doing

them a favor. We're just doing our part of the bargain, and they're doing us a favor if they bring us an opportunity to put our one little ingredient, which is money, into some thing all the other ingredients of which are present. So that our part, the thing we can kick in, is going to be a key factor in doing something that's really very badly needed.[1]

Thieves, on the other hand, are either completely cynical about the grants system or else they think of themselves as Robin Hood, righteously nabbing their fair shares of the bucks for a client group that may actually not exist. Thieves are very suspicious of the funder's motives, since they project into grantors their own distrust, often attributing to funders nothing more elevated than a desire to escape taxes. They are also adept at skirting the strings attached to grants. Thieves are inclined to go after any available money, often by wrenching their program objectives—if there are any—into a shape that they imagine will please the funder. Otherwise, the thief spends a lot of time on the prowl, looking for the perfect funder, one who gives without conditions.

YOUR FUNDER IS YOUR FRIEND

If somehow the beggar or the thief does get funded, chances are very good that his relationship with the funder will sour. Refunding plans will fail and the beggar-thief will leave the grants field muttering bitterly. Why? Because he overlooked the partnership that is intrinsic in the grants exchange and secretly feels that asking for money is somehow demeaning. If he's a beggar, he turns the sense of alienation inward; if he's a thief, he turns it outward. Neither understands the logic and integrity of the grants transaction. Both fail to learn that the funder needs them just as much as they need the funder. The proper role of the grantsperson is that of partner with the funder, who complements the funder's role by transforming the enormous potential of the granting process into specific designs for change.

Good funders understand that their true role is that of a guardian, who stands along the border between the grant preserve and the larger world, watching to prevent imposters or frauds from

[1]The Regents of the University of California, *Bay Area Foundation History,* Vol. 1., The Bancroft Library, University of California, Berkeley, 1976, p. 97.

entering, but also waiting to open the gates to those who approach correctly, with insight, confidence, and dignity.

What does this mean for you, the grantsperson, who must find a way to gain access to the funding world? It means that you must become the counterpart of the guardian, a steward, one who is entrusted to help bring the power of grants to bear in the real world. If you properly understand and embody the knowledge that grants come from all of us and must be returned to us all, to try and help improve our common lot, you will find that your way into the grants world is open.

What it all comes down to is this: You have an obligation first to be convinced of the genuine merit of your project, and then second, to educate your funder as to its value and its potential for promoting real change. As John May points out, sophisticated funders recognize their need to be open to new ideas, and they seek opportunities to become excited and challenged by an applicant's vision. So, the most powerful attitude to adopt in approaching funders is not one of out-guessing the funder, of "getting your fair share of the bucks," but the slightly more audacious one of educating them to the value and need for your project.

FROM GENUS TO SPECIES: A FUNDER TAXONOMY

Although they share a common role, funders vary, and an appreciation for their individual styles is necessary if you are going to be able to communicate with them, to convince them of the significance of your purpose. You will encounter an endless variety of individual styles in your funder contacts that can be placed into one of the four general types of funder: Corporate, Private Foundation, Community Foundation, and Government. These four paradigms fall neatly into distinct places along a continuum, ranging from the most private funders on the left to the most public on the right.

Corporate	Private Philanthropic	Community Philanthropic	Local, Regional, State, Federal Government
Granters	Foundations	Foundations	Funders

←——private sector——→←——public sector——→

In the remainder of this chapter, we consider each of these kinds of funder. In each case, we describe the characteristics of each particular funder type, followed by a profile of a sample member of that funder category, and conclude with a description of the tools and resources that will help you find your own grantmakers in that branch of the funding world. Remember that this information is just a beginning that helps you go directly to the process of developing your own individual working relationships with prospective funding partners.

CORPORATIONS

Corporate giving is the smallest but in some ways the most intriguing component of the private philanthropic sector. The Filer Commission (the Commission on Public Needs and Private Philanthropy) has called it "the last major undeveloped frontier for private giving to philanthropic causes."[2]

The basic facts about the corporate giving record are these: About 2 million corporations currently file income tax forms in the United States. Each one is entitled and encouraged to deduct up to 5 percent of its profits (pretax net income) for donations to tax-exempt, nonprofit organizations. However, although corporations control far, far more wealth than foundations do, in 1976 the total amount thus deducted by all American corporations put together was only about $1.3 billion, or roughly two-thirds of the amount granted that year by American foundations. Because most of these foundations were in strong tax positions already, each dollar that they *did* give only "cost" them about 50 cents. So they were really giving only about 33 cents for every dollar that was granted by a foundation. Finally, almost all corporate granting is done by a very tiny fraction (about 1/2000th, or roughly 1000) corporations in operation and these tend to be the giants.

Furthermore, the corporations that make grants tend to consistently do so at about 20 percent of the level allowed them by the Internal Revenue Service. Instead of deducting the full 5 percent, their contributions are down at about the 1 percent mark and have

[2]*Giving in America,* op. cit., p. 154.

remained more or less stuck at that level since World War II. (One Treasury Department official, Gabriel Rudney, former Committee Coordinator of the Treasury Advisory Committee on Private Philanthropy, agrees that although corporate giving levels are rapidly rising in absolute terms, as net income rises, he predicts that this percentage will continue at roughly the same level for the foreseeable future.) The cash grants that are made tend to be small—averaging about $500 or so—about half the size of the "average" foundation grant. Also, corporations tend to give to the most well-established, secure, noncontroversial applicants.

Critics argue that the corporate giving record is dismally poor. The Filer Commission itself, hardly a radical body, has stated: "The record of giving by the corporate world as a whole in the mid-70's is . . . ultimately an unimpressive and inadequate one."[3] Other commentators, reviewing the figures above and comparing them to the grantmaking activities of foundations and government agencies, have come to the conclusion that corporations are shirking their social responsibilities. They point out, for example, that by not taking their full 5 percent deduction, corporations are in effect passively letting the government tax processes decide where their money will be spent, rather than making the most of an opportunity to exercise control over what their money goes to support. They are abdicating their right to direct the focus of their philanthropic contribution.

Or are they? Other analysts contend in response that corporations are very properly simply leaving the government's business, social welfare, up to the government. Who is right? This is a good question and a very complex one. Let's take a closer look at the issue.

First, it is important to understand that legally, there were until the early 1950s definite sanctions against mixing business with philanthropy. Based on the argument, formulated in the mid-nineteenth century, that corporations were first and foremost instruments of profit and that they exerted a positive influence on society by concentrating wealth and then redistributing it to shareholders, it was strongly felt that assigning them the responsibility for solving social problems would be dangerous. This point

[3]*Giving in America,* op. cit., p. 157.

of view held that the business of business is business and we all benefit most by not inhibiting the free play of market capitalism. In fact, there were legal barriers to any significant philanthropic involvement by corporations unless they could show that the action was of "direct benefit" to the corporate well-being.[4] Eventually these barriers to the free play of corporate generosity were broken by a landmark suit engineered in the early 1950s by Standard Oil of New Jersey over a grant to Princeton University. Why the dispute? It was partly intended to block proxy fights brought on by shareholder resentment of corporate giving programs. It was also because SO wanted to place control of its corporate philanthropy programs firmly in the hands of corporate management. Since then corporations have had a much freer hand to run their granting programs as they see fit, whether out of the goodness of their hearts or as a relatively surefire and inexpensive public relations vehicle. But, as we have already mentioned, the erosion of the direct-benefit stricture did not produce a sudden boom in the levels of corporate donations. Nor did the civil rights struggles of the 1960s, which generated a flurry of empty talk on both sides of the corporate wall. Although these events did give rise to an occasional public interest lawsuit and the rare socially responsive investment program, the bottom line has remained unchanged for over three decades.

What is different about the kind of grants made by corporations? For one thing, corporations have a recent record for supporting the ongoing operating expenses of social service projects, an event that is nearly unheard of in the foundation world. Corporate grantmakers are much more likely than any other kind of funder to make donations in the form of services and products, which have ranged in the past from pharmaceutical supplies to motorcycles to obsolete but still serviceable office equipment, job training programs, and professional and technical assistance provided by corporate personnel, often on company time. As of this writing, one large Midwestern corporation is reviewing a request made by a small rural school for a tractor for its agricultural classes.

[4]This topic was extensively covered in an issue of the *Grantsmanship Center News,* 1977, Vol. 3, No. 5, pp. 35–38.

It has been suggested by a prominent research firm that the value of these in-kind donations is at least equivalent to the value of the cash contributions reflected in corporate tax returns.[5] In other words, if it were possible somehow to account for all of the activities that a corporation undertakes for philanthropic purposes, through some kind of "social responsibility audit,"[6] corporate giving might be found to match and possibly even exceed the aggregate giving levels of philanthropic foundations.

In comparison with foundations, researchers note, corporations tend to favor support for civic activities. Both foundations and corporations tend to place an equal and relatively strong emphasis on grants for educational and health purposes. Until recently, few corporate grants went to scientific research or to large-scale capital improvement projects, but there are some signs of change in these areas.

One suggested interpretation of these differences is that those corporations making grants feel a stronger sense of commitment to the immediate community they operate in and a sense of responsibility to improve the quality of life in the cities where they are headquartered. Their interest in educational granting may also stem from a position of enlightened self-interest, since they often support programs for employees and their families and for the immediate labor pool from which future corporate employees will come.

There are solid arguments both for and against the status quo in corporate granting, as well as strong indications that many corporations have taken the Filer Commission's comments seriously and are now working to upgrade their granting programs. Let's take a look at a representative corporate program and see how it exemplifies what we have learned so far.

[5] *Giving in America,* op. cit., p. 153.

[6] At least one large Research and Development firm claims to have already developed the necessary accounting technology for just such an audit.

Profile of a Corporate Grantmaker: The Abex Group, Inc.

The Abex Group,[7] headquartered in Chicago, is one of the giants of America's corporate community. With worldwide sales of nearly $3 billion annually and a total staff of nearly 20,000 in branches all over the world, its potential for active, effective granting is enormous.

Abex originated in the 1920s as a wholesaler of grains and cereals. After World War II, it expanded into a number of retail markets and began to grow at an astonishing rate. Today it comprises four separate subdivisions, including a land development group, a chemicals and pesticide branch, a food processing and retailing group, and a drug company, each of which is located in a different part of the country.

The Abex Foundation was incorporated as a private foundation in 1938. It was originally intended to support research into ways to improve insecticides and to offer fellowship support to students who intended to pursue careers in related research fields, particularly in biochemistry and entomology. It remains a private foundation today, despite the fact that the Tax Reform Act of 1969 made this particular organizational structure a less flexible vehicle for corporate giving than before. For example, whereas a corporation can directly buy plates at a fund-raising dinner, a corporate foundation cannot.

The Abex Foundation tends to restrict about half of its giving to the greater Chicago area; managers in each of the four major corporate subdivisions also operate independent giving programs in their respective locations. The headquarters office will also occasionally make grants to groups with a national scope, since it recognizes that its own status as a business of national prominence implies some obligation to respond to national problems.

Jim McKinnon, the manager of the Abex Foundation, has been with the Abex Group for six years. He contends that there are a number of clear-cut differences between corporate and foundation giving practices. "We are in existence to make a profit. The people who run corporations are business people, not professional altruists, and they make no apology for the fact that their first alle-

[7]This is a fictional composite drawn from numerous real-life models.

giance is to make as much money as possible for their shareholders or owners. Philanthropy is not at the top of their list of priorities."

However, cautions McKinnon, that does not mean that the Abex commitment to its philanthropic program is not a serious one. "We recognize," he says, "that you can't operate a health business in an unhealthy community, so we're very interested in seeing that our grants go as far as possible toward alleviating the problems that anyone living in a contemporary urban American setting has to contend with." During the calendar year 1977, the Abex Foundation received well over 1,000 applications. It awarded less than one out of every ten it received, for a total number of approximately 90 grants, ranging from a low of $200 to a high of $15,000, and averaging around $2,000 each. The four autonomous subdivisions of Abex had contributed an additional $50,000 or so in their respective communities. The value of the various other types of contributions made by Abex, such as in-kind and United Way donations, brought the value of its total philanthropic contributions to nearly $950,000. Only about one-sixth of this figure was due to direct cash grants made by the headquarters foundation.

Most of Abex's grants go to the support of educational purposes, though the focus of support available has broadened since the foundation's inception. Abex makes grants of scholarship funds to children of Abex employees; it matches employee gifts to higher education institutions for amounts up to $500; and it participates in a student loan program administered by an independent, nonprofit insurance agency. McKinnon frankly admits that corporate giving tends to gravitate toward educational programs precisely because they are relatively noncontroversial and they appeal to corporations' natural instinct for self-interest, since they improve the quality of the work force and help promote better internal employee relations.

Beside grants for educational purposes, which account for 32 percent of the Abex giving program, the corporation also makes health and welfare grants (15 percent), civic grants (13 percent), cultural grants (13 percent), a few international grants (2 percent), and a large number of miscellaneous grants (25 percent), such as one for $500 to a national ecology institute.

McKinnon notes that one major difference between private philanthropy and the kind of corporate giving that he conducts is that corporations are quite willing to contribute to the ongoing operating expenses of nonprofit groups, usually those with a credible, established track record. Most foundations, by contrast, tend to shy away from this type of request and to look for highly promising new funding opportunities instead, or for relatively complete programmatic areas to underwrite.

However, McKinnon cautions that this is by no means a hard and fast rule, and he cites a clear exception to it from his list of 1977's miscellaneous grants. This particular donation, for $6,000, went to support a community juvenile relations board working in one of Chicago's ghettos. The group's objective was to promote a less severe alternative to outright jail for juvenile criminal offenders, as well as to enlist broad community support for, and involvement with, their efforts. The program worked like this: When the police apprehended a first-time juvenile offender, they gave him a choice: either to be taken to juvenile court or to appear before a community board composed of adults from the youngster's own neighborhood. The board attempted to settle disputes and redress crimes on an informal basis. For example, if kids were caught joyriding, they were required to pay for any damage to the car or other expenses and to apologize to the owner, but they were not arrested or formally charged. The Abex grant helped to pay for the costs of professional mediation training for prospective board members. The program has thus far been quite successful and has attracted the attention of the Department of Justice, which may set aside funds for its continuation within the next fiscal year. The fact that the grant applicants had the foresight to plan for future financial needs, which will probably be met by these government funds, was a definite factor in their winning Abex support, McKinnon believes.

Apparently responding to criticism by the Filer Commission and others about lackluster corporate granting performance since World War II, Abex is taking a new look at its giving program and is planning to increase its contribution percentage. "Abex," McKinnon adds, "is well aware of the price it pays for not running its own giving program as actively and efficiently as possible. We want to exercise as much control as possible over what our donations support."

According to McKinnon, there are also a number of specific types of applicants that Abex is very reluctant to make grants to, including individuals, religious groups, controversial social or political groups, and any organization that already receives extensive tax or United Way support.

Fiscal rectitude counts heavily with corporate grantmakers in weighing grant requests. Abex requires that applicants submit audited financial statements for the two years preceding the request. It also looks for the standard descriptive material: a general statement of organizational background and purpose, a description of the specific activities and budget for the grant requested, and a list of the organization's Board of Directors. In addition, all applicants must have tax-exempt status. Finally, Abex likes to know who the intended client group is and what kind of track record the applicant has.

Funding decisions are made every two months by a three-member Board of Trustees, all of whom are corporate officers.

How should applicants approach Abex? McKinnon says the same thing every other funder does: First get on the phone. Since corporate contributions can be handled by any one of a very large number of different corporate officers, including community affairs, public affairs, public relations, legal, the corporate secretary's office, or even the corporate treasurer, the best bet is to pick the corporation's general information number out of the phone book, call it, and ask whoever answers to connect you with the person who handles the company's philanthropic activities.

Finally, McKinnon urges grantseekers not to overlook one other very important type of granting: in-kind contributions of products, materials, equipment, and staff time and expertise. "The only thing that we have that foundations don't is plenty of people, products, and skills," he says.

For example, one very common type of in-kind contribution made frequently by Abex is printing services. McKinnon cites the example of a suicide-prevention group that needed to have bus cards designed and printed for display on Chicago's mass transit system. Once it learned of their request, Abex located a graphic artist on its staff who was interested in volunteering his time. The cards were soon designed, printed, and delivered back to the nonprofit group, a job that would have cost them thousands of dollars had they gone to a commercial printer. According to McKinnon, it is not at all uncommon for a large corporation to have a full-time in-house volunteer coordinator on its staff, whose job is to match outside requests and needs with available in-house skills and interests.

Researching Corporate Funders: Tools and Resources

If you are not a member of a well-established, national, highly visible, health-oriented service group, such as the National Council on Alcoholism, there are two main things to remember about corporate giving: (1) About 50 percent of it is highly localized, and (2) it depends heavily on personal contact. Unless your proposed project is in the same regional area as the corporate office or plant, you are probably not going to gain much support from the company.

As McKinnon points out, your first step is to get on the phone, call every corporation in your area that is big enough to have a philanthropic program, and make contact with whoever is handling it in each company. Describe your project briefly and try to get some immediate sense of whether it's worth your time and theirs to proceed to that next step, that of sending in a short discussion paper (see the sample below).

New Facility for Triumph Industries

A Discussion Paper

SUMMARY

Triumph Industries, a workshop for the severely handicapped, proposes the expansion of its present facility in South Seattle from the 26,000 square footage of its current leased site to 65,000 square feet in a new building. Costing an estimated $1.4 million, the construction would more than double the number of clients served by Triumph, but what is perhaps more important, it would also convert the workshop into a research, development, and training facility that would demonstrate effective management practices to sheltered workshops throughout the northwest region.

Recognized since 1957 as a leader in cost-effective organizational procedures, Triumph in its new site will apply its model program to new areas of industrial and commercial production to show how the severely handicapped, when properly supervised, can enter promising areas of employment now thought to be closed to the disabled. Funds for this project will be obtained from a combination of loans, government grants, and private contributions. The planning phase is scheduled to begin soon; final construction and phase-in of new programs is scheduled for completion at the target date of January 1982.

To get a broad overview of trends in corporate granting, you might want to contact the Conference Board, Inc., 845 Third Avenue, New York, N.Y. 10022, which is a nonprofit research firm in the area of business economics. It has a section on corporate philanthropy and has published several small books in the field, such as *Corporate Philanthropic Public Service Activities.* In 1976 the Board began a series of annual surveys of corporate contributions based on interviews with over 700 of the leading corporate donors.

Finally, you should know about one interesting new source of corporate granting: the chambers of commerce. The national U.S. organization has set up its own foundation, called the National Chamber Foundation, which is now working with 2,500 local affiliates, 1,300 professional and trade associations, and 68,000 corporations to develop and systematize donation programs. Their first step will be to hold a series of regional conferences where participants can meet and share information.

If you are not sure which corporations in your area are likely prospects, or even which corporations operate in your area at all, there are a couple of standard reference works that will give you all the information you need to start the search: *Standard & Poor's Register of Corporations, Directors, and Executives,* and *Dun & Bradstreet's Reference Book of Corporate Management.* The first, published each year, contains information on 35,000 corporations and about the same number of officers, directors, and other corporate principals. The second focuses on officers of those 2,400 corporations whose revenues account for 80 percent of the Gross National Product. It contains such biographical tidbits as the individual's age, educational background, experience, and business affiliations.

Also, *Fortune* magazine publishes an annual list describing the

500 largest corporations in the United States. Your library will surely have a well-thumbed copy.

Although relatively few corporations operate foundations, you will still want to check the *Corporate Foundation Directory.*[8] This work lists corporate foundations and foundation officials (both directors and trustees) in a series of indexes, arranged alphabetically by the foundation name, by state, by the field of interest, by the parent company (not all corporate foundations have the same name as their sponsoring corporation), and by the types of grant made.

PRIVATE FOUNDATIONS

Foundations are institutions established by individuals, families, and some communities that are able to promote the common good by using their advantageous tax status to redirect the power of privately accumulated wealth into programs of social research, invention, education, and application.

There are approximately 30,000 foundations in the United States today. They annually disburse funds—about $2 billion in 1976—that represent only a very small fraction of those distributed each year through government granting programs, but which are relatively free of the complex strings that are invariably attached to government grants, and which are sizable enough in absolute terms to hold the potential for sparking substantial social changes.

Among the many issues that the Filer Commission investigated were the specific ways in which foundation funding differed from the patterns of government funding.[9] Stated succinctly, the Commission concluded that:

1. Despite the surge of governmental support for biomedical research in the 1970s, foundations still place great emphasis on medical education and training and certain specialized areas of research.

[8]Jean Brodsky, ed., Taft Corporation, 1000 Vermont Avenue, N.W., Washington, D.C. 20005

[9]In particular, see Michael S. Koleda, Daniel Bourgue, and Randall Smith, "Foundations and the Federal Government: A Look at Spending Patterns," in the Commission's *Research Papers,* Department of the Treasury, 1977, pp. 1679–1688.

2. Foundations proportionally earmark a far greater percentage of their grant dollars for higher education, particularly for private education, than the federal government does, especially for research, capital investment, and training. Most federal support for higher education takes the form of student loans, which, since they are rarely repaid, might more accurately be considered student grants.
3. Foundations emphasize scientific training and capital improvements, especially construction projects, more than the federal government does.
4. While government may soon get the upper hand, foundations outspend it for arts and humanities projects, both absolutely and proportionally.

Although it represents only a tiny fraction of the total grants made in any given year, foundation giving is more flexible than government granting, since it is not obliged to contend with large political constituencies, vociferous special interest lobbies, bureaucratic civil service empires, and elaborate rules and regulations developed for implementing government grant programs. On the debit side, private sector spending, whether it is done by corporations, private foundations, or affluent individuals, is much more susceptible than government granting is to very personal biases.

Despite the fact that there is less money available, there are definite advantages to be gained in exploring private rather than public grant-making sources. For one thing, the application process is usually much simpler than it is for applications to a government agency. The funding priorities of private funders are often less rigidly defined than those of federal and state programs, and staff members of private foundations are often more responsive, since they are not insulated by densely compacted layers of a bureaucracy. People in the private granting world usually have a refreshingly direct and active sense of responsibility for their grant programs.

Also, the small private funder tends to respond more quickly to grant applications. The time lag between submitting an application and learning the response to it is much shorter than it is for government sources, most of which operate according to firm submission deadlines. Private grantors, on the other hand, are much more open to considering "unsolicited" proposals, which can be submitted at any time.

Finally, if a foundation or corporation has an ideological bias of one kind or another, it is usually made quite a bit more obvious sooner than government agencies can afford to make theirs.

There are three major subdivisions of the general category of philanthropic foundation. About half of all foundation grants are made by *general purpose foundations.* These are the largest funding agencies in the foundations world, and the most well known. The Rockefeller Foundation, for example, is a general purpose foundation.

There are also a number of large foundations that can best be described as *special purpose foundations,* which simply means that they have a strong or exclusive interest in making grants in a specific programmatic area, such as health research. The Robert Wood Johnson Foundation is an example of a special interest foundation.

By far the majority of the 30,000 philanthropic organizations in the United States are very small, private foundations. Most of these are *family foundations.* They tend to have limited financial resources, no staff, and to be controlled closely by the donor or the donor's family, whose personal interests are often reflected in their funding patterns.

Until fairly recently, there was a discernible geographical bias in the distribution of the grants made by large philanthropic foundations. Most of their granting was concentrated in the heavily urbanized areas of the Northeastern United States and the Great Lakes area.

Profile of a Private Foundation: The Rosenberg Foundation

For forty years, San Francisco's Rosenberg Foundation[10] has been one of the pacesetters of philanthropy. Founded in 1935, the foundation was established as a way of focusing the Rosenberg family wealth, acquired through a fruit packing business, on ways to help improve the quality of life for the people of California's rural areas. Over its lifetime, the foundation has achieved a strong

[10]There are about two dozen Rosenberg Foundations across the country.

record of support for early childhood development projects and projects addressing the role of the adolescent in society. It also has a firm tradition of involvement with migrant farmworker issues in California.

Rosenberg grants consistently tend to accomplish the ultimate result that the granting system is designed for: significant social change. For example, during the mid-1950s the foundation played a central role in the creation and maintenance of a migrant health program, one that has now expanded to the national level, with a federally supported network of about 300 facilities in rural locations across the country. In effect, the Rosenberg Foundation's initial support for this solution triggered the establishment of an entirely new health service delivery system.

As another example: In 1956, a school administrator working in one of California's richest agricultural regions, the San Joaquin Valley, came to the Rosenberg Foundation with a problem. Simply stated, he was having trouble with children who were disrupting classrooms and hindering the educational process. They had been diagnosed as having learning disorders, usually due to emotional stresses caused by unstable family situations. What the administrator wanted was what we would now call a counseling service, one that would involve parents and school staff members as well as the troubled children themselves—not a new idea in the 1970s, perhaps, but a radical one in the 1950s in a rural California community. The overall goal of the program was straightforward: Get the children back into the classrooms, back to studying and, hopefully, learning.

The project that the foundation eventually funded was also relatively straightforward, with one cost-cutting exception. Since the school really had no need for a full-time psychological counselor, it was decided to use an expert consultant at periodic intervals rather than add unnecessary staff costs to the project budget. A prominent child psychiatrist was retained to help establish and guide the program. On an as-needed basis, he flew to the project site from his home in northern California. Thus the paradigm of a rural medical service delivery system—one that imports expertise only when needed—was born, one that is just now beginning to receive national and international attention.

One of the first of its kind in the state, the program was an unqualified success. The California Legislature was sufficiently inspired by its example to enact laws making special education counseling available in other California schools. A Special Education Department was established at a major San Francisco area university, again with the help of Rosenberg support; it continues to offer a very highly regarded degree program.

Other examples of areas where the Rosenberg Foundation has been at the forefront of social trends are probably countless. They include crisis phone lines for runaway teenagers, art workshops for institutionalized children, rural family counseling services, drug rehabilitation programs for teenagers, and better grievance procedures for juveniles involved with crime. In most cases, the eventual impact of the initial Rosenberg grant has been unpredictably far-reaching, a phenomenon that ex-Rosenberg Executive Director Ruth Chance calls "the serendipity effect."

If there is one word that best describes the role of current director Kirke Wilson in Rosenberg-supported projects, it is *commitment.* For example, noting the difficulty that spontaneous grass-roots efforts have traditionally encountered in attracting and sustaining long-term financial support, especially from government and school district budgets or from United Way organizations, Wilson described in some detail his current efforts to propel the best projects funded by the foundation into positions of greater eligibility for "hard" funding. For instance, he has persuaded the United Way branch in San Francisco to create a "provisional" category for service projects, one that is used to designate those that are qualified in every respect for United Way funding but have not yet actually been brought into its funding cycle. Wilson also has begun using a system that projects future revenues and costs for projects in an effort to pinpoint more accurately just when they will probably begin to run into cash flow problems.

"And," Wilson added, "it's not just a problem of bringing the newer projects up to snuff. The problem of hard funding is even more complex because it's difficult to predict where long-term support will be available in the future. Government budget priorities change. Budget committees for the United Way–type funders are recomposed every year, so you have no real idea what next year's priorities will be."

Wilson made it clear that he expects the difficulty of securing long-term funding to lead to the emergence of proportionally more short-term, ad hoc grant projects, especially advocacy projects, intended solely to expose existing institutional deficiencies and urge appropriate changes. This type of project is effective only as long as the inequities it attacks persist; once change begins to take place, it phases out, having accomplished its objectives. As Mrs. Chance puts it, in these cases "to be short-lived is not necessarily to fail."

Both Wilson and Mrs. Chance agree that the mushrooming of governmental grant programs in the last two decades has imposed a new task on private philanthropies, that of taking more time to assure that foundation grants do not simply duplicate the support available from federal or state tax resources. For example, foundations have tended to withdraw from criminal justice areas in the last few years because the Department of Justice's Law Enforcement Assistance Administration has been pumping money into the kinds of social service projects aimed at juvenile and adult offenders that attracted foundations in the 1960s. However, adds Wilson, it is entirely conceivable that foundations may again be drawn into these areas if government funding begins to dry up again. From his point of view, the object is to see that relatively scarce foundation dollars go where they are most effective: to support the most potentially valuable social change experiments, especially those that are so new or radical that they would have trouble finding grants from other sources.

Although foundations are usually careful to avoid *duplicating* government funding programs, most of them, like the Rosenberg Foundation, are open to proposals that suggest a collaboration between public and private funders, one in which each grantor complements the resources of the other. For example, a Rosenberg grant supported a cabinetmaking workshop that was designed as a separate, self-contained employment training component of a Self-Help Housing Program for migrant farmworkers in the 1950s. The other components were entirely supported by two federal agencies, and the program was quite successful. Most foundations will also consider making direct grants to supplement the budgets of government agencies if the need is great and the lack of alternative resources can be convincingly demonstrated.

Wilson also described an instance in which the Rosenberg Foundation played an instrumental role in helping a small nonprofit community action group cut through intermediate-level, governmental red tape to gain access to a federal grant program that they knew they needed and could qualify for. The grant began with a sophisticated move by a local nonprofit group, that of educating their prospective funder. They approached Rosenberg and pointed out that the San Francisco school district was the only one in the entire nation of any size that was ignoring a federal formula grant program that had money available for school breakfasts for elementary school students in disadvantaged neighborhoods. The community itself knew of and wanted the program, and the federal agency involved wanted to make the money available, but the program rules and regulations required that the application come from the Local Education Agency, which was, in this case, as in most others, the local school district. That is where the bottleneck was, in the district office, where a mid-level bureaucrat simply would not move ahead with the application.

Once alerted to the problem, Rosenberg began working closely with community leaders. Community needs were carefully documented; the program's suitability for area residents was thoroughly established; and Wilson himself provided some minor but necessary technical assistance, helping to fill out the necessary application forms. With the coordinated push made possible by Rosenberg support, the application was completed and submitted; the funds were released; and the program was launched.

Its efforts to maximize the effect of its grants also mean that there are some funding areas the Rosenberg Foundation consciously avoids. For example, one role that the foundation will not undertake is that of the local "match," the community source that makes it possible for a group to qualify for federal grants by putting up a portion of the requested budget, usually ranging from 10 to 50 percent. According to Wilson, the view of the Rosenberg Foundation is that contributing a matching grant, although it may indeed free sizable chunks of federal money, places the foundation in a less effective, reactive posture.

The foundation also declines proposals for grants for medical research; grants to individuals; grants to support the ongoing operating expenses of an established nonprofit organization; grants for capital or endowment expenses; and grants in highly specialized technical areas, where the authenticity of the project's potential contribution cannot be accurately assessed by the well-informed, intelligent lay person, such as those who make up the Rosenberg's staff and board.

Unlike many funders, such as most corporations, the Rosenberg Foundation *will* consider making grants known as "expenditure responsibility" awards. These are grants made to newer projects and groups that do not yet have tax-exempt status. Because making a grant to such a group can mean additional programmatic and financial reporting requirements for the funder, most grantors require that applicants already have obtained their tax-exempt status, so as to avoid possible liability if the grant is misused, but the Rosenberg Foundation does not feel especially concerned about this stricture. For that matter, the IRS itself is on record as stating that grant recipients must either have obtained tax exemption *or be eligible for it* [emphasis ours]. In other words, already having the papers is not absolutely necessary, from the point of view of the IRS. Most funders, however, feel safer granting to those who are already certified as tax-exempt. Occasionally, the Rosenberg Foundation will initiate a joint funding arrangement with another funder, such as the San Francisco Foundation, whose status as a community foundation allows it to make grants without having to comply with the expenditure responsibility requirement.

What is the scale of Rosenberg grantmaking? As of the end of 1976, according to *The Foundation Directory* (which we discuss in detail in the following section of this chapter), the Rosenberg Foundation had assets amounting to about $16 million. During the calendar year 1976, which was also the foundation's fiscal year, it distributed a total of almost $700,000 to forty-three separate grant projects, ranging in size from $500 to $50,000. This was not the foundation's biggest year. In 1971, it allocated $824,590 in sixty-eight separate grants.

Because it is a private foundation, the Rosenberg Foundation is subject to a 4 percent "audit" tax on revenues from its investments. It is also obliged to pay out in grants each year an amount equal to either all of its investment revenues, or a fixed percentage of its assets, whichever is larger. This creates pressure, according to Wilson and other philanthropists, to make wise investments, those that will meet IRS tax and payout requirements from revenues rather than capital. Many foundations are also concerned that their investments be made in socially responsible areas. The Rosenberg Foundation, for example, has a Financial Policies Committee that reviews the social appropriateness of its investments.

For some years after its inception, the Rosenberg Foundation would probably have been best categorized as a family foundation, since its assets remained in the Rosenberg business, the board was composed of Rosenberg family members, and its funding interests were determined by family inclinations. This is still the case with many private foundations today, and it can lead to very narrow, self-serving funding patterns. But not necessarily, as Wilson is quick to point out. It is equally true that some of the most enlightened, risky, and innovative granting being done in the country today is done by family foundations.

The central role of the Rosenberg family waned rather quickly. New members to the board were appointed from outside its ranks, and the funds were redirected into other investment areas. Today, the foundation would most likely be classified as a small, special-purpose, private foundation, one of the most effective in the nation.

Although Rosenberg once prided itself on responding to all inquiries with a personal reply, the sudden increase in the volume of applications since the 1960s has forced it to develop form letters to manage the flow of correspondence. The alternative of hiring additional staff members was rejected because this would reduce the amount of money available for grantmaking.

For every applicant that the foundation eventually funds, it receives at least 10 other proposals that it declines and an uncounted number of additional preliminary informational calls and inquiries. The total number of submitted proposals averages about 400 to 500 a year, but relatively few of these actually even fall within Rosenberg guidelines.

Wilson recommended that individuals or groups contemplating applying for funds from any foundation call first and briefly discuss their project idea with the director or another administrator. If the foundation is staffed (many small private foundations are not), this initial contact can give applicants a quick sense of whether their project is one that the foundation will even consider, thus saving them the wasted time of preparing and submitting a futile proposal. In the case of the Rosenberg Foundation the staff will ask a number of questions to see if the proposed project falls within Rosenberg guidelines, and will either invite further contact or discourage applicants from consideration of the Rosenberg Foundation as a potential funding source.

The foundation does prescreen applications through a sort of informal triage system. If you have already submitted a proposal elsewhere, you will be asked to refrain from submitting it to the Rosenberg Foundation until you've heard from your other prospective funder. This resistance to multiple proposal submissions is common in the grants world, and it points out the value of doing your homework first. Proposals that move from funder to funder get shopworn, and that decreases their chances of getting funded.

Once a proposal has been received by the foundation, it is reviewed by the staff. If the proposal seems to fall within Rosenberg guidelines and looks like something that the board will want to consider, a "face sheet" is prepared. This is a short (three-to-six-page) summary, written from the perspective of the foundation staff member, outlining the field, the concept, the applicant's background, and the plan of the proposed project.

Proposals are submitted to the board chronologically in the order in which they are received at the foundation's office. There is often a time lag of some months before proposals can be considered—no foundation should be approached as though it were a source of emergency funding; some lead time is always necessary.

Consideration by the board is the critical stage of the proposal review process. Unlike many foundation boards, who meet only once every three months, Rosenberg board members meet monthly. Wilson underscored the quality of their involvement in current issues and directions. They are not remote, insulated figures of authority.

Although the foundation's stated areas of priority interest are rural California, early childhood and adolescent socialization, Wilson cautioned against interpreting these categories too literally. As an example, he mentioned solar energy proposals. Although the general topic of energy research and application might at first seem quite unrelated to the Rosenberg's professed priorities, he explained that since the foundation has a long record of supporting migrant farmworker housing projects, it is entirely conceivable to him that a solar proposal linking its objective to the foundation's interest in improving the socioeconomic conditions of farmworker children could receive Rosenberg support. In short, foundation funding categories can be quite elastic, as we shall discuss in more detail later in this chapter. Declared priorities are a good first indicator of its likely initial interest in what you want to do, but they should not always be accepted rigidly.

In conclusion, Wilson strongly endorsed the idea that a foundation can and should be educated—particularly those that have limited staff resources. He, for one, welcomes imaginative and thoughtful expositions of new, emerging areas of potential for good grantmaking.

Researching Philanthropic Foundations: Tools and Resources

Unquestionably, the best starting point for research on funding prospects from philanthropic foundations is a review of the various publications and other resources of the Foundation Center. The Center is a nationwide, nonprofit organization that collects, analyzes, and disseminates information on philanthropic foundations. Its services and resources fall into three basic categories: publications, libraries, and computer data bases.

Publications

You may want to begin by reading *About Foundations: How to Find the Facts You Need to Get a Grant,* a Foundation Center booklet (forty-eight pages, plus two annotated bibliographies) that gives an explicit, step-by-step overview of the research process necessary for identifying potential funders. As an introduction and guide to the Center's information resources, *About Foundations* is invaluable. Other important Center publications are:

The Foundation Directory, 6th ed. This is a reference work that contains brief entries on the 2,818 largest U.S. foundations, that is, those with either at least $1 million in assets or that award at least $100,000 annually in grants. According to the Center, foundations included in the *Directory* make 80 percent of the grants awarded by U.S. foundations.

Each entry includes the foundation name, phone number, address, statement of purpose, total assets, amount of grant dollars awarded, range of grants made, names of officers and trustees, frequency of board meetings, and grant application steps. *Directory* information is indexed by the grant subject, foundation name, state, city, donors, and trustees/administrators.

Foundation Center Source Book Profiles. This is actually a subscription service, offering subscribers comprehensive three-to-six-page profiles on larger U.S. foundations. The service, which began in August 1977, includes foundations granting at least $200,000 annually. Information given on each foundation includes an analysis of giving patterns by grant type, recipient, and subject area; additional financial data on assets and grants awarded; sample grants; background information; application procedures; contact person; and officers and trustees.

Subscribers receive approximately 40 to 45 new profiles each month, as well as all those previously distributed (about 500 as of July 1978). A monthly subject index is also included.

Foundation Grants to Individuals. This is a specialized directory of the 1,000 foundations that the Center has been able to identify as making grants to individuals as well as nonprofit organizations. Entries represent grants to over 40,000 individuals, amounting to more than $56 million. The work is arranged by program area and contains a comprehensive subject index, as well as additional detailed information on each funder.

The Foundation Center National Data Book (2 vols.). In terms of the sheer number of foundations covered, this is by far the most comprehensive of the Foundation Center's many publications. Brief listings are included for *all* of the 22,000 or so active grantmaking organizations listed in 1976 and 1977 by the IRS as being private foundations. Volume I lists foundations alphabetically; Volume II arranges them by state and in descending order by the amount of grants annually awarded, that is, the largest giver to the smallest. Using Volume II, grantseekers can identify local foundations of a particular size operating in their zip code area or city.

The Foundation Grants Index. The *Grants Index* is a list of actual grants of $5,000 or more made by approximately 400 foundations that voluntarily report their grants to the Foundation Center. This is an extremely useful tool for identifying foundations active in a particular subject area. Although the *Grants Index* does not include all grants of $5,000 or more, it covers many of the larger, more active foundations. The Center currently estimates that the *Grants Index* covers 35 percent of all foundation funds awarded in a given year and 65 percent of all grants of $5,000 or more. The *Grants Index* is available in several different formats:

1. Current grant lists are printed in the bimonthly journal *Foundation News,* published by the Council on Foundations. Grants are arranged by foundation and by state. A key-word/phrase index and an index of recipients allow easy identification of specific grants of interest.
2. All grants reported to the Center during the year are also published in an annual volume. (*Grants Index, 1978,* is the latest edition.) Many of these grants have not been published previously in the *Foundation News.* Again, grants are arranged by foundation and by state with both a key-word/phrase and a recipient index. The annual volume also includes a broad subject index that indexes grants by geographic region.
3. The Center has used the *Grants Index* data base to generate computer listings of grants made in any one of 57 different subject categories. (See the complete list of available categories below.)

Each of these *COMSEARCH Printouts* lists all grants reported to the Center in that particular subject category during the year of record; 1978 is the latest year for which the printouts have been generated. Again, the grants are arranged by foundation and by state.

Foundation Center COMSEARCH Printout Categories

COMMUNICATIONS

1. Films, documentaries, media, and audiovisuals
2. Television, radio, and communications
3. Journalism and publishing

EDUCATION

16. Public primary and secondary education
17. Independent primary and secondary education
18. Higher education—buildings and equipment
19. Higher education—general support
20. Higher education—special projects
21. Higher education—scholarships
22. Higher education—fellowships, loans, and other student aid
23. Libraries
24. Educational research, administration, and personnel development
25. Vocational counseling, and career and adult education

HEALTH

31. Medical education
32. Medical research
33. Dentistry, nursing, and public health
34. Hospitals—buildings and equipment
35. Hospitals—programs
36. Medical care, rehabilitation, alcoholism, and drug abuse
37. Mental health

HUMANITIES

46. Art and architecture
47. Dance, theater, and performing arts
48. Music
49. Museums
50. Historical projects

POPULATION GROUPS

61. The aged
62. The handicapped
63. Women
64. Minorities—general
65. Blacks
66. Native Americans, Hispanics, and Orientals

PHYSICAL AND LIFE SCIENCES

76. Agriculture, biology, and nutrition
77. Chemistry, physics, and mathematics

78. Environmental programs, and marine and earth sciences
79. Computer technology and engineering

SOCIAL SCIENCES

86. Economics and business
87. Government and political science
88. Legal programs and law schools
89. Psychology and sociology

WELFARE

91. Public interest, citizen participation, and consumerism
92. Urban development, housing, and transportation
93. Community funds
94. Crime and delinquency
95. Social agencies
96. Family services and population studies
97. Child welfare
98. Young men's and women's associations
99. Boy(s) and Girl(s) Scouts and clubs
100. Youth programs
101. Animal welfare
102. Rural development
103. Recreation, camps, and athletics

OTHER CATEGORIES

105. International grants—domestic recipients
106. International grants—foreign recipients
107. Religion—welfare and theology
108. Matching and challenge grants
109. Conferences and seminars

Libraries

In addition to distributing numerous types of publications, the Foundation Center also maintains three different types of foundation-information libraries around the country: national collections, field offices, and regional cooperating collections.

The Center's home offices in New York and Washington, D.C., both have a national collection of documents covering a wide array of pertinent topics on all U.S. foundations. The Center's two field offices in San Francisco and Cleveland each have collections that focus on their respective eleven-state areas, but which also include information on national and regional foundations.

Finally, the Center has established regional cooperating collections in over sixty public, foundation, or university libraries around the country. (See the list in Appendix A for exact addresses.) These regional collections primarily cover the foundations located in their state. Each regional Center library has a complete set of Foundation Center publications, foundation annual reports, and copies of the information returns that private foundations are required to file annually with the IRS. All Center libraries are open to the public free of charge.

Computer Data Bases

Three of the published volumes described previously—the *Grants Index,* the *Foundation Directory,* and the *National Data Book*—also have computerized counterparts that are updated continuously and can be highly flexible tools for acquiring current, customized information oriented to a specific funding interest. Access to these data bases is available either by directly contacting Lockheed's DIALOG Information Retrieval Service,[11] or by employing any local, computer-equipped information service to make the Lockheed contact for you.

If you are a member of the Foundation Center's Associates program, you receive, among other services, direct access to, and assistance with, custom computer searches.

In addition to the extensive information available from the Foundation Center's sources, you may want to cross-check your state's Registry of Charitable Trusts, which is customarily administered by the office of the attorney general of the state. Any nonprofit, tax-exempt organization will be listed there, in most states; access to these files is usually free and open to the public.

COMMUNITY FOUNDATIONS

Community foundations are public organizations serving a specific geographical area: a city, a local metropolitan region, or even

[11] 3251 Hanover Street, Palo Alto, Calif. 94304.

an entire state. They represent a small and specialized sector of the nongovernmental funding world that has been growing rapidly over the last decade. There are between 200 and 250 community foundations in the country today; almost every major urban area has at least one. Although community foundations currently control less than 10 percent of the total assets of private philanthropic institutions in the country, their share of these assets has been growing rapidly over the last decade. The Grantsmanship Center predicts that at their present rate of growth, community foundations may control as much as one-quarter of all foundation assets in the United States within the next decade.[12] Norman Sugarman, a contributor to the Filer Commission's *Research Papers,* notes that combined U.S. and Canadian community foundations made grants totaling $60 million in 1973.[13]

Community foundations differ in significant ways from both private foundations, on the one hand, and from regional or local chapters of fund-raising groups like the United Way, on the other. Unlike foundations, community foundations are usually classified as *public,* tax-exempt organizations by the Internal Revenue Service under the provisions of Section 501(c)(3) of the 1954 Internal Revenue Code. Thus they are not obliged to pay the 4 percent "audit" tax on their income from investments and endowments and, whereas private foundations are required by the IRS to pay out annually an amount equal to 6 percent of their assets, no such requirement is imposed on community foundations, though most do in fact, according to Sugarman, distribute their total revenues within a very short time—two years or so—after they are received. In order to qualify for this favored standing, community foundations are required to be much more accountable to the public in the geographical area that they serve than are private foundations. Also, a percentage of their annual income must come from public or government sources, and they must make an effort to inform the public about their giving programs, for example, by publishing annual reports. They must also be named after the area they serve. Finally, the distribution of grants by a community foundation must be managed by a committee or board that is representative

[12]*News,* Vol. 3, No. 4, pp. 29–51.

[13]*Special Behavioral Studies, Foundations, and Corporations,* Vol. 3, pp. 1689–1712.

of the community it serves, a fact that has served as a pressure for the same representativeness in many private foundations.

Community foundations also differ from more traditional fund-raising groups, such as United Way, primarily because they do not organize annual fund-raising drives, and they are not oriented toward relatively long-term support for a fixed group of service agencies. Community foundations rely heavily on bequests and endowments from affluent individuals and, like private foundations, distribute their funds on the basis of competitive proposal applications. Furthermore, community foundations are legally entitled to alter the terms of a bequest to suit it more closely to a community's needs if the original terms become outmoded or anachronistic. For example, a New England trust originally established in 1842 to benefit the crews of canal boats has recently been modified so that it can be used to benefit truckdrivers.

One highly characteristic aspect of most community foundations is that they have a clear and strong separation between the function of receiving, investing, and managing the endowed funds, which is usually handled by a bank, and the function of distributing the income from these funds in the form of grants. That means that no single person is in control of the foundation's funds. Most community foundations are organized either as mere trusts or as full-bodied nonprofit corporations, or a mixture of both.

Essentially, the differences between community foundations and private foundations are that (1) the community foundation must be accessible to and accountable to public interests, and (2) the community foundation be oriented toward supporting service projects within a specific geographical region.

Although the concept of the community foundation is at least half a century old, having originated in 1914 in Cleveland, it has become especially prominent in the last decade or so due to 1964 and 1969 tax law rulings that specifically favor the community foundation model over that of the private foundation. In fact, the IRS is on record as recommending to those private foundations that are unwilling or unable to meet tax and payout requirements to terminate by placing their assets at the disposal of community foundations in their areas. Sugarman cites data gathered in 1973 by the Council on Foundations showing that nearly half of the sudden jump in the growth of community foundations in the early 1970s seems to have been due to such terminations: about twenty community foundations responding to the survey indicated having received a total of about $60 million from ninety-one terminated private foundations.[14]

Profile of a Community Foundation: The San Mateo Foundation

San Mateo County is a prosperous, largely suburban area just south of San Francisco. It contains Stanford University, a large part of the nation's electronics industry, some of the most affluent residential areas in the San Francisco Bay Area, and all the problems of steadily increasing urbanization.

The San Mateo Foundation was established in 1964 to serve the area's 600,000-plus population. Its first full-time executive director, Bill Somerville, was named in 1974. Since he has been in charge of the Foundation, it has taken a number of dynamic new directions.

The San Mateo Foundation is supported by gifts, private foundations, corporations, and, primarily, the income received from 16 separate trust funds, amounting to $3.3 million in assets, which are managed by the eight major banks in the county. In 1977, the Foundation made 47 grants and authorized 12 more, for a total of 59 separate grants. The total dollar amount authorized equaled $326,013. An additional 31 donor-advised or designated grants, which the Foundation accepts only with some reluctance, added $26,969 to that sum.

The Foundation's gifts and income from investments were $402,652 in 1977, and its administrative costs for the same period were $66,000. Aside from its own operating expenses, all of the Foundation's income from investments and gifts was distributed or authorized in the form of competitively awarded grants.

Grants made by the Foundation in 1977 ranged in size from $50 to $20,000. Typically, according to Somerville, San Mateo Foundation grants fall into the $5,000 to $20,000 range, though the Foundation has made grants in the past as large as $60,000.

[14]Ibid., pp. 1691–1692.

The Foundation makes grants for nearly every purpose, except research, the creation of films and publications, and political activities, which are barred or carefully limited for every tax-exempt organization. Few of the Foundation's grants go to the support of capital expenditures, although it has helped local groups restore buildings of historical value in the past; Somerville notes that the Foundation is really still too small to seriously consider large capital allocation requests. The Foundation does make grants for the purchase of equipment on occasion, and it will consider furnishing the local share of a matching grant, but the major thrust of its distribution activities is directed at supporting the operating expenses, primarily salaries, for grantee organizations working in the human services field. The Foundation also makes grants to individuals, particularly to students for educational purposes, but such grants are only made through a nonprofit channel, such as a church.

There is only one other full-time staff member beside the executive director. In addition, one or two unpaid college-age student interns often work with the executive director. The Foundation's administrative costs, which cover salaries, insurance, phone, rent, equipment, travel, and a comprehensive library of funding resource material that is open to the public, amount to about 16 percent of its total annual revenues. Somerville notes that although this may seem like a high percentage from some points of view, he could easily distribute sixty times the amount of grant money each year that he does at present with no increase in administrative costs. It should be understood, he states, that a foundation with limited assets is generally more expensive to operate, on a relative basis, than one with very large assets.

The San Mateo Foundation's annual report states that it serves San Mateo County and the Palo Alto area. This definition is interpreted somewhat liberally, since Somerville acknowledges making occasional grants in communities that lie outside these boundaries. He cautions applicants in other communities to refrain from sending him proposals, since the vast majority of the Foundation's grants are made in the San Francisco peninsula area.

Following the usual organizational model for community foundations, the function of managing the investment program, which is handled by participating trustee banks, is clearly separated from the grant distribution function, which is handled by a distribution committee made up of five individuals, all long-time residents of the area and outstanding citizens. All have extensive experience with philanthropic activities; all are affluent; and all are white. Two of the committee members are appointed by the presidents of local higher education institutions; one is appointed by the Presiding Judge of the County's Superior Court; one is appointed by the President of the San Francisco Superior Court; and one is appointed by the trustee banks. The distribution committee meets quarterly, in February, May, August, and November of each year.

In order for a proposal to be considered by the Foundation's distribution committee, it must pass through a number of screening steps. First, according to Somerville, prospective applicants should simply call the foundation, and either request a copy of its application guidelines, or, preferably, speak with Somerville or his assistant, describe briefly the nature of the project for which they are seeking funding, and ask if it falls within general guidelines for consideration by the foundation. Once a proposal has been received by the foundation and reviewed, Somerville makes a site visit and talks with the applicant group. He also likes to consult with professionals working in related fields and to research the need for the proposed activity and the credibility of the applicant in a number of additional ways. "Essentially," he says, "I like to make grants because a project is good, and I have the means to find out if it is in fact good."

Finally, he prepares a two-to-three-page writeup of his findings, decides whether to recommend funding or rejection of the proposal to the distribution committee, and submits his findings to the committee three weeks in advance of each quarterly meeting. Out of forty proposals received, Somerville may recommend ten of these for funding consideration by the distribution committee, and perhaps five to seven of these ten will be funded. *Most proposals are turned down because they should not have been submitted to the Foundation in the first place,* like that submitted by an applicant from Ottawa, Canada.

The distribution committee has available to it *all* proposals received by the foundation for the quarter under consideration, including those that Somerville has recommended should be declined as well as those that he feels should be funded. They have the option of reversing any of his recommendations; in his four years of tenure as the Foundation's executive director this has not happened once.

Many things set the San Mateo Foundation apart from most other grantmakers; by and large, they stem directly from Somerville's own views on grantmaking. First and foremost, he emphasizes his preference for hearing an applicant describe the kind of world he or she envisions the grant will help to create. He is not interested, he stresses, in discussions that revolve solely around problem solving. "Americans," he asserts, "are far too problem-oriented. We're dealing with creative, energetic people here and I want to hear their positive, active views, not their proposed orientations to an impending crisis."

The foundation makes a point of making available information on funding sources and the grants process. It regularly, for example, sponsors community workshops on such topics as fund raising, proposal writing, the use of volunteer staff, and the location of prospective funders. The foundation also sponsors a funding resource library, available for consultation by the public.

Also, Somerville is not hesitant about actively looking for new ideas or promising grantees, and then initiating the grants process himself. "I do not see my job as just sitting back and answering the mail," he says. For example, asked to describe a project that he felt was a particularly innovative one, he told of reading in a local newspaper about a group that started a community computer center in East Palo Alto, which has a large minority population. Sponsored only by minimal bank loans at first, the members of this group rented a storefront, furnished it with cushions, and installed a simple computer. Then they began to invite grade-school classes to the community center to learn something about computers. Their overall objective was simply to demystify the computer, to make math and deductive reasoning processes more enjoyable and familiar to children by using progressively more complicated computer games to teach them something about using computers, and, for especially proficient students, even something about learning to program them. When he read about the group, Somerville got interested, so he called them up and asked if he could come over and look around. He liked what he found, and the outcome was a $6,000 grant from a source they had not even known existed before Somerville's visit: their local community foundation.

Although the foundation is not concerned about where participating banks invest its funds, it is, according to Somerville, legally obliged to insist that trustee banks strive to maximize the rate of return on these investments. He insists that banks not invest the foundation's assets conservatively. In mid-1978, the goal quoted by Somerville was an average annual interest yield of 7 percent.

Like most other grantmaking officials, Somerville is not only interested in finding new ideas to fund, but also in getting the most for his grant dollar. This translates into two concerns: (1) a desire to see that there is sound coordination between human services funding agencies in San Mateo County, thus reducing the risk of wasting precious grant dollars by unnecessary or pointless funding duplication, and (2) by carefully evaluating programs once they are underway.

Somerville points out that funding duplication is not inevitably bad: a project attempting to alleviate basic, critical needs for an enormous or severely deprived population probably needs all the funding it can get. But he does maintain continuous and careful liaison with other funders in the San Mateo County area, including private foundations, the United Way, corporations, and local government agencies. He was also instrumental in urging the county to establish a "partnership program," funded by an HEW grant, that allows human services groups to meet monthly under county auspices to discuss their programs with one another.

To properly evaluate grant-supported projects, Somerville feels that one must look first at who among all potential grantees *should* be getting grant support, and then second at how effectively and efficiently those groups who do receive it actually spend it. His own evaluations depend heavily on surprise site visits, which give him a chance to assess the strengths and weaknesses in a project. Somerville also reads local newspapers extensively to keep track of community activities, asks to be put on project mailing lists, and requests them to send him any reports that may be compiled on their program activities. A great deal of his time is also spent in contact with others working in related fields. From all these sources, says Somerville, he is able to get a good intuitive feel for how any project is doing.

Another part of Somerville's job is looking for new funds for the Foundation. "I probably only spend about 15 percent of my time on this end of the job," he says, "and that's not enough. I hate to ask for money, but I love to give it away." To attract potential donors, Somerville maintains continuous close contact with local probate attorneys and with bankers. He distributes press releases to local media organizations to keep the community informed of the Foundation's grantmaking activities. The Foundation prepares and makes available an annual report, as do most community foundations; one section of this report states: "The Foundation is supported by the community it serves. It actively seeks bequests and gifts from living donors. The Foundation's staff would be pleased to meet with prospective donors or their attorneys to discuss the creative use of donor funds and the tax advantages of charitable giving. Gifts to the San Mateo Foundation can include anything of value. Donors may give gifts of any size through cash grants, wills, trust agreements, life insurance, or transfers of property. Living gifts are as welcome as bequests. Suggested phraseology for utilizing the San Mateo Foundation by Will and other information for attorneys is available upon request."

As well as distributing annual reports, the San Mateo Foundation periodically distributes an announcement describing recent grants, something that relatively few other grantmakers do.

We asked Somerville about his failures: In what areas, we wondered, had he found the Foundation's grantmaking to be frustrating or ineffective. His response was twofold. First, he conceded that few of the projects supported by the Foundation, especially the new and innovative projects, had yet been able to achieve self-sufficiency. Some, of course, are not intended to last for more than a year, a month, or even a day. But others, such as the community computer center already described, not only had held the potential to become autonomous, but also, in Somerville's opinion, deserved to find long-term support. Thus far, however, not one Foundation-supported project has been able to find or develop hard, long-term funding. The computer center no longer exists.

The second part of his response was more nebulous and more disturbing. According to Somerville, not only do many grantees turn out to be inexperienced at managing simple business accounting, record keeping, and other procedures, but they will also refuse assistance in these and other areas when it is made available to them. Offers to grantees by the Foundation of various kinds of technical assistance have repeatedly fallen on deaf ears. In one case, according to Somerville, he had to send out three repeat mailings to school counselors in the San Mateo area to get any responses at all to an announcement about a funding workshop in an area pertinent to their field. In another case, three-quarters of his letters to grantees informing them of the availability of a retired county official who was experienced in establishing productive federal and state funding contacts went unanswered. "At best," asserts Somerville, "our grantees have lousy business instincts."

Finally, Somerville has some simple and explicit advice for those interested in applying for funds from community foundations in their areas. "Call," he says, "and don't bother looking at the annual report first: Just call, describe your project and find out if it is likely to be given further consideration. Then ask about guidelines for submitting the proposal."

Researching Community Foundations: Tools and Resources

Since community foundations must be accessible to the public, they are legally obliged to promote and maintain strong channels of information so that they can reach prospective applicants. The burden is very definitely on them to make sure that their community becomes aware of their existence, objectives, and grantmaking activities. This is why community foundations *must* name themselves after the community or geographical area they operate in, and why they *must* distribute annual reports. If you cannot find a community foundation named after your area listed in the phone book, try contacting the trust department of a local bank, the editorial offices of a local newspaper, or even a local probate attorney or two, to try to identify the community foundations located near you.[15]

However, once you have a name and a phone number, bear in mind that 80 to 90 percent of the 200 or so community foundations in the country today do not yet control even $1 million in assets, and, since it takes at least $3 to 5 million in assets before a foundation can afford to support full-time paid staff members, most try to make do with part-time volunteer administration. This means that a community foundation can seem surprisingly unresponsive to your efforts to contact it. But persevere. Once you make contact, describe your project, ask about their areas of interest, and see if you can obtain guidelines for submitting your proposal. Do not be discouraged when, after reaching the staff member, he tells you that he cannot fund your $10,000 project, since their maximum grants are for $3,000. Keep pressing: Does he know other foundations in the area that specialize in your subject matter? Can he help you get a loan instead? Are there local government programs that could help?

You may be surprised at how comprehensive his answers are. You see, community foundations and their staffs often play a network and clearinghouse role among local funders. They often coordinate regional associations of foundation executives, which usually meet at monthly luncheons in which an enormous amount of grants gossip is exchanged, including all-important information on who wants to fund what (see Appendix B for a list of regional associations). Some local foundations that can't afford their own staff often rely on the community foundations for knowledge about granting. So the staff members often get on the phone to put grantees and grantors in touch with each other or to arrange joint funding agreements among several.

GOVERNMENT FUNDERS

Although there are nearly 40,000 separate government bodies in the United States, most of which have some grantmaking role,

[15]The Council on Foundations, 1828 L Street, NW, Washington, DC, 20036, can provide you with a list of all the community foundations in the country and their addresses.

government funding is overwhelmingly dominated by the federal level's 1,400-odd Federal Domestic Assistance programs, which annually distribute billions of dollars to nonprofit organizations in every corner of the country. Estimates of the current total amount of these allocations range from a low of $40 billion to well over $100 billion, annually.

Where does it all go? The Social Security Administration figures that half of all federal, state and local taxes go to support social services, such as health clinics, subsidized housing, aid to the elderly and the disabled, food stamp subsidies, unemployment compensation, educational support, and veteran's benefits. HEW, the largest of all government grantmakers, had a budget of $128 billion for Fiscal Year 1978. It annually makes grants to over 50,000 separate recipients, most of whom are state and local governments, school districts, hospitals, and research institutes. In FY 1977, HEW *wasted or lost* between $6.3 and $7.4 billion, roughly three times as much as all the foundations in the country combined *granted.* It goes everywhere.

As federal grant programs have mushroomed since World War II, the underlying assumptions about the grantmaking role of the federal government have gone through some informative changes. The earliest function was crisis intervention. The creation of a new granting program went something like this: The liberal public would become alarmed at an impending disaster, and then various government agencies would pour out funds until the problem was resolved. It was a way of appeasing the interest groups that claimed to speak for the problem.

This method did not work. Before long everyone involved realized that we were simply treating different symptoms of the same disease, and that the gap between powerful and powerless, affluent and poor, was plainly not narrowing and in many cases was even growing wider despite, and sometimes because of, the operation of federal granting programs. Furthermore, the inception of a new grant program too often meant that vast new administrative fiefdoms also appeared, which then bitterly competed with each other because of overlapping program areas.

A number of responses emerged from the dissatisfaction. First, programs were consolidated to avoid duplication and to allow for better coordination of services for a given client group, such as juvenile criminal offenders.

Also, demonstration programs were launched to expand our understanding of what works and what doesn't. Much more emphasis was placed on local determination of funding priorities. It became routine for federal grants to require that some portion of a grant project's budget—ranging anywhere from 10 to 50 percent—be provided by local sources, as a measure of local involvement in the project.

In some problem areas, ambitious programs were undertaken to forestall the development of social problems in the first place. In childhood education, for example, Head Start was conceived of as a way to prevent the tenacious effects of childhood cultural deprivation from ever forming at all. Follow-up programs were then devised, based on these efforts, to assure that the benefits of these programs would persist.

Our very recent national concern about an impending "era of limits" has stimulated the introduction of a number of programs designed to make greater use of available institutional resources by putting old things to new use and by reorienting existing services to make them more relevant and thus more effective. For example, Governor Jerry Brown of California recently inaugurated a program in Oakland that is intended to help alleviate high unemployment among minority youth by enlisting them in the National Guard. The training they receive while in service will qualify them for jobs in the private sector that have already been pledged by local firms.

One central issue that has continued to re-emerge as a topic of debate is where in the hierarchy of governmental entities—from local to county to regional to state to federal level—should decisions be made about allocating governmental grant funds. During the 1960s, the prevailing tendency was for decisions made centrally in Washington to have a direct impact on local recipients without much intervention by the regional, state, and local bodies encountered along the way. At best, such intermediary levels functioned only as pass-through agencies, taking funds in one day and redistributing them the next. This "top-down" kind of grant became known as a "categorical" grant, since it was already earmarked in Washington for a specific purpose that fit into one narrowly defined category. Accounting for about $51 billion in 1977, it is still the predominant type of federal grant. However, categorical grants came into disfavor when it was understood that they ran counter to the thrust of local planning, which emphasized the need to avoid duplication of programs and to incorporate broader local input into the design of local programs. It was simply unworkable for bureaucrats in Washington to arbitrate among local needs. So there developed a strong federal trend to return decision-making powers to the state and local levels, to decentralize the process of making federal grant allocations.

With decentralization came a slight shift away from categorical to "block" grants, which simply means that the money arrives at a local or state level in one more-or-less undifferentiated chunk. It became the duty of local officials to make the tough decisions about who got what. Block grants now account for about one-quarter of all federal aid to state and local governments.

Often called New Federalism, the philosophy that the local community knows better than the federal or even the state government how tax money can best be used in its jurisdiction led the Republican administration in 1972 to enact Public Law 95–512, *The State and Local Fiscal Assistance Act of 1972,* commonly known as General Revenue Sharing (GRS). This law mandated the return of about $30 billion, collected from federal income taxes, to virtually every state and local governing body over a five-year period.

Although ultimate distribution of the funds for each community was left to local discretion, a formula was devised by the Treasury Department, which manages the GRS program, based on population, the average per capita income, and the level of local income tax contribution so as to measure relative need. The objective was to return more money to those communities with the poorest residents, who are often also the most heavily taxed, in proportional terms. Certain restrictions and priorities were established for eligible programs, including health, social services, public safety, recreation, environmental protection, financial administration, debt retirement, and capital improvement. The only thing local officials could not do with GRS funds was subsidize welfare payments, general education, or use GRS dollars to make up the local match for other federal grant programs. This type of grant is quite logically known as a formula block grant.

When it expired in 1976, the GRS legislation was extended for another three and three-quarter years to September 30, 1980. A total of $25.5 billion is to be spent over this period. The total of combined federal aid to states and cities, primarily attributable to GRS legislation, will approach $86 billion in Fiscal Year 1979. Twenty years earlier, in 1960, this figure was about $7 billion.

Under the second extension of GRS, some changes have been introduced that make the distribution of the funds at the local level even more flexible. There are no longer any priority categories, like health or public safety, into which funds must be channeled. General Revenue Sharing is no longer distributed on a poverty basis—only population is taken into account in the distribution formula. In some cases, GRS funds can even be used as the match for other federal assistance programs.

There have been criticisms of the GRS program. The strongest one is that local authorities are often neither as effective nor as impartial as the federal government when it comes to giving out money. The GRS program has led to bitter lobbying and devisive community struggles in more than one instance, particularly where the debate poses human service advocates against capital improvement supporters. Others point out that GRS is part and parcel of an attitude that tends to quash healthy competition among grantees. Under consolidation, all too often the Old Guard becomes entrenched and eventually stagnates.

Although much federal granting, like GRS and other block grants, is done on a formula basis and is initially directed at local governments rather than individual nonprofit groups, Washington does manage an extensive competitive granting system as well, based on selection from among project proposals. Most are cash grants, naturally, but there are also opportunities to compete for equipment, office space, and even various kinds of services.

To some extent, block granting did away with grantee competition, since the recipient government body or agency was able to put the money into its own budget. But some block granting merely transferred the competition to a local level, where private nonprofit groups competed with government agencies to become part of a federally financed service delivery system.

Rather than become simpler, federal funding processes have gotten more and more confusing. One new expression of their complexity is the apparent arbitrariness about whether funding is handled through grants or contracts.

What is the difference between a grant and a contract? Basically, it is a matter of who takes the initiative in identifying the problem and then proposing a solution. Searching for a grant means that you, the conceiver of the project, ask a funder to join you in your program. Going after contracts means that the funder advertises a need; you recognize your ability to meet the need; and you offer to join the funder in its program. The difference is often summarized like this: Grants are made to *support* services or research; contracts are made to *procure* them.

Because contracts are initiated and defined by the funder, who presumably knows what he wants for his money, they ask for more extensive and more specific information than do most grant proposals. They also tend to come with more strings attached, like narrow cost boundaries, detailed methodologies, and the required involvement of staff members with particular types of expertise. They are usually subject to more rigorously spelled-out implementation and evaluation procedures.

Contracts have more commercial overtones than grants. Contractor service providers may have less of a feeling that they have a personal stake in the service they are providing, viewing themselves not so much as social change agents as businesspeople providing a service in an area of need.

They also have greater overtones of exclusivity. Quality standards imposed by the funder are usually more rigorous than those applied to grant recipients because grants are considered to be intrinsically riskier and more open-ended; grants tend to focus on more nebulous and open-ended issues than do contracts. There is greater selectivity on the part of the funding agency about who may be invited to bid on a contract. Contracting agencies and departments usually have a pretty good advance idea about who has the qualifications and experience needed to adequately provide the desired services, and they will make a special point of seeing to it that the Contract Opportunity Notice (CON) is brought to the attention of these groups.

The process of selecting a contractor to provide the service begins with the decision by a governmental body to study a particular problem or to meet a specific need. Once the money is firmly allocated by the department, and perhaps by Congress, a team headed by a project officer prepares the CON or Request for Proposal (RFP) describing in substantial detail the problem or need, the methods to be used in researching or meeting it, and the general cost boundaries. The CON is then published in Washington's shopping list, the *Commerce Business Daily* (CBD), which we describe in more detail later in this section. Interested groups receive copies of it for study. If they feel like going after the contract, they prepare a proposal along the guidelines set forth in the *CBD.*

After the proposal submission deadline has passed, the contracting agency convenes technical and cost review panels, looks over the proposals, winnows out those that are obviously not competitive, and begins to further investigate those that seem promising. Site visits to these applicants may follow, and additional negotiation between the two or three most likely prospective contractors and representatives of the review panels may take place. A "best and final" offer is made by the competing contractors, the review panels make their final recommendations, someone reaches a decision, and the contract award notice is sent out and published in the *CBD.* The project formally begins.

Although there is more money available in Washington for contracts than for grants, there is relatively less competition for contracts because the application process is more demanding and requires greater investments of time, money, and energy. However, if your group is experienced, and wants to move ahead toward greater fiscal self-sufficiency, contracts can be a very attractive funding resource.

Profile of a Government Funder: Appropriate Technology

The current attention to appropriate technologies stems largely from a rejection of the unquestioned American adherence to growth at any cost and to an awareness that many of our technologies are inappropriate to the environment. Responding to these shifts in social orientation, the 1977 Authorization Act (Public Law 95-39) of the Department of Energy (DOE) called for development of programs to stimulate small-scale, appropriate energy technologies. In his subsequent energy message, President Carter also endorsed the need to explore these "high-risk" technologies and to promote greater individual and small-business involvement in this search. As one official later noted, it was an effort to "tap the grass-roots brain power of the nation." In early 1977, DOE established the first pilot Appropriate Energy Technology (AET) program. Initially, $500,000 was set aside for grantmaking purposes, and it was determined that Region IX, comprising California, Nevada, Arizona, and Hawaii and the other U.S. islands in the Pacific, would provide a highly suitable area for the program's trial run. All went well in Region IX, and the AET program has been expanded gradually in other areas of the country until it is now operating at a nationwide level.

In February 1977, Web Otis, an experienced federal administrator, was selected to manage the Region IX pilot program. Shortly thereafter, he was joined by Tom Chester. From that point on, working only with half-time secretarial support, these two individuals constituted the entire AET program staff for Region IX.

Otis' first task was educational. He needed to inform pertinent agencies in all parts of Region IX about the existence of the AET program and what its goals were; he also needed to enlist their active cooperation in helping to see that information about the program got to the people it was intended to reach, the individuals and small businesses at the local level, the backyard inventors who would be the program's source of new ideas. The first job, in short, was to get the word out as thoroughly as possible.

Several months were also spent during this initial period determining more exactly what the term *appropriate* should mean in the specific context of this program. Although it has widely accepted connotations of simplicity, neighborhood scale, extensive use of human labor, and conservation and recycling of natural resources, the concept needed more elaboration.

Eventually, Otis and Chester arrived at the following description:

In terms of resources, Appropriate Energy Technology:

- Makes best use of available renewable energy sources.
- Conserves nonrenewable resources.
- Depends largely on human labor.
- Maximizes use of local materials and labor skills.

In scale and efficiency, Appropriate Energy Technology:

- Is efficient in its use of energy and other resources.
- Is simple to install, operate, and maintain.
- Is compatible with community regulations.
- May employ scaled-down industrial technology.
- Employs novel applications of existing technologies.
- Emphasizes decentralized technologies.

In relation to the end-user, Appropriate Energy Technology:

- Satisfies local needs.
- Increases community energy understanding and self-reliance.
- Is environmentally sound.
- Results in durable, recyclable systems and/or products.

Another important priority during the first six months of the program was to develop a comprehensive, clear, easily understood application form. This process, involving repeated consultations with the DOE contract, legal, patent, and public affairs staff, was highly successful. The resulting application was organized around only a few questions, in stark contrast to the reams of forms usually required for a federal grant. And yet all the key questions were asked:

- Provide a summary of your proposed energy-related project, identify needs (technical, economic, social) to be addressed, the approach to meeting those needs and objectives, anticipated results, and benefits of the project.
- Describe your proposed energy-related research, development, demonstration, technology, or process. Also describe construction methods if this is a factor.
- What is your time schedule to complete the project?
- Who will work on the project and what are their qualifications? Provide brief résumés. How much time will they devote?
- Indicate the proposal's environmental compatibility. Problems? Pollutants, esthetic?
- Are there difficulties of a nonresearch nature: social, economic, legal? If yes, explain.
- Is this work being funded or supported by any other source or have you submitted this or a similar proposal for funding to any organization other than DOE's Appropriate Energy Technology program (For example, The National Center for Appropriate Technology, National Bureau of Standards, state and local governments, private groups)?

On September 15, 1977, the program was announced publicly, through newspaper notices, direct mailings, and announcements to local groups and agencies. Eligible applicants included nonprofit organizations, state and local government agencies, small businesses, native American tribes, and, in a radical departure from the overwhelming majority of both public and private grant programs, individuals.

Grant requests were not to exceed $50,000 per year for a maximum of two years of funding.

As is always the case in the grants world, the response far exceeded the feasible scope of the program. By the time the final application submission date—November 21, 1977—had passed, slightly more than 1,000 proposals had been received, requesting a total of $22 million. In reaction to the enthusiastic response, DOE officials in Washington allocated an additional $800,000 to the grants budget, bringing it up to a total of $1.26 million.

Even with the additional funds, only about 100 of the applications were funded. As do most funders, DOE freely admits that many qualified proposals were rejected. Isn't that unethical: forcing the mule to trot around the track chasing the carrot over and over again with never a chomp? The mule may get healthier but it might also get soured on the chase and get cynical about any future carrot-chasing. Isn't it self-destructive to set up grant programs that raise expectations and yet cannot meet the demand they generate?

The Department of Energy says no. The Department officials think that their AET program is building leadership and skills in the emerging AET community. "So they don't all get funded. They may not yet have a track record, but now they know what running on the track is all about. By putting together a proposal, they have done what most inventors would be too hesitant to do without a competition like this one. Now they have thought through their project and they have a proposal that's marketable. It's in good enough shape to take to a bank for a loan or to another agency that can give them technical assistance. Probably more appropriate technologies will be spawned by the rejected applications than by the accepted ones," one candid official said.

Once all eligible proposals had been received, they were reviewed by different groups for compatibility with program goals, for technical feasibility, for economic feasibility, and for congruence with local needs. In California, DOE contracted technical review functions out to the Lawrence Laboratory in Berkeley, and the California Office of Appropriate Technology was asked to evaluate the match between proposals and the state's own previously identified AET needs and goals. Similar procedures are being followed in other areas.

The purpose of the economic review was simply to determine if the budget request was reasonable, that is, if it seemed likely that the proposed activities could be completed for the amount requested. As often as not, it was found that applicants had asked for *less* money than they really were likely to need, rather than more.

Of the 1,115 proposals submitted, the 108 eventually selected for funding ranged from $238 for a Hawaiian solar beeswax melter to $49,000 for a scale model of a barge carrying "turbines, generators, and electrical equipment which can be anchored in, and produce electricity from, any moving body of water," proposed by a small business located in Santa Monica, California. About half of the proposals received were from individuals, and about 45 percent of the grants made were allocated to individuals.

Region IX grant awards were announced on April 1, 1978. Grantees receive 60 percent of the grant in advance, 35 percent when they reach the halfway point, and 5 percent at the completion of their project.

In terms of administrative costs, the Region IX program has been highly efficient. Eighteen months after the program started, for every dollar granted, it had spent about 12 cents on its own costs.

Otis and Chester are also assuming responsibility for continuous follow-up as well, to help recipients with implementation and business management procedures. As Otis puts it, "This is not a 'leave the money on the doorstep and run' type of program." Efforts are also being made to explore possible avenues to self-sufficiency for grantees, particularly those that offer the potential for making the grant project commercially marketable. As Tom Chester puts it, with tongue firmly in cheek, DOE is interested in helping grantees "viabilize" their projects.

For example, in an effort to encourage commercial application of appropriate products, the program found an ingenious use of patent rights. The Department of Energy insisted on holding patent rights for all products. After the grant terminated, they asked certain inventors to develop a plan to market their discoveries. If this was done, DOE would then return the patent rights to the inventor. However, if the inventor failed to become an entrepreneur, DOE reserved the right to commercialize the product itself.

Researching Government Funders: Tools and Resources

The basic tool for the search for federal funds is the *Catalogue of Federal Domestic Assistance (CFDA),* which contains extensive information on the objectives, eligibility requirements, application process, grant range and average grant size, accomplishments, and information contacts for well over 1,000 federal grant-making programs (see p. 123 for a typical *CFDA* listing). Programs in the *CFDA* are cross-indexed by agency program, by eligible applicant, by function (i.e., subject), and by popular name.

But referring to the *CFDA* is only a start, since much of the financial information is already out of date by the time the catalogue gets distributed: Money may have run out or even never have been allocated in the first place. Programs can change drastically, and you may find that, despite the description in the catalogue, eligibility requirements are far more restrictive than it would seem to indicate.

Once you have checked the *CFDA* listing, contact the local or regional office listed under *Information Contacts,* if there is one, and find out just what the current status of the program is, and whether or not it applies to the kind of project you have in mind. If it does, make an appointment to meet with a program or agency staff member to talk about specifics. There is almost always someone on the staff whose job is just that: to help applicants—including representatives of local, regional, and state governments—understand program guidelines in order to keep their funding applications and project operations in compliance with federal regulations. The amount of help you get will largely depend on how much you can interest this staff member in what it is you want to do.

Remember that this initial phone call or visit will be your most important source of up-to-date leads. This is how you find out, for example, that the Vocational Education program for neurologically handicapped adults is no longer operative but that a similar program is now being administered by the state and the person to call is. . . . (This is *very* valuable information; when you call a regional or local federal office to find out more about an attractive *CFDA* listing, be sure to get all the leads you possibly can from your contact, including a list of recent grant recipients in your area if possible. Also remember that dropping a brief thank-you note in the mail afterward can help smooth the way for renewed contacts in the future.)

You will frequently find that the *CFDA* listing shows, as in our sample here, that there are *no* regional or local offices for your program. Unfortunately, this means that you will have to write or call the Washington, D.C., contacts for more information. Neither of these choices is very satisfactory: Getting a reply to a letter usually takes a long time and trying to reach the right person to speak with in a Washington government office can be a nightmarish and expensive process, despite the fact that contact phone numbers are included in the *CFDA*. If the deadline appears to leave you enough time to write—a month or more, at least—compose a letter of intent along the lines of that shown on page 193. Then, when you receive a response, contact your respondent by phone for more information.

The *CFDA* is issued annually and updated between issues. It costs $18 and can be obtained from government bookstores located at federal regional offices or from the Superintendent of Documents, U.S. Government Printing Office, Washington, D.C. 20402. Most libraries also carry a copy, and you can sometimes get free copies by writing to the Office of Management and Budget, Washington, D.C. 20402.

A companion publication for use with the *CFDA* is the *Federal Register*, which you can get from most government libraries, and from the development offices of many educational and contract research institutions. The *Register* is a newssheet, published every working day that either the House or the Senate is in session. It contains current information on everything being legislated in Washington, including rules, regulations, and allocation decisions pertaining to federal granting programs. Information in the *Register*

OFFICE OF HUMAN DEVELOPMENT*

13.600 CHILD DEVELOPMENT —HEAD START

FEDERAL AGENCY: Office of Human Development, Department of Health, Education, and Welfare . . .
OBJECTIVES: To provide comprehensive health educational, nutritional, social and other services primarily to preschool economically disadvantaged children and their families and involve parents in activities with their children so that the children will attain overall social competence.
TYPES OF ASSISTANCE: Project Grants.
USES AND USE RESTRICTIONS: 90 percent of the enrollees in a program must come from families whose income is below the poverty guidelines as established. . . .
ELIGIBILITY REQUIREMENTS:
Applicant Eligibility: Any public or private nonprofit agency which meets the requirements may apply for a grant.
Beneficiary Eligibility: Full-year Head Start programs are primarily for children from age 3 up to the age when the child enters the school system, but may include some younger children. . . .
Credentials/Documentation: Nonprofit organizations which have not previously received OHD program support must submit proof of nonprofit status. . . .
APPLICATION AND AWARD PROCESS:
Preapplication Coordination: The grantee, policy advisory group, and the Head Start community representative participate in a preview to develop plans and priorities. . . .
Application Procedure: The Office of Child Development/Head Start regional representative will provide each applicant agency with a completed check list form showing exactly which items must be completed by each applicant and delegate agency. . . .
Award Procedure: All funds are awarded directly to the grantees. Funds for local Head Start programs, some experimental programs and some career development and technical assistance programs are awarded by the Regional Offices. However, funds for the following are awarded by OCD Headquarters: Indian programs (reservation only); Migrant programs; evaluation studies; some experimental programs and some career development training and technical assistance programs. . . .
Deadlines: Applications for new projects may be submitted at any time. Applications for continuation grants must be received 90 days prior to the start of the new budget period.
Range of Approval/Disapproval Time: 90 days from submission of application to Governor's approval.
Appeals: The grantee may appeal adverse decisions to the OCD office which makes the decision. . . .
Renewals: HEW Regional Offices will inform grantees of the application procedures for renewal.
ASSISTANCE CONSIDERATIONS:
Formula and Matching Requirements: 20 percent non-Federal share must be supplied. . . .
Length and Time Phasing of Assistance: Summer Head Start—minimum 120 hours. . . .
POST ASSISTANCE REQUIREMENTS:
Reports: Quarterly financial and program progress reports are required.
Audits: All Head Start grantees must arrange for an annual audit due 120 days after the end of the year.
Records: Grantee must maintain an accounting system adequate to meet the purposes of the grant.
FINANCIAL INFORMATION:
Account Identification: 75-1636-0-1-500.
Obligations: (Grants) FY 76 $432,-598,000; TQ $140,889,000; FY 77 $475,-000,000; and FY 78 est $485,000,000.
Range and Average of Financial Assistance: $30,000 $14,000,000; (Estimate of average is not applicable).
INFORMATION CONTACTS:
Regional or Local Office: Regional Program Director, Office of Child Development, Office of Human Development, HEW Regional Offices.
Headquarters Office: Office of Child Development/Head Start, Office of Human Development, Department of Health, Education, and Welfare, P.O. Box 1182, Washington, DC 20013.

*Excerpt of a typical *CFDA* listing.

tends to be more relevant to those seeking grants rather than contracts. Note that since it is a running indicator of current legislative activity, it will contain news about a particular program only if a change is being made in it, and it will print this news only *once.* Therefore, you should not go first to the *Register* to find out where to look for federal funds.

When you do consult the *Register,* look for the sections entitled "Notices, Rules, and Regulations," and "Proposed Rules and Regulations," pertaining to the grant-making agencies that operate in your field of interest. That last section, Proposed Rules and Regulations, is the most fruitful listing to follow, since this is where details about proposed granting programs first appear in print for public consumption. If you see one that interests you, and you follow up on it, you may be in the luxurious position of being able to actually plan your proposal writing process in some leisure. All the programs that eventually appear in the *CFDA* first publish their guidelines, *once,* in the *Register,* so you can stay a step ahead of the game if you have the time and fortitude to keep close track of this publication, which runs to about 70,000 pages per year.

One thing you will not be able to find, however, is good advance information on just how much money may actually be available at your level, since that is always subject to last-minute alteration by Congress, the Executive Branch, and the grantmaker itself.

The *Federal Register* can be ordered from the Superintendent of Documents, U.S. Government Printing Office, Washington, D.C. 20402. It costs $45 per year, or $5 per month. You can usually find it carried in larger public libraries, business libraries, law libraries, and some university libraries. There is also a handy time-saving monthly Index, which costs an additional $8 per year.

A similar publication, the *Commerce Business Daily (CBD),* is another daily newssheet that contains comprehensive, if obscure, listings on everything the federal government is interested in procuring, so it is read religiously by organizations looking for government contracts.

Remember also that federal agencies often operate their own information offices, which issue newsletters, magazines, program announcements, grant awards descriptions, and a host of other literature on program funding and deadlines. Once you have narrowed the field down a bit, check with agencies in your area of interest about other publications you can subscribe to.

A few years ago, the Department of Agriculture initiated a computerized counterpart of the *CFDA,* called the Federal Assistance Program Retrieval System (FAPRS). Originally intended for use by rural communities who were suffering losses of grant funding because of their geographical isolation, the system is now run by the Office of Management and Budget and is being expanded to include programs of interest to urban areas. However, it is primarily intended for use by city and county governments. As recently as early 1977, FAPRS had not yet been programmed to include the same scope of programs covered by the *CFDA,* so you may find that your area of interest is not one that it can handle yet. But if it is, FAPRS can deliver a printout on pertinent funding programs in a fraction of the time that it will take you to plow through the *CFDA,* and the cost is usually nominal. Also, FAPRS entries are updated monthly.

Once you have located a terminal, either at a public governmental agency or at a private computer time-sharing service, chances are the operator will ask you to provide data such as that asked for on the FAPRS applicant sheet below.

FAPRS Applicant Sheet

I. COMMUNITY FACILITIES

1. Community water supply
2. Community sewage treatment
3. Solid waste management
4. Public buildings
5. Hospitals and health related facilities
6. Recreation
7. Land acquisition
8. Public roads and bridges
9. Utilities
10. Historic preservation
11. Federal surplus property
12. Flood prevention and control
13. Emerg. preparedness and disaster relief
14. Fire protection
15. Research and development

II. BUSINESS AND INDUSTRIAL DEVELOPMENT

16. Operating capital assistance
17. Construction and equipment assistance
18. Small business
19. Site acquisition
20. Environmental health/safety compliance
21. Economic injury and natural disaster
22. Minority business enterprise
23. Research and development

III. PLANNING AND TECHNICAL ASSISTANCE

24. Data and information
25. Community facilities
26. Business and industrial development
27. Natural resources
28. Agriculture
29. Human resources
30. Transportation
31. Education
32. Housing

IV. HOUSING

33. Construction or purchase of structures for private housing
34. Construction or purchase of structures for public housing
35. Repair, improvement, or rehabilitation of housing structures
36. Rental or leasing supplements, mortgage assistance payments, etc.
37. Land acquisition
38. Site preparation for housing
39. Property or mortgage insurance
40. Research and development

V. EDUCATION

41. Curriculum
42. Demonstration
43. Emergency assistance
44. Facilities planning, construction and equipment

45. Libraries and related information service
46. Planning and technical assistance
47. Program development
48. Resource development and support
49. Scholarship and other financial assistance
50. Training
51. Research and development

VI. EMPLOYMENT

52. Facilities planning, construction and equipment
53. Information services
54. Job placement
55. Occupational safety and health
56. Planning and technical assistance
57. Program development
58. Services
59. Training and education
60. Research and development

VII. HEALTH

61. Demonstration
62. Education and training
63. Emergency and disaster
64. Facilities planning, construction and equipment
65. Information services
66. Occupational safety and health
67. Planning and technical assistance
68. Prevention and control
69. Program development
70. Services
71. Research and development

VIII. SOCIAL SCIENCES

72. Demonstration
73. Emergency and crisis assistance
74. Family and child services
75. Home services
76. Information and referral services
77. Legal and advocacy services
78. Nutrition
79. Prevention
80. Recreation and physical fitness

81. Rehabilitation
82. Training
83. Research and development

As you can see, the listing of program areas gives a general sense of the kinds of subject areas that can be searched with a FAPRS terminal. Note that the 83 subcategories are grouped under 8 major headings: Community Facilities, Business and Industrial Development, Planning and Technical Assistance, Housing, Education, Employment, Health, and Social Services. However, there is no mention, for example, of programs for the aging, or of arts programs such as those presented in the *CFDA* listing shown before.

There are a number of private counterparts to the FAPRS system. Several companies, such as Lockheed, computerize grants information onto tapes and then sell the tapes to public and university libraries, as well as to private commercial time-sharing services. User fees for these services vary enormously. They may cost $10 to $15, or they may run upwards of $200 to $300, depending on the firm or agency offering the service.

Contracts and the Small Business Administration

The Small Business Administration (SBA) does a lot more than just give loans for small businesses. It also provides a wide range of technical assistance services. For example, the SBA's Senior Corps of Retired Executives (SCORE) working in conjunction with another SBA group, the Active Corps of Executives (ACE), offers free management counseling and information workshops for small business firms, including service contractors. Topics covered include accounting, record-keeping, retail merchandising, personnel management, tax procedures, and so on. The quality of assistance available from SCORE/ACE varies enormously—some of its members are highly knowledgeable and helpful, but others will know less than you do about grants and contracts once you have finished this book.

Over the last decade, the SBA has actively focused its training and technical assistance programs, particularly its Section 8(a) Business Development Program, on "Disadvantaged" firms, with the goal of making them more competitive. Eligibility for "Disadvantaged" status is determined in each individual case by an SBA official, who considers the size of the firm, its management history, earning power, credit rating, earning history, and the background of its owners/directors.

A number of specific ways in which the SBA can help would-be contractors compete for federal business are:

1. Deciphering the *CBD,* which is laced with bureaucratese and technical jargon.
2. Charting *CBD* trends.
3. Providing information about sole-source contracts and other inside tracks to federal business.
4. Actually taking over the management of negotiations with government agencies to help new businesses win contracts.
5. Serving as prime contractor to a federal agency, and then subcontracting with the disadvantaged firm.
6. Helping new firms get on government bid lists, so that they do not have to scrutinize the *CBD* constantly to learn about new contract opportunities.

Unfortunately, the SBA 8(a) program has had its problems. Questions have been raised about the effectiveness of its assistance to disadvantaged firms, especially as measured by the number (less than ninety in over ten years of operation) of those who have "graduated" to full self-sufficiency. In some cases, SBA 8(a) programs seemed not only to perpetuate client dependency, they were also showing signs of outright corruption. Large and by no means "disadvantaged" businesses had established dummy corporations and had employed minority representatives to front for them. Consequently, as of February 1978, the SBA is now stipulating that the principals of firms applying for 8(a) assistance must be involved full time in day-to-day operations of the applicant business and must be the primary recipients of the program's activities.

THE TEN FEDERAL REGIONS

If you happen to live near one of these ten cities,

- Boston (Region I)
- New York (Region II)
- Philadelphia (Region III)

- Atlanta (Region IV)
- Chicago (Region V)
- Dallas (Region VI)
- Kansas City (Region VII)
- Denver (Region VIII)
- San Francisco (Region IX)
- Seattle (Region X)

you are in close proximity to regional offices of all major federal agencies and departments, such as HEW and DOL. A few make their own grants, but most merely act as regional advisory outposts for money allocated in Washington, and their primary job is interpreting rules and regulations. In either case, you need allies on the staff who can act as brokers between you and the funding decision makers.

Federal Regional Councils

There is also in each region a group called the Federal Regional Council (FRC), which principally operates at upper levels of local government and regards its primary contact as the chief executive officer in each locality. However, FRCs also make special commitments to specific client groups, such as the elderly, veterans, native Americans, migrant farmworkers, so that a contact in the FRC can be invaluable.

The FRC system was established in 1972. It is chaired by the Deputy Director of the Office of Management and Budget and is managed by the Deputy Directors or Under Secretaries of the major federal departments and agencies.

The essential function of the ten FRCs is to assist state and local governments in coordinating federal program grant operations by (1) improving the short-term delivery of the benefits of these programs, (2) helping to integrate programs and funding plans with governors' offices and with local chief executives, (3) encouraging state and local collaboration on joint grant applications to federal programs, and (4) evaluating programs to determine more effective ways of allocating federal resources to help meet long-range state and local needs.

This responsiveness on the part of the federal side of the granting system filters down through state and local government bodies. Get a copy of the FRC work plan for your region and see if it has assumed a commitment to your area of interest. Federal Regional Council meetings, which are usually held monthly, are open to the public.

State and Local Government Funders

Although state governments do administer their own grant programs, as well as offer advisory and information services, scholarships, and loans, most of the grant money that is distributed by the states is actually federal money that is "passed-through" state agencies. The Federal Advisory Commission on Intergovernmental Relations calculates that 35 percent of combined state and local revenues came from federal sources in 1977. In 1978, the total amount of federal aid to state and local sources exceeded $80 billion. Of all the federal money flowing to state and local sources, 30 percent goes directly to municipalities, 30 percent is passed through the state governments to the local level, and 40 percent remains at the state level.

Most states publish their own funding guides, usually modeled on the *CFDA.* It will usually be available from both major municipal libraries and the official state library. If you are not sure whether your state has such a guide, call the general information number for state offices and ask for the agency that handles information on state granting programs. If that does not work, ask the reference librarian in the state library. When these options fail, plead your case directly to someone in the governor's office.

There are also two or three other keys that can give you access to more information about state funding activities. One way to get a fairly detailed idea of just where the federal money has been going in your state is to write to the National Technical Information Service[16] and ask for a copy of *Federal Outlays in (Name of Your State)* for the previous fiscal year. There is a small charge for each report.

These reports show domestic allocations of all federal funds, by county and major metropolitan areas, under each of the 1,400 appropriations or programs listed in the *CFDA.* Spending levels are

[16]U.S. Department of Commerce, Springfield, Va. 22161

also summarized at national and state levels by program and function, so you can get a sense of how outlays in your area compare with others. If you are writing a grant to the National Endowment for the Humanities, for example, you can find out who NEH has already funded in your area. Then call them up and find out who got the grant and for what. You may even want to see if you can take a look at their proposal.

For many federal programs, the states are required to operate clearinghouses under the federal Office of Management and Budget's A-95 review program. Briefly, A-95 review, required for about 200 federal granting programs, is a mechanism that allows a preliminary review of proposals by a range of government and private nonprofit agencies that are given an opportunity to comment on whether, in their opinion, applications conform to civil rights and environmental protection laws or state plans, and most importantly whether they seem to duplicate an existing service. Check with the clearinghouse in your state; it is located in the governor's office. It should be able to provide you with information on the general categories and total recent expenditures in those categories for state-administered federal grants.

As well as requiring A-95 clearinghouse review, many federal programs that channel grants through state government agencies stipulate that these funds be allocated according to a state plan for each program category. Thus, if you're looking for funds for a project to serve the aging, you should check the state plan of the state Office on the Aging—assuming that your state has one, of course, as most states do—to see if the kind of service that you wish to provide is covered in the state plan. If it is, the state has in effect already declared its commitment to your service area, and you stand that much better a chance of getting funds.

In a similar way, it can be invaluable to refer to a copy of the state budget. It won't outline the dimensions of specific grant programs for you, but, as with the state plan and the A-95 review information, it will help you gain some insight into the conformation of the state's intended investment in various service areas.

Stepping down from the state level, you will find that there is also a regional A-95 review process. This service is more powerful, since it is integrated into the activities of Councils of Governments, composed of coalitions of city and county governments within a specific geographical region. Many regard COGs as the first step toward abolishing state and county governments and moving to a new system of regional governments matched to natural ecological and sociopolitical demarcations.

The main activity of COGs is regional planning. The task of COG planners is to manage future regional growth. They must develop transportation systems, pollution control systems, water supply systems, and most important for this discussion, they must design something called "human services delivery systems." That means that they must look around to see where needs are, what resources exist to fill them, and, if they're found to be lacking, how to add new services without duplicating old ones.

The A-95 service fits neatly into their mission, since it provides them with a way of assuring that new grant projects conform to future regional needs. Not all COGs have the same power. In some regions, they are mere rubber stamp agencies that are generally considered to be nuisances, at best. In any case the future influence of such regional governing bodies will increase. That is why it is important for the grantseeker to know how to use them.

Call your local mayor's office and ask if you are part of a COG. If not, ask which local agency handles the regional A-95 function for your area. Then call them up and ask for a meeting with the A-95 coordinator or a member of the planning staff who is familiar with grant programs.

When you meet, these are the types of questions you should ask:

- Which agencies locally are working in my area? (Get names, phone numbers.)
- What are the problems that those agencies have had?
- What are their reputations with the funders? Which are considered exemplary? Which are being audited? Why?
- What kind of regional planning has been done in my area?
- What are the civil rights and environmental factors that regional planners will look for in examining my project?
- Are there regional associations that could be of use to me?
- Who are the best technical assistance providers in my area?
- Is there some way that my project could be designed so that it will help to implement a regional plan?

MISTAKES TO AVOID IN APPROACHING THE FUNDER

Now that you have all this information, you have what everyone else has. What do you do next? First, you avoid making two typical mistakes that most novice grantseekers make:

1. When you set about approaching the funder, do not take his funding subject categories too literally so that you end up only going after the most visible funder, the obvious one for your area, the one that everyone else in your field is going after.
2. Avoid making the mistake of assuming that all you can get from a funder is a yes or no decision on whether you will receive the dollars. There is a whole range of information, assistance, and insights that funders and others in the grants world can offer to grantseekers, all of which comes under the heading "technical assistance."

We now explore both of these points.

Avoiding the Category Trap

Most information systems that you will encounter in your grants search categorize grants and grantmakers by subject area like those described on page 000. Usually, these subjects are derived from the problem areas the funder has an interest in resolving, and they indicate the type of activities it is willing to support. This is obviously critical information for you to acquire, since you do not want to waste your time proposing a rural alcoholism treatment center to a funder who is exclusively devoted to urban transportation research.

There are funders, it is quite true, who are rigidly and exclusively devoted to grant making in one specific area, and you certainly want to be able to reject them as potential supporters for your project if it doesn't happen to coincide with their areas of interest. But many funders, especially foundations, establish only very general areas of interest, and are willing to consider applications that at first glance would seem to be very remote from their declared priorities.

There is no denying that the information available under these broad headings can be very useful if you understand that it is only a starting point. Not only is it always at least a month out of date, usually more, but the categories shift. The grants system is a large, fluid, and highly pragmatic one, and it is constantly changing. You are quite likely to find, if you try to use these subject categories as a map into the briarpatch, that the clear points of entry they once charted are now completely overgrown.

Say you want to find a funder who will subsidize the construction of a sculpture that you want to build near a stream in a public park. Nothing could be more tempting than to go straight to the Foundation Center's listing (page 97), run your finger down the column until you come to number 46—Art and architecture, look up the funders making grants under that category, fire off a letter of inquiry to the most promising of them, and then sit back and wait for the application forms to roll in.

Let's say you send off a half-dozen letters, and you settle back to wait for a response. Since the Foundation Center keeps track of only the largest grants and foundations in the private funding sector, which are well staffed, you can probably expect to actually get replies from the people you have written to. If you were applying to any of the small foundations that make up by far the largest percentage of the 30,000 or so private foundations in the country, you might never hear any word at all from them, since very, very few have any staff members whatsoever.

As the weeks pass, you do begin to receive replies. The first one thanks you for your interest in the Noah Vale Foundation and informs you, apologetically, that it only makes grants in the Greater Boston Area, not Los Angeles, where you live. You would have known this earlier and saved yourself a little time, postage, and misplaced expectation if you had concentrated on doing your homework before you sent out your inquiries. The second foundation tells you that it now emphasizes support for the performing arts, and thanks you for your interest. The third and fourth say that your project sounds exciting, but that they have a six-month backlog of requests for funding that they will have to consider before they can get to yours, and they invite you to contact them again later. The fifth politely wonders if you have investigated government funding programs for artists—like CETA—and the sixth doesn't answer your letter at all. The replies you do get sound like form letters. You feel a sense of hopelessness welling up in you.

By not digging a little deeper, you may in fact be doing yourself an enormous disservice, as well as severely limiting your opportunities to actually connect with a funder. How? Well, you decided not to bother looking for a government funder until the private foundation mentioned the CETA program. Sure, you knew that the National Endowment for the Arts has been around for about fifteen years now and that it makes grants to artists. You even sent away for a copy of their guidelines, but you are shrewd enough to know that they get a lot of applications and they don't hand out all that much money, so you figured, why bother, what other government agency would give money away to artists?

The Department of Labor, for one. In fact, there is currently more money for local artists available from Labor's CETA (Comprehensive Employment and Training Act) program than from any other funding source at all. "Fine," you say, "now that I know that, I'll send them a letter of inquiry too." But it's not quite that simple. Because the CETA program has different objectives than do most private foundations, it makes money available to artists in an entirely different way, by funding public service jobs. This means that you will have to convince someone that your sculpture is a matter of civic interest, then get hired by a CETA program, which will pay you a monthly salary. It's more like becoming a temporary civil servant, with some latitude about the kind of work you do, than like receiving a lump sum to spend as you wish. In other words, the DOL game plan is so different from the (Blank) Foundation's that getting a grant means something very different in each case. The point is that the subject category is only the tip of the iceberg. You limit your granting prospects if you rely on it exclusively to produce the right funder for you, just like that.

At this point, you may say, "That's all very interesting, but the last thing I want to do is become a city employee, even if it means that I would get to do my sculpture in the park." Federal funding sounds like too much of a hassle.

So there you are, fuming and gnashing your teeth, asking yourself what is a poor starving artist to do? You are in imminent danger of becoming yet another tattered casualty of the funding case. You haven't exactly lost ground, since you can now say for sure that there are half a dozen unlikely funding prospects for your project, but you haven't made much real headway in identifying more promising prospects either. It looks like your only choice is to become a petty bureaucrat or keep on hunting.

The point is that guidelines that seem to exclude you at first glance may turn out to include you when you take a closer look.

Inside Technical Assistance

Beside passively receiving and judging proposals, many funders are beginning to take on an active and even initiatory role to promote what they feel to be the most promising grant ideas. They are becoming keenly aware of the extent to which it is in their best interests to fund the best designed proposals, submitted by groups that are best equipped to deliver the services described in the proposal. Through offering technical assistance, the funder often gets quite involved in shaping the content of a proposal. For example, through technical assistance the following project might have been changed from one that taught people to fish to one that trained its clients in the art of tackle making: "Give a man a fish, as the saying goes, and you are helping him a little bit for a very short while; teach him the art of fishing, and he can help himself all his life. On a higher level: Supply him with fishing tackle; this will cost you a good deal of money, and the result remains doubtful; but even if fruitful, the man's continuing livelihood will still be dependent upon you for replacements. But teach him to make his own fishing tackle and you have helped him to become not only self-supporting, but also self-reliant and independent."[17]

Many granters now understand that if they do not provide active assistance to unskilled applicants, they are in effect shutting the door on many conceivers of projects who have good ideas, experience, strong practical skills, and the emphatic support of their client populations, but relatively little familiarity with typical processes in the grants world, such as program development, technical writing, and budget preparation.

What kinds of help can technical assistance (TA) providers offer? It ranges from just giving out formal information to actually

[17]*Small Is Beautiful: Economics as if People Mattered,* E. F. Schumacher, Harper & Row, New York.

playing a strong advocacy role for you, with a lot in between. We have identified these fifteen categories.

1. *Guidelines.* They can give you the guidelines that will tell you the format for proposals and that will generally include three kinds of basic "how-to" information: budget data, narrative descriptions, and legal criteria.

2. *Other Printed Material.* If the funder is a corporation or private foundation, it may give you its annual reports or other descriptions of what it did last year and how much money it has. If it is a government funder, practically all its written communications are accessible to you because of the Freedom of Information Act, including copies of the public laws that authorize the grant program, which will give you a sense of its overall intention; copies of the *Federal Register,* which will give you deadlines, award processes, etc.; and brochures that should answer any other questions you may have about the formal realities of the agency.

3. *Program Objectives.* The funder's technical assistance people will explain the priorities of the grantmaker to you. They will usually go beyond the stated objectives of the program to describe what they want in detail.

4. *Review Process.* They will tell you who makes what kinds of decisions. Usually, there are three kinds of reviews that your proposal will pass through: administrative (a check to see if you filled everything out and that you are eligible), technical (expert opinion on your project—which can do you in if your method conflicts with the expertise of the reviewer), and a final review. A proposal submitted to certain federal grant programs will be cycled through the local A-95 process to see if it duplicates other programs or violates environmental or civil rights statutes.

5. *Next Steps.* Technical assistance providers can outline the steps you will have to go through before your proposal is funded, including how it will be channeled through their and other offices.

6. *Money Matters.* They can also give you the real financial picture, which is one of their most important functions, since library-based information doesn't have up-to-date financial data. If it's a federal program, for example, it may be authorized to make grants but in fact have no money. You can also find out how much to ask for, what to budget for, and what format to use in preparing your budget.

If they feel it's worth their time, TA people can go farther and fill in the spaces between and beneath the rules and regulations, telling you the practical realities that exist in their world.

7. *Secrets of Decision Making.* It may be that the decision makers have an agenda all their own that differs sharply from the formal criteria. Since they themselves do not make decisions but are aware of the process, TA people might tell you frankly if you stand a chance or what you will have to do to fit into the propensities of the funders. Do local elected officials use their role as CETA funders to return political favors? Do family members of the deceased philanthropist tie up grant money on pet projects? Do the grantees of a Community Action Agency form an Old Boys' network by using their political contacts to keep any of them from being dropped from the budget, or conversely, to prevent any new agencies from getting money? Are the corporation's grants used exclusively as a form of public relations? Do the funders have an ideological axe to grind? Are they into low-risk funding (i.e., do they give to only one type of grantee that they can depend on) or are they oriented toward high-risks (i.e., so they support experimental, unpredictable grantees who might possibly not have the administrative capacity to manage a grant)?

8. *How to Raise Your Credibility.* Technical assistance people may be able to tell you what you need to do to raise your own credibility in order to become more acceptable to the grantmaker. That could mean, for example, that you might have to collaborate with the grantees who were funded last year so that your proposal fits into the pattern of investment of that agency. Your grant could help shore up a grant project that they had previously funded. The TA provider will point out which are their exemplary projects and may suggest that you visit them so that you can model yours after theirs.

9. *New Contacts.* If the agency does not have money at the present time, its TA provider may be able to inform you where money for your type of project is, and can put you in touch with other TA people who are closer to the dollars. In government agencies, these kinds of contacts have two forms: vertical and horizontal. A TA person gives you vertical contacts when he points you toward people higher up, perhaps in Washington, D.C.,

or lower down, perhaps at the city or county level, where the real discretion over how to use the money might lie. Horizontal contacts are those that are in a different agency or department but who deal with your project area.

10. *Preliminary Review of Your Proposal.* If the TA people really believe in your idea they may even "broker" your project and do more to help you. They may give your proposal an early reading (if you get it to them in time!). They can also pass it on to experts on staff who will react from their perspectives. Incorporating their ideas into the proposal design will enable them to buy into your project. There is no better way to turn them into advocates.

11. *Site Visit.* You might ask a TA provider to come to your turf. They will then convey their impressions to the decision makers.

12. *Joint Funding.* If the funder likes your project but cannot put up the full grant amount, its TA people may be willing to call up contacts in other funding agencies to ask if they might chip in for a share of your costs.

13. *RFP's.* If the TA people say "No money at this time," it could be that they will have it later. Ask them to put you on their mailing list for RFP's announcing their next grant or contract opportunities. If you can convince TA people that you are the only person for a specific job they want to fund, they may actually write an RFP tailored to your special qualifications so that you are virtually guaranteed the work.

14. *Read Old Proposals.* TA people can also show you old copies of successful proposals funded last year to help clarify what you need to do to develop a winning proposal for them. If you claim that you do not have the time, skills, or fearlessness necessary to write your own, TA people have been known to write proposals for applicants, or pay for them to be trained in proposal writing, or pay for a consultant to help them.

15. *Not Just Money.* Finally, your TA provider and you might decide that money isn't your only need, that you also need management support: help with setting up a nonprofit corporation, legal advice, grass-roots fund raising, media help, loans, accounting, or someone to help you work out a marketing plan. They can then put you in touch with other TA people who specialize in those areas or with public interest agencies with consultants who do that sort of thing.

New Approaches in TA

The newest approaches to technical assistance go far beyond merely providing rules and regulations to new inquirers, an approach that is coming to be considered too narrow and literal and which is often motivated as much by a need to discourage the largest possible number of applicants as by a desire to give all applicants a fair chance. Some examples of newer and more active approaches to technical assistance include these:

1. Denver's Piton Foundation assigns consultants to work with promising applicants to develop their proposals. Following this same line, the Department of Housing and Urban Development is experimenting with a program for giving a "preliminary grant" of $60,000 just to assist a nonprofit group's development of an application for a larger housing grant.

2. Technical assistance staff members in some state departments of education will sometimes invite a coalition of representatives from several educational agencies to collaborate on the design of a single project that is, in effect, "pre-funded." (Many funders are known to dispense with their end-of-year unexpended funds in this way.) Many CETA funders tell specific agencies, "If you can come with such-and-such a project, we'll fund it."

3. Chicago's Sloan Foundation stopped giving away money five years ago and now only "grants" technical assistance. Similarly, the reorganization of HEW has resulted in stripping many of its offices of their granting (and contracting) powers. These offices are now predominantly a technical assistance service designed to help nonprofit agencies gain access to the funders in Washington.

4. The National Institute of Mental Health regularly receives, reviews, and comments on some applications before they are formally submitted.

5. Since 1970 the Ford Foundation has made grants for technical assistance activities (accounting, management planning, and budgeting) that dovetail with the SBA's push for loans to minorities and help assure the success of the enterprises for which the loans are made.

6. Boston's foundations have paved the way in collaborating on technical assistance by pooling their efforts in a regional association called the Associated Foundations of Greater Boston. The

association has the best grants library in town and is staffed as a clearinghouse of grants information. It serves as a vehicle for joint funding of summer camps for disadvantaged youths and for investigation of ways to make an impact on federal granting patterns. The AFGB model has since been adopted by other regional groups of funders around the country.

The term *technical assistance* is beginning to appear in some surprising places. For example, Andrew Young, America's controversial former Ambassador to the United Nations, was recently speaking to a group of new Peace Corps volunteers who were about to begin their missions in foreign countries. Young told his audience that what they were setting off to accomplish was just what the Cubans in Angola were doing—technical assistance. Said Young, "They are working in the field to promote the economic development of those rural villages and so are you."

For others, however, technical assistance is old wine in a new bottle. Here is a description of a prototypical form of technical assistance that was being practiced in the Central Valley of California in the 1930s.

Bard should be an immortal. He's an extraordinary man who, although he did not speak Spanish, simply sat around where the farmworkers gathered, and listened. He's a whittler (really a sculptor—his things are beautiful), and he would whittle while he listened to see what these people wanted—what did they want to do?

Bard McAllister was the catalyst in bringing water into Teviston, for instance, and that was years before most of those places got water. The people had to haul the water they needed for every purpose. As soon as Teviston brought water in, others saw that it could be done, and later various federal programs helped them.

. . . He was interested in progress—in helping people learn to do it themselves. They went through prolonged stages of developing the confidence that something could be done and that they could do it, and then listing what they wanted to do, and learning how to take the steps, and, finally, taking them. That's the enabler role, and it takes a lot of patience and skill to help people believe that things aren't hopeless for them, and that something could be done. It's part of what we call technical assistance now, when technical assistance is done well; but I'm talking about a time before the civil rights movement when many very poor people from minority backgrounds really didn't think they could improve their situations.[18]

Further Resources

Grants: How to Find Out About Them and What to Do Next, Virginia P. White, Plenum Press, New York, New York, 1975.

This is easily one of the most comprehensive and well prepared of a number of recent books on grants. The author, currently Director of the Office of Sponsored Research at the City University of New York, covers basic information sources, government granters, foundations, and grant sources in the corporate world. She also discusses, in lucid and carefully prepared detail, how to select and approach the most suitable funder for your project, how to prepare the different parts of the typical proposal, and what happens once the grant has been declined or awarded.

The book also includes a number of useful appendixes, including a list of Public Health Service grant programs and a list of definitions of the many kinds of grants that may be applied for.

GRANTSPEOPLE, INC., 1027 Twenty-third Avenue East, Seattle, Washington 98112.

This is a national nonprofit training organization that educates grant seekers and grantmakers through its regional centers in Denver, Boston, Atlanta, and Seattle. Separate workshops are held for community-based and research-oriented grantseekers. A comprehensive set of local resources and contacts are given to each participant. Write for a schedule of training events.

The Grantsmanship Center News, The Grantsmanship Center, 1015 West Olympic Boulevard, Los Angeles, California 90015.

No serious student or seeker of grants should be without a subscription to this publication by this organization which also conducts training. For $15 you receive four to six issues of this well-written, -researched, and -designed magazine. You can also order, at a fee, reprints of key past articles.

Foundations Under Fire, Thomas C. Reeves, ed., Cornell University Press, Ithaca, New York, 1970.

This is one of surprisingly few books that came out of the extensive Congressional scrutiny of foundations provoked by the Honorable

[18]Ruth Chance, *Bay Area Foundation History,* Vol. 2, The Regents of the University of California, The Bancroft Library, Berkeley, Calif., 1976, p. 85.

Wright Patman's investigations in the late 1960s. Both pro and con arguments on a number of fundamental issues—public responsibility, venture capital, propaganda and politics, CIA involvement, and taxes—are represented in the selections in this book. Since much of the last decade's legislation regulating foundations arose in this era, reading this book will give you a good appreciation of the arguments surrounding issues that are still very much alive today.

Giving in America: Toward a Stronger Voluntary Sector, Report of the Commission on Private Philanthropy and Public Needs, Department of the Treasury, Washington, D.C., 1975.

This work is the summary result of inquiries conducted from October 31, 1973, to December 6, 1975, by a private commission, initiated by John D. Rockefeller III and set into motion at a meeting held at the Brookings Institution. The object of the commission was to study the role of philanthropy in American society and to make recommendations for change. The effort to establish and operate the commission was strongly supported not only by a number of prestigious private foundations but also indirectly by the Department of the Treasury, especially by such individuals as George Shultz and William Simon, and by Congressional leaders, notably Wilbur Mills.

Chaired by John H. Filer, of the Aetna Life and Casualty Company, the commission (which soon came to be known as the Filer Commission) was composed of a broad cross section of American society, including a group representing grant recipients. The commission sponsored, during the course of its investigations, ninety-one research studies, held numerous interviews, conducted extensive surveys of public attitudes and practices, convened hearings, meetings, and discussion sessions across the country, and extensively analyzed and synthesized the enormous amount of data gathered in the course of its research efforts.

The first section of the book summarizes over a dozen conclusions reached by the commission in regard to philanthropic activity. These comment on the dangers, particularly economic, that face the philanthropic sector of the economy and the relationship of private to government giving. They also recommend (1) that all taxpayers, including those who simply take a standard deduction, be allowed also to deduct charitable donations; that the amount of these deductions be doubled for families with incomes below $15,000 a year and increased by 50 percent for those with incomes ranging between $15,000 and $30,000 a year; (2) that corporations be encouraged to give at a level of 2 percent of their pretax net income; (3) that all grantors, with the exception of churches, issue annual reports and that larger grantors hold annual public meetings to explain their programs and priorities; (4) that expenditure responsibility be solely the concern of the grantee; (5) that funders and nonprofit organizations strive to make their boards representative of new needs and viewpoints; (6) that philanthropic organizations avoid business dealings with profit-oriented organizations that their board members or staff may have a financial interest in; (7) that federal regulations be developed for charitable solicitation; (8) that nonprofit organizations be allowed to politically lobby in the same way that business and trade groups do (the restrictions on political lobbying have been loosened since the Commission's recommendations were published); and, finally, (9) that a permanent commission on the nonprofit sector be set up.

The balance of the book discusses the scope and nature of the nonprofit sector of American society, including its primary funding sources, beneficiaries, motivations, objectives, potential vulnerabilities, economic pressures, the increasing role of government in philanthropic activities, tax issues, and additional alternatives for preserving and expanding the bases for private giving.

Research Papers, sponsored by the Commission on Private Philanthropy and Public Needs, Department of the Treasury, 1977, six vols.

This, the companion work to *Giving in America,* is a collection of the research studies supported by the Filer Commission during its two-year existence. The six volumes contain ninety-one separate studies covering a wide spectrum of grant-related issues in health, education, welfare, religion, culture, social change, community change, and public policy, roughly distributed as follows:

Vol. I: History, Trends, and Current Magnitudes
Vol. II: Philanthropic Fields of Interest—Areas of Activity (Part I)
Vol. II: Philanthropic Fields of Interest—Additional Perspectives (Part II)
Vol. III: Special Behavioral Studies, Foundations, and Corporations
Vol. IV: Taxes
Vol. V: Regulation

Setting National Priorities: The 1978 Budget, Joseph A. Peachman, ed., The Brookings Institution, Washington, D.C., 1977.

Each year the Brookings Institution produces this definitive analysis of major issues involved in the upcoming federal budget for the next fiscal year. Since the federal budget is, in the Institution's words, "the basic planning document of the federal government," and since the Institution itself attracts a very high caliber of public policy analyst, you can usually gain a very good insight into growth and recession trends in federal granting for the next fiscal year by reading this book. It does not deal with grants per se, but the 1978 edition covered such highly pertinent topics as welfare reform, cities, energy, employment and training assistance, Social Security, medical care costs, and budget prospects and process. Brookings also reviews federal budget trends on a ten-year basis, in separate publications.

IV

Becoming More Believable: How to Use Third Parties to Support Your Project

Put yourself in the funder's shoes for a moment. There you sit, with $340,000 left in your grants budget, five months to go in your fiscal year, and some grants to make. As usual, you want to make them count, to be as sure as you possibly can that when you pick a proposal to support you are going to be getting the most return for the dollar. And because you are well aware that you are going to have to depend on the grantee to help you realize your goals, you want to pick someone you can trust. But there's the rub: Out of the hundreds of proposals that come in every month, you do not know more than 10 percent—if that many—of the applicants at all, and few of those are more than names and faces. So you take a risk every time you make a grant, and you would like as much assurance as possible in advance that the project you have decided to support is not going to go sour or blow up in your face.

What do you do? Out of this flood of proposals that never stops streaming in, how do you pick the ones that you feel you can rely on? Is it a horserace? A matter of blind luck? Are there definitive criteria that can help you analyze these proposals? Or is there some other way to make your selection?

Fortunately, some proposals you can reject immediately, since they obviously come from applicants who haven't done their homework. Here's one, for example, from a character who lives in Florida—and you only make grants in Chicago. You can set that one aside, shaking your head in mild amusement. And here's someone who wants to get a grant to develop some kind of Buck Rogers machine for cutting down trees with sound waves. Here's another from a retired teacher who wants your help in the development of a phonetic alphabet. You discard those, since neither one is remotely connected to your own funding priorities. And then there is one from a nonprofit agency located in one of the city's worst ghettos that has been running on federal funds for almost a decade now, but its last evaluation was sharply critical. It is on the way to being defunded and wants you to step in to make up the difference. Even though you have some affinity for what the applicant group is trying to do, you tell yourself, we are not in the salvage business. . . .

But even when you have weeded out the hopelessly inappropriate applications, you are still left with a substantial pile of possibilities, and a half-dozen of these look very good indeed. You have deadlines, too, though. Your board meets tomorrow and you have to make recommendations on which project is the best, which looks like the next best, and so on. Fortunately, you have an active, involved board . . . one that will make up its own mind —it always does—but you can't kid yourself, your recommendation is going to carry a lot of weight and your job is always on the line. The last person in your position funded too many turkeys and got the boot.

So, you are on the spot. You need to figure out, from the information you have in front of you, which of these six to go with, which to trust. What do you look for? What makes the critical difference?

Let's assume that all six of the best proposals look equally good from an internal point of view. Each is focused on a real problem; each outlines a well-conceived project to help resolve the problem; each is well-designed, appropriately staffed, and skillfully budgeted. Judging from the project plans alone, all these applicants seem to be on an equal footing. You have met each one and chatted with him or her briefly, but you don't know any of them well enough to predict how well they would handle the grant. What do you look for next?

FOUR KINDS OF BELIEVABILITY

1. First, the right philanthropic *credentials:* nonprofit, tax-exempt status. If the proposal comes from a source with these qualifications, you know that your state's attorney general, the Franchise Tax Board, and the IRS have vouched for the applicant's authenticity as a bona fide charitable, educational, religious, scientific, or literary group. If you give money to them, you can be reasonably sure that they are not going to use it to buy a new car or fly to Paris.

This concern makes it especially difficult, as you know, for individuals to get grants. Fewer than one out of every thirty foundations and only a very few governmental granting programs are willing to consider proposals from individuals. In practically every field of granting activity, it is rare to find grants made to one person rather than to an organization. Only for certain limited granting programs in the arts, for some areas of scientific research, and for scholarship and fellowship programs could it be considered normal for grants to go to individuals who have no organization affiliation, and even in those cases there is often an institution, like a university, hovering in the background somewhere.

The reason for this common reluctance on the part of funders to make grants to individuals is simply that there are long-standing historical and legal strictures in the philanthropic world against private gain. The spirit of grants is one of advancement of the human condition; money placed in one person's hands, it is feared, can too readily be misused. The IRS has codified this taboo in a number of ways. For example, donors who make gifts to private individuals do not realize the same tax advantages that they do if the gift is made to an organization that has been reviewed by the IRS and granted tax exemption. Another IRS constraint, known as expenditure responsibility, holds private foundations responsible if they make grants to individuals or groups who then use the funds for something other than philanthropic ends, and imposes extra financial and programmatic reporting requirements on them.

So you decide to scrap the two proposals that lack mention of any kind of affiliation with a tax-exempt nonprofit organization. Time is pressing, after all, and you have to make some decisions. It's too bad, you tell yourself, they were intriguing proposals. But without that basic guarantee, the right credentials, they just were not competitive. A little more investigation might have told you that they came from groups that *would be eligible for tax exemption if they applied,* and that is actually all that the IRS demands, but like most funders you feel that you should go with the safest risk. This just isn't one of those times when you want to put in the extra hours to set up some kind of joint-funding arrangement with a community foundation so that you won't have to deal with the expenditure-responsibility reporting requirements.

2. What do you look for next, as you shuffle through the remaining four proposals, trying to make up your mind? *A track record.* Some indication that the applicant has the experience to do what he says he wants to do in the proposal. The experience may not be in precisely the same field, or directed at quite the same problem, but it should be close enough so that the skills are transferrable. You don't want to fund someone's learning experience if you can help it; you want your dollars to get to the problem as efficiently as possible.

Funders like proven performers, perhaps too much: About 90 cents out of every grant dollar goes to proven service groups rather than to completely new organizations. And this is fairly understandable: Few experiences are more galling for a funder than to take a large hand in launching a very promising and highly innovative program, only to be forced to stand sadly on the shore and watch while it founders from lack of experience and mismanagement. The fact that a funder wants to get the most (social) benefit for its investment, like any other investor, combined with the fact that it cannot actually recover its money or repossess the project if the services are not performed, just increases the funder's emphasis on credibility. It is one thing to get a funder excited about your project, but quite another to assure him that your organization has the skills and resources needed to do the job right, and to do it in such a way that the grant yields as high a social return as possible.

If you are new to the grants field, you must be feeling, having read the last few paragraphs, that you just stumbled on yet another example of Catch-22: Funders will not fund inexperienced applicants, but how can you get any experience unless you get funded? Well, first of all, most people who apply for a grant already do have some experience in a related field, perhaps as an employee rather than a grantsperson, but that experience counts. So the answer to the puzzle is really quite simple. Meeting the funder's emphasis on a track record is the role of the sponsor and of other third-party groups who collaborate with you to meet the funder's requirements. Sponsors are generally groups, agencies, and institutions with visibility, established performance in your field, a record of solid accomplishment, and thus high-quality credibility. Often you will find that they are already quite familiar with the funding source that you are thinking of contacting and can give you valuable advice on making your approach. Universities, for example, have for years served as sponsors to a wide spectrum of new, unproven grant projects. In fact, if the statistics showing that 90 cents out of every funded dollar goes to well-established groups were to take into account the prevalence of sponsoring arrangements, under which new groups qualify for grant money under their sponsor's name, the 90-cent figure would drop sharply.

Three of the four proposals have strong track records. The fourth is a little weak, and you start to set it aside along with the other rejects, but then something catches your eye. You remember that this one sounded a little far out when you first read it, and you never heard of the applicant before, but you have since found your mind slipping back to it, attracted by its audaciously innovative aspects. Now as you read through it again, you see that the applicant has worked out an arrangement with a well-established, stable nonprofit organization—the YMCA—to sponsor the project. The YMCA will act as fiscal agent, taking the money from you and then allocating it to the applicant, as well as keeping track of the project's expenses. It has also agreed to provide some office space and a phone for the project. In return for acting as the sponsor, the YMCA wants a small percentage to help cover its overhead costs.

With the YMCA acting as fiscal agent, this proposal suddenly looks very good to you. It has the right balance of two kinds of credibility: that of the established institution plus that of the latest thing on the block. With this proposal, you can have your cake and eat it too. The risk of losing is nil, since the YMCA is willing to put itself on the line as the fiscal intermediary. You can also see that if the project succeeds, its impact on the problem could be tremendous and it could also cause credit to rebound to you from having had the vision to see the potential of this proposal. It begins to look better and better to you.

You quickly flip through the other three remaining possibilities. All have some affiliation with a reputable nonprofit outfit, but two are from large universities that have a reputation for sticking the applicant for an arm and a leg in indirect costs, so you set them aside, tentatively consigning them to the reject pile. You do not want any more of your precious grant dollars to go for paying huge institutional operating costs than you can help.

3. So you really have two contenders left. They both have the right credentials, but the one you are really excited about has a slightly less impressive track record. Although you are inclined to favor this proposal, you are not convinced yet that it is the best place for your grant. But, as you flip through it, you find that you had overlooked an attachment at the back of the proposal, containing three very enthusiastic *letters of support,* one from a professional association in the applicant's field, one from an eminent professional working on similar problems, and one from a large group that has been delivering services in a related field for some years. All three letters not only endorse the applicant's proposal, they offer to actively support the project in specific ways. The professional association commits itself to helping disseminate the project's accomplishments. The eminent professional attests to the sophistication of the project's design and states his willingness to consult with the applicant, at a reduced fee, on its implementation. The service organization states that the project will complement rather than duplicate its own services and offers to make its outreach workers available for the applicant's work. Flipping to the budget section, you find that both the consultant and the outreach workers' time are shown as an in-kind contribution to the project's costs, and your opinion of the applicant's sophistication rises.

4. You are definitely impressed now. If there were also, on top of the credentials, the track record, and the letters of support, *more evidence that the community and the clients themselves were strongly behind this proposal,* your decision would be almost automatic. As it is, you will prepare strong recommendations for both of the top proposals and let the board decide. If it goes the way you hope it will, you'll be

drafting a letter to your favorite choice tomorrow, saying that it is your pleasure to inform him that. . . .

So you, the grantsperson, can see from this hypothetical example that there are four kinds of credibility that will strengthen your proposal:

- Nonprofit, tax-exempt status.
- Track record.
- Letters of support.
- Evidence of community support.

HOW TO FIND A SPONSOR

It is almost essential that you find a willing sponsor, technically called a fiscal agent, if you are not applying as a nonprofit, tax-exempt organization. Otherwise a funder will be reluctant to trust you with a grant. The most persuasive credibility mix is one that combines risk and innovation with a stable, established, and prestigious sponsor.

One excellent way to find a sponsor is to use your technical assistant contacts to figure out who is already being funded in your field of activity or is providing services that have an obvious relationship to what your project is designed to do. Go to these organizations, talk to them, and find out if they might be in a position to sponsor your project.

An alternative is to seek out people who have a professional reputation in the field that you want to work in. Ask them for tips on who is working in the same area, and who is getting funded. Or go to traditional nonprofit organizations, groups like hospitals; churches; colleges and universities; social welfare agencies; Junior Leagues; public television stations; the Friends Service Committee; the YMCA and YWCA; professional, trade, and service groups; civic organizations; benevolent associations; and so forth. Keep buttonholing people until you have some good leads.

Shopping Around: What to Look for in a Sponsor

Once you have narrowed the field down to a few prospects, meet with them and raise these issues:

- Do you have credibility with your funding sources? What is the background of your relationship with your funder(s)? (Also go to the funder, if possible, and double-check the responses you get.)
- Do you have the trust and respect of your clients, as well as the cooperation of the local political structure? What is the attitude of indigenous community leaders toward you?
- Do you need the services I want to provide? Why? Do you have a formal plan or needs assessment and a list of priorities? Where would my project fit in with these priorities?
- What is your history of efforts to meet the needs defined in your needs assessment?
- Are your key decisionmakers responsive to my project?

The best sponsors will work to help you strengthen the financial and programmatic reach of your project, and will tend to view it as a benign extension of their own efforts, a Research and Development device that can help them serve a wider population more effectively. They will see the quid pro quo in your functioning as their Research and Development in return for their offering you credibility and indirect support. They will be interested in the sense of new possibilities that your presence may imply, and they will have a healthy curiosity about your methods and content. They may even help you attain eventual fiscal independence.

Seven Reasons Why a Sponsor Needs You

When you go looking for a sponsor, avoid the beggar mentality. Because you need a sponsor's credentials does not mean that you are being done a favor. As with the funder, the proper arrangement is a partnership, and there are a number of possible benefits that a sponsor can realize by supporting you:

1. *Spread the Overhead.* Your sponsor usually gets a small percentage of your grant to help pay its overhead (indirect costs). Negotiating this percentage and what you will get in return for it can

be a very tricky process. Be sure that you and the sponsor both clearly understand, down to the last paper clip, just what supplies and services you will get in return for the indirect cost percentage that you are giving up.

2. *More Return for the Dollar.* Both you and the sponsor may increase the cost-effectiveness of your respective services by combining functions, space, and perhaps even client populations. You may be offering a service component that will dramatically improve their overall program design and enhance the impact of their service delivery system.

3. *Fresh Blood.* In agreeing to support your project, the sponsor may feel that it is obtaining new skills and energy that will pep up its program.

4. *The Limelight.* If you have convinced the sponsor of the feasibility and the innovativeness of your project, it may support you because of the potential for the reflected prestige that will come its way if your efforts are a resounding success. They may also see a way to turn enhanced visibility to their advantage.

5. *New Turf.* You may be addressing a problem or serving a client group that they had recognized in the past but were unable to muster up the resources or the insight to try to deal with yet. By supporting your project, they open up the possibility of expanding their operational territory.

6. *Pre-Empt Competition.* They may recognize that you *are* the latest thing on the block and if they fail to get on the bandwagon and support you, someone else will, possibly nudging them out of the service picture over the long run.

7. *New Funders.* You may also be opening up links to new funding sources for your sponsor. There is an almost universal need among nonprofit, service-oriented organizations to diversify funding sources so that if one terminates or fails to renew a grant, they are not forced to close their doors.

Example: In 1967, the Ford Foundation decided that the lack of experienced minority managerial-level professionals in business was a serious obstacle to economic development in the inner city. Of the 13,000 graduate students enrolled in business schools that year, Ford could find only 50 who were black. However, the problems inherent in making grant money available to each individual MBA program were serious, especially since Ford rarely gives small grants. So, when Dr. Sterling Schoen, Professor of Management at Washington University in St. Louis, devised a consortium of business schools—involving the University of Southern California, the University of Indiana, Rochester University, and the University of Wisconsin—that would act as a central sponsor for all participants and would recruit and offer financial support to potential minority MBA students, Ford was interested.

The program was initially funded for just over $100,000. Following its demonstrated success, a larger coalition of schools adopted the same model, winning a $3.9 million grant from the Sloan Foundation, which also picked up the Washington University program after the Ford support ran out.

Each of the seven advantages briefly described here was realized by participating university programs. They spread their overhead, got as much as they could out of their funds, moved into exciting new educational areas, won a little recognition for their pioneering work, expanded their educational horizons, attracted students who would eventually have gone on to other opportunities, and opened up links to new funders.

ALTERNATIVES TO FINDING A SPONSOR

If you cannot find a sponsor that meets your needs, consider one of these alternatives:

- Start your own nonprofit organization. It will not have much of a track record, but it will be more closely related to your own special goals than anything else around. If you choose this route, remember that it takes time, usually from three months to one year, to qualify for tax-exempt status.
- Organize a community grant-getting consortium. Bring together all of the grantseekers who need money and work out a mutual agreement. Each successful hunter contributes a little something to the common pot, and all can avail themselves of whatever services your consortium's umbrella can assemble.

  The National Center for Atmospheric Research, located in Boulder, Colorado, was established in this way. When NASA issued the original announcement calling for this center, it was immediately evident to the scientific community that only a handful of universities in the country had the expertise and experience in atmospheric studies to respond to the notice adequately. Rather than compete with one another, twelve of them banded together to form a coalition, and *then* responded to NASA as a unit. The presidents of these twelve universities now form the board of directors of NCAR.

- Check out your current organization. Be sure not to miss the trees for the forest. If you are already part of a service-oriented nonprofit organization, it could be to your mutual advantage to have a little reorientation of roles, particularly if it looked like you might be in a position to bring some money into the organization.
- Work out a subcontract or subgrant with an institution to provide the services you want to seek a grant for. This is not the same as being sponsored, but it is close. It does, however, put you one step closer to being an employee of the contracting agency.

CONSUMER PROTECTION: WHAT TO WATCH OUT FOR IN A SPONSOR

Before finalizing an agreement with a sponsor (including your own organization, if it seems to have this potential) you should be aware of potential conflicts that can result from a difference of opinion between you and the sponsor:

- There may be management constraints: You may be expected to tailor your personnel, budget, and expenditure functions to suit their regular procedures.
- You may find that your sponsor becomes jealous of your independence and energy; it may try to shift your priorities toward its own, particularly if you do not have a separate budget.
- It might also try to make you a scapegoat, a safety valve for its own mismanagement, someone at which its disgruntled clients can blow off steam.
- Most sponsors, even the best, are wary of projects that may

compete with their own programs or that may develop a separate power base; there is as much territoriality in the nonprofit, human services world as in any other and it is usually made worse by inadequate budgeting.

- Most sponsors will be concerned, as are most funders, about your plans and their responsibilities once your funding runs out.

Sponsoring arrangements can backfire. For example, we know an enterprising and industrious researcher with a solid background in both engineering and sociology, as well as expertise in solar energy research. Noting the intense public debate over future energy needs, he decided to commit a great deal of his own energy to convincing the head of his state's energy council that funding an Alternative Energy Futures Conference, to which the best minds in a wide spectrum of energy fields would be invited, would help that agency's long-range planning. He knew that the results of such a conference would be essential for government agencies, libraries, newspapers, colleges, businesses, schools, and so forth.

The idea met with considerable enthusiasm on the part of state officials, but problems developed over the precise nature of the role that our entrepreneurial friend was to play in the convening of the conference. He had, of course, an understandable desire to reap some professional rewards for his part in originating the conference, and he also wanted reasonable compensation for his work.

It was the issue of compensation that led him astray. Three alternative models for his participation were offered: (1) He could be hired as a temporary state agency staff member, (2) He could be employed on a short-term basis as a consultant for a fixed daily rate, or (3) He could arrange a contract with the state. Because the third choice seemed to offer him the best combination of autonomy, professional stature, and the most remuneration, he chose it.

But all contracts above a relatively small amount with most government agencies must be competitively bid, unless, as is true in some cases, there are grounds for a sole-source contract, where only one individual or firm has a monopoly on the expertise needed to furnish a particular service. That unfortunately was not true in this case, so a Contract Opportunity Notice was drawn up by the state agency and published in the *Wall Street Journal.*

Wanting to strengthen his credibility, our friend contacted his strongest competition, a large and well-established research institute, and proposed a joint venture with one of them subcontracting to the other. Following hard-nosed discussions, it was decided that the team stood the best chance of winning the contract if the institute submitted the bid and then subcontracted to our friend. In essence, the institute agreed to act as his sponsor. One very compelling reason for this arrangement was the sheer, if overrated, reputation of this particular research institute. Another was its ability to charge a much lower overhead rate—13 percent—than our friend's, which, once he had established the necessary facilities, hired the right assistants and arranged for the necessary support services, such as accounting, legal help, and computer time, would probably have exceeded 30 percent.

The deadline approached, twenty-seven proposals were submitted, and to no one's surprise, our friend's "partner" was awarded the contract. But somehow, when it came down to defining hard and fast roles, he found that the project didn't really belong to him anymore. The institute's own staff, always on the lookout for developing new research areas, had already moved prominently into the picture, and his role had been reduced. Out of a total budget of $240,000, he was slated to receive about one-twelfth: $20,000. He had been gobbled up by his own sponsor.

He could have avoided this problem if, in addition to working out the actual proposal, he had developed a separate contract, such as the one shown below, specifying exactly who will do what, when, and for how much, during the different phases of the project.

Letter of Agreement
between
Fred Solar
and
Bandwagon Research Institute, Inc.

This letter describes an agreement reached between Mr. Fred Solar and Bandwagon Research Institute (BRI), represented by Ms. Rhonda Roberts. It specifies mutual responsibilities and rewards accruing to each of the two parties during their collaboration on the proposed Alternative Energy Futures Conference. These agreements pertain to four phases of the project's development: (a) proposal design and writing, (b) negotiation with the funder, (c) rewriting and redesign of proposal in the event that the funder grants less money than initially requested, and (d) implementation.

(a) PROPOSAL WRITING

Mr. Solar will be responsible for writing and making all decisions pertaining to the narrative and technical sections of the proposal. Bandwagon Research Institute will prepare the complementary business sections. The two parties will jointly develop the project's schedule, itemize the tasks of the program plan, and prepare the budget.

(b) NEGOTIATION

Both parties must be represented in all negotiation sessions with the funder, whether in person or by telephone. Both parties must sign off on all grant, contract, or subcontract documents.

(c) REWRITING

Mr. Solar has complete responsibility over altering the proposal in the event that the outcome of negotiations with the funder require redesign of the project. BRI has the power of review.

(d) IMPLEMENTATION

The Work Statement as written in the proposal will provide the basis for actual implementation of the project.

Signatures:

____________________	____________________
Mr. Fred Solar	Ms. Rhonda Roberts for Bandwagon Research Institute, Inc.

BEYOND CREDIBILITY

You may have noticed that most of the strategies for building your credibility discussed here are basically defensive: They seek to assuage the funder's natural cautiousness by proving to him that you can be trusted with his grant money. This is a necessary part of operating in the grants world.

But there is also a more powerful way to persuade the funder that your idea is one that deserves his support. Essentially, it involves carrying the concept of collaboration that underlies sponsorship, letters of support, and community endorsement one step further into the realm of coalition building. If this is done skillfully, you move away from limited, two-party exchanges with your funder and toward a position in which, having mobilized many different elements of the service community around your idea, it begins to seem that it is emerging from a collective recognition of real need, and you become simply its spokesman, or agent. The funder then no longer sees himself as entering into a somewhat risky relationship with you alone; instead he feels that he is becoming just one more partner in a broad community package, one that you have provided the catalyst for. This places you in a much more powerful, and fundable, position.

There are a number of specific ways to start building a coalition. Basically, they boil down to *reducing costs* and/or *increasing impact,* or, to put it in a nutshell, getting the most return for your dollar.

Reducing costs begins by playing scavenger: As you build contacts with other service agencies working in your field or in a related area, keep your eye out for anything that they might be able to contribute to your project that could appear on your proposal budget as an in-kind contribution. One agency might have a little extra office space that you can use. Another might be willing to carry you on its WATS line. A third might have a van that it would be willing to let you borrow to serve your clients now and then. A fourth might be willing to lend you its accountant to help you set up your books. A fifth might be able to steer you toward a printer who will donate time and materials to putting together stationery for you. Everything you can show as a local in-kind contribution on your budget when you eventually submit it to the funder will further convince him that you really do represent a coalition of agencies all joining in one way or another to attack a problem.

The concept underlying increasing impact is basically this: If your project is originally designed to serve 30 people but by talking to another agency you recognize that what you want to do could also tie in with their services and benefit their 300 clients, then instead of asking your funder to help you help 30 people you could conceivably wind up building a coalition that would pool clients and allow you to ask the funder to help you help 330 people. The more ripples you can cause in the service delivery system, the more people and impact you can affect, the lower your per unit (i.e., client) costs will be and the more efficient you will become.

As another example of identifying a secondary or an expanded population for your services, you might find that your meditation project for prisoners works just as well for stress-ridden executives and that the Red Cross is willing to cut you in on the clients of some of its stress-prevention classes.

Another way to increase your impact is to cross subject boundaries. You may have set yourself up as a health project (reducing stress). It could be that by affiliating with the local Community College you could add an educational component that would allow your clients to learn prevention techniques as well. By doing so, you have deepened your impact on them.

Or you may find that your collaboration with another agency could sustain your impact on your clients even after they have left your care. For instance, if your bilingual education project is geared toward preschoolers, it will help your program to link up with the kindergarten or first-grade teacher in your area, who could build on your own curriculum after your children move on at the end of the year.

Or you may want to build links with the parents who pick the children up at the end of the day. You have them from 9 to 3; the parents have them from 3 to 9. By building parent components into your project design, you extend the reach of the project and carry its potential impact on to maybe double the coverage it would otherwise have.

Building a coalition means entering into the network of service providers and funders—government agencies, private nonprofit and public nonprofit organizations, and even for-profit individuals and organizations—that spring up all around any clearly defined problem and identifiable client group. The generic name for these networks is service delivery system. All of us, whether we recognize it or not, are already thoroughly familiar with a multitude of conventional service delivery systems (SDSs), simply because they constitute an integral part of any complex urban society. Education, health, criminal justice, employment, research, minority rights, environmental preservation, youth, community development—these are just a few of the fields of complex activity about which an elaborate, constantly changing system of getting services to legitimate users exists.

The handicapped SDS is a good example. Within any large metropolitan area, there is now a vast aggregate of services that exist to meet the needs of the handicapped and to promote their autonomy. They may at times overlap, but there is, as with any SDS, a concerted and continuing effort to see that they complement rather than duplicate one another, insofar as is possible. Some are concerned with the special health problems of the handicapped, others with their housing needs. Some focus on providing information and referral services, others on advocacy of handicapped causes at state and federal levels, still others with special handicapped counseling procedures.

Service delivery systems come in all shapes. The foremost, and in many ways the most logical, is an arrangement that clusters service delivery agencies by major client need, such as education, housing, job placement, transportation, health, counseling, and advocacy. But there are many other ways to take a slice of any SDS, and these overlap. You may, for example, find that the SDS for your client group is already set up by age groups, particularly if you work in an education field. Some SDSs are strictly local; others are national. Some are entirely public; some are private; and some are curious hybrids of the two. Some are rigidly hierarchical and bureaucratic; others are loose and rather amorphous.

Many SDSs follow the lines of local government jurisdictions: Your city may provide one component of a particular client group's needs, while county, state, and federal levels try to fill in other areas. As long as there is good coordination between government levels, this is feasible, but political groupings are inherently highly territorial. Jealousy about their respective prerogatives can undermine collaborative arrangements, cause duplication of effort, or, more likely, leave important client needs unmet simply because they may get shelved as the providers are fighting over whose responsibility it is to respond to this particular group. This is, of course, what happened to the displaced homemakers of Chapter 2. Until Tish Sommers came along, no one was acknowledging responsibility to do something about a dispossessed and victimized sector of the population. The same holds for Joan Cooney and CTW: The education SDS simply had not hooked up with the power of TV as a learning tool until she provided the entrepreneurial catalyst for the connection. Hank Rasé is in on the ground floor of efforts to establish one of the most significant SDSs in the nation's history, one that will eventually make solar energy available to all of us.

Most SDSs are in a constant state of flux, and, furthermore, it takes only a very slight shift in the perspective of the grantseeker to bring a whole new kaleidoscopic pattern of the service network into focus.

HOW YOU CAN RELATE TO THE SDS

Once you do your own research into a service delivery system that relates to your project, you will be able to develop a strategy for complementing rather than competing with its network of services. The point is to interpret your project as a service to *them,* as a way of helping them fulfill their goals. The more you know about the dynamics of the SDS, its strength and weaknesses, the better you will be at figuring out how to fit into it.

It will help you to know that there are at least nine ways that you can argue that your idea can mesh with the SDS:

1. *Missing Link.* The SDS has services that are doing just fine in their own way. The problem is that these services are not properly linked up so that they work together efficiently to eliminate problems. Your idea is not to replace these services but to connect them so that they better solve the problem that is the chief concern of the SDS.

Example: A halfway house for exmental patients to provide a link between mental institutions and various employment and training services.

2. *Symptom to Cause.* You complain that the service delivery system is not really dealing with the heart of the problem that they

are supposed to be addressing. You claim that the existing services are Band-Aid approaches that deal with symptoms but not with causes. You see a possibility of an alternative approach that could eliminate the problem altogether rather than simply treat its effects. So your idea is to demonstrate to the existing service providers the efficacy of another approach that would ultimately serve the function of shifting the service delivery system toward preventive rather than reactive care.

Example: You propose a demonstration project to test out biofeedback as a way of dealing with the underlying stress of hypertension, seeking to prove to the medical profession an effective alternative to the drug-based response to hypertension that is now prevalent in the service delivery system.

3. *Old Message, New Medium.* You understand that the service delivery system is doing good work, but the problem is that certain critical populations of clients are being missed by the prevalent approaches. This neglect is not due to any conscious oversight but occurs simply because the services were not designed with these groups in mind. So, you propose to tailor a message to a specific population by putting it into a new medium so that it communicates effectively.

Example: Your project reduces the isolation of deaf persons by captioning important television programs, like presidential speeches. Or you develop a telephone system for the deaf, a system that not only allows the deaf to communicate with each other but also to reach such emergency services as police and fire stations.

4. *Old Idea, New Population.* You are impressed by a service that has been applied to one distinct group within the service delivery system, but you want to see if it will be transferrable to a new context and a new target population. You want to see how you would have to change this idea for it to be enthusiastically adapted to a new setting. This approach would mean taking a service from one SDS and applying it to another.

Example: You conduct a research study to determine if a relaxation technique which has been successfully used to help executives reduce the risk of cardiovascular disease could be used to help former drug addicts now dependent on methadone taper off.

5. *Anticipate Crisis.* You suspect that the service delivery system

is going its merry way in complete ignorance of a major new factor which is going to render irrelevant or obsolete much of what it is doing.

Example: A study was recently funded by a NASA grant to analyze the possibilities that a canister brought back from Mars with soil samples might contaminate Earth with a virulent, unknown disease. The study concluded, among other things, that the chances of massive plague could be enormously reduced if retrieval of the canister was made outside the Earth's atmosphere, rather than after it had fallen to the surface of the planet.

6. *Consolidate Resources.* You realize that the service delivery system is very inefficient. In some cases, two services are providing nearly the same services for the same small group of persons. In other cases, the target populations are so small that the programs are not cost-effective. You propose to consolidate and streamline some of the services so that costs could be saved and grant money freed up for services that are not presently being provided.

Example: A group developed a community memory project, an information and referral project that replaced the duplication of telephone switchboards, counseling services, and information centers, previously in operation. The project greatly improved the communications channels among nonprofit groups.

7. *Revitalize Markets.* You complain that government-funded service delivery systems are taking over some functions that ought to be generated on a self-sufficient, fee-for-service basis. In fact, you see that, with the proper stimulus, a business climate could be created that would reverse the present trends toward increasing dependency on the public dole. So you propose a grant to cover the startup costs of a new business enterprise that will stimulate new and appropriate economic development.

Example: You propose the refurbishing of a dilapidated, downtown area of a rural community that would have the effect of establishing a tourist trade, staving off complete abandonment of the community by business interests.

8. *Discover a New Population.* You examine the service delivery system and conclude that the service providers have built failure into their methods, since they have chosen the wrong categories to use to look at the problem. Without being able even to see the problem, they are unable to diagnose the clients correctly and

prescribe remedies. Furthermore, they group clients incorrectly, lumping apples and oranges together when they should be separated. So you decide that you want to isolate a specific group that represents, in your judgment, the appropriate treatment category. Then your project would be able to design a learning project intended especially for, and in some cases by, that same group. You argue that the extra costs entailed in separating out this new category are more than justified by the effectiveness of the future results.

Example: You realize that in special education classes at the grade-school level, the brain-damaged children are being mistakenly lumped together with slow learners. The school district is unknowingly stigmatizing these children and creating retardation in those who are actually quite bright. Incensed, you create a diagnostic and placement service which would assure that the children are grouped according to real needs and then grouped in such a way that teachers can work with them successfully.

9. *Discover a Promising New Idea.* You look at the SDS and conclude that the attempts to solve the problem are not quite on target. But you are not sure that you could put your finger on exactly what is wrong. Perhaps you feel that the prevailing approaches lack inspiration. So you propose to throw away the preconceptions that are conventionally accepted in the field and approach the problem in an altogether open-ended way, rather than set yourself up for doing the same old thing. Instead of working toward a predetermined goal, your idea is to help establish an open-ended environment in which new and promising discoveries could be made that are simply not possible in the SDS as it now stands.

Example: You propose to establish an Institute of Biomedical Research to bring together scientists who are innovators in the field. Rather than prescribe outcomes, the grant will simply pay them to continue doing what they do but in a more intensive environment with much more support than is possible while isolated in their respective universities.

All the examples given here are already off to a good start. They have already stated the problem in terms of proposing an advancement not just for you or your "clients," but for the whole field that you are a part of. That means that you are not just speaking for yourself but for the entire community of service providers, who are all trying to learn about the problem and contribute to the evolution of shared learning experiences.

But in this discussion we should not neglect to emphasize that it also must be *your* idea. It should make perfect sense from your own personal, self-interested point of view. Otherwise it is like trying to give your last pair of shoes to the cause, forgetting that to work for it successfully you need to be able to march.

V

Packaging: The Grantseeker as a Proposal Designer

Strange things happen to people when faced with a proposal deadline. Their hands cramp up; their brains turn to oatmeal. They suddenly find a thousand more important things to do, like cleaning the Xerox machine or making a fresh pot of coffee. Procrastination, anxiety, boredom, frustration—all come flooding in.

Why is writing a proposal such a miserable process? Because we sense the power of well-conceived and -written proposals, but we cannot always grasp how they come about. We know there is something there, an organizing principle that can help structure our thoughts and communicate them persuasively, but we are not sure what it is or how to tap into it. We feel confused and hesitant, with the result that we postpone doing it until we are pressed by deadlines, and in the end we may botch it.

Partly, this is a problem of attitude. Either we are too new to the process and we just do not feel confident enough to take charge of something as overwhelming as writing The Proposal, or we are too familiar with the process—we are burned out and cynical—and we tend to dismiss the proposal itself as a relatively insignificant part of grantseeking, insisting that contacts and connections are all that count.

There is a little bit of truth in both these views. Novice grant-writers usually are not forceful enough or daring enough to attract the right kind of attention; they usually do not as yet have a sufficiently fluent command of the funder's language. Instead, they tend to waste a lot of time trying to respond as literally as possible to every blank on the funder's guidelines, filling in every box on the application form and making sure that they have done everything right. And it is also true that *who* you know is often as important as what you say or how well you present it, but when the cynic tries only to tell the funder what he thinks it wants to hear, the process becomes an empty ritual of compliance rather than a genuine attempt at conveying one's inspiration in written form.

Ironically, actually getting the grant can be a disaster in either case because the bad faith or anxiety that underlie the proposal writing will be mirrored in the project. Lack of foresight, careful planning, and sincere commitment will lead to confusion and apathy. Once it has lost touch with its own integrity, the project usually gets side-tracked and either speeds up feverishly to cover up its lack of purpose or slowly grinds to a halt. Ultimately, the lack of attention to the proposal design process leads to wasted potential for change.

It's more than just a matter of attitude. The proposal itself, whether a 3-page letter or a 300-page volume of forms, narratives, work statements, contracts, schedules, budgets, charts, biographies, and appendixes, is a complex and demanding document, an important intersection where at least five major functions converge.

THE FIVEFOLD FUNCTION OF THE PROPOSAL

1. The Proposal as a Sales Piece

The first thing a good proposal must do is build a link between the funder's orientation and yours, between what he needs and what you have to offer. In other words, it needs to sell. Typically, this is done by demonstrating how your project will help fulfill the funder's mission. You should relate your concept to the problems he is interested in resolving or the activities he wants to support, and the rationale for your project. Is he in business to save the whales? Then your proposal for a marine mammal sanctuary will at least get past the secretary and into the executive director's hands.

2. The Proposal as a Concept Paper

Second, the proposal should tersely describe your concept: why, what, and how. This is the broadest function that the proposal serves, that of plain description of what it is you have in mind, why it is important or interesting, who will benefit from it, and why it is the best possible approach to making the changes you want to bring about. Next year when the newly hired project secretary asks, "What the devil is going on here?" you should be able to answer him by just giving him the proposal to read.

3. The Proposal as a Plan

Third, a proposal is a step-by-step working plan, showing in as much detail as necessary what objectives you will be shooting for, the specific tasks these objectives imply, how long it will take you to accomplish them, what kind of organizational structure and staffing you will need, and what the whole process will cost. It should stand out as a way of guiding the project's implementation.

4. The Proposal as an Agreement

Fourth, the proposal is a legal agreement, almost a contract, outlining specifically what the funder will be getting in return for writing out a check.

5. The Proposal as an Evaluation Design

Finally, the proposal constitutes the basis for evaluating the project. Since it gives a clear and detailed picture of your intentions, it is the most logical yardstick to use when the project is underway and once it is ended to judge how well you have measured up to expectations.

Understanding that these are the basic functions of any proposal will prepare you to communicate with others about your project in a much more fluid way. It gives you command over the range of possible perspectives that may be brought to bear by funders, sponsors, clients, and staff members on what you are doing. It gives you access to their points of view and allows you to interpret the raw material of your vision appropriately for different audiences. Some will be interested in the whole package, in all five functions. Others will zero in on one specific topic, such as how you intend to accomplish your third objective in three months, or what you plan to do once your current funding runs out, or how they can help you set up the most suitable accounting systems.

There must be, above all, an appropriate balance in the relationship among these central elements and your treatment of them. If you place too much emphasis on the sales function, the design will finally come across as weakly planned, not implementable, and perhaps cynical. There is a tendency for proposals like this to become overly dependent on one funder.

If you give too much emphasis to the concept, the proposal will seem too remote from practical, "do-able" reality.

Too much emphasis on the plan, the systematic nuts and bolts of grantgetting, will make your proposal too rational. You will lose the all-important elements of inspiration and surprise.

Understanding the many facets of the proposal places you in the center of its design, a position from which you will be able to turn to meet new questions, speak meaningfully to divergent points of view, and coordinate the participation of others who may join you in the writing. Instead of handing out pat answers and cookbook directions, you will be able to convey the intrinsic dynamics of the entire process.

STRUCTURE: WHY, WHAT, AND HOW

Proposals come in all shapes and sizes, but each and every one, if effective, is organized around a simple yet powerful framework of Why, What, and How. If you ground yourself in these three terms, explained below, you will have no trouble translating your grant request into whatever specific format a funder may require.

The Why Section: The Pitch

The first section, the Why section, builds a bridge between your world and the funder's. It gets your foot in the door. That is not to say that it has to be pushy or flashy, but it has to let the busy foundation director know as quickly and succinctly as possible why he or she should take the time to give your proposal a serious reading soon. The fact of the matter is that anyone with money to give away, regardless of how narrowly defined his mission, target population, or geographical area of operation may be, is deluged with proposals. Since a majority of these should not even have been submitted in the first place, usually because they bear little or no relationship to the funder's interests, he naturally develops a highly critical screening process in sheer self-defense. Anything that looks as if it came from someone who hasn't done his homework instantly gets a polite letter of rejection, if that, in the return mail. This means that even before you think about sending your proposal to a funder you have to know that it addresses a problem he is disposed to take an interest in, that it offers to work in the geographical area he has selected for grantgiving and that it asks for an amount of money that is not too far removed from his customary giving range.

The Why section of the proposal goes by a number of more conventional names: Needs Assessment, Problem Statement, Background, and Rationale. It can be divided logically into four major subsections.

1. General Problem

This is the general need, as perceived by the funder. Here you get his attention by discussing his interests. Often this section includes a profile of the broad target group that you intend to serve. Describe its needs and characteristics. Don't try to educate the funder yet.

2. Hone Down

The second subsection hones down your discussion of the client group to a more manageable level and zeros in on the specific way in which you intend to solve at least part of the problem. This is where you inform the funder about ways to solve his own problem that he could not have envisioned without you.

You can do this in any of three ways: (a) by describing your client group as an acute example of the larger problem, implying that by studying it you will solve more of the problem than by choosing another sample; (b) by arguing that your client group is typical, so that what you learn from studying it will be more transferable to the entire population than another case; and (c) by arguing that *your method* is the most promising one for either solving or "shedding light on" the problem.

3. What Has Been Done

The third subsection makes you more believable by showing your familiarity with past efforts to resolve this same problem or meet the needs of the client group set forth in the first two subsections. Having already described the subtleties of the problem itself, you now need to discuss in detail the history of approaches to solving it: What has worked, what has not worked, and how the community of people aware of, and responsive to, the problem has evolved. Whether you discuss the history of past projects or review the pertinent literature, what you need to do here is establish your grasp of what has been learned from past attempts to resolve the problem. In other words, avoid making the naïve mistake of issuing a blanket condemnation of everything that has preceded you.

4. Introduce Yourself

In the last step of the Why section, not before, introduce your organization. You have built a connection with the funder's interests, shown how your clients relate to his mission, and identified yourself with the history of previous efforts to deal with this problem. Now you need to show what it is about you that makes you the best candidate to carry the learning process on to the next step.

This is the place to toot your own horn. Talk about your track record. Or, if you do not have one yet, talk about the special qualifications of your staff members or your consultants. Explain what you have already learned about delivering services to this particular population.

If you are part of an already successful project and are looking for continuation money, this is where you tell your prospective funder just how successful you have been in the past and what you plan to do to expand your success or to reach even more clients with similar unmet needs.

If you do this right, you demonstrate to the funder that you have inherited a learning process, one that has evolved from past solution efforts, and that you are exercising a sense of discrimination in your project design by discarding the unworkable and building on the positive. You also demonstrate to the funder that the services you will be providing will *complement,* not duplicate, existing services. In short, you show that you are not about to reinvent the wheel. In doing so, you not only avoid looking naïve, you also establish your service credentials in the funder's eyes.

Describe your readiness for the proposed project in such a way that you clearly give the funder the idea that you are coming to him with a pre-existing commitment to working on this problem, but that you cannot take the next logical step without more money. On the other hand, you also have to be careful to show him that once you get the money you will not continue to need fresh infusions of cash, that what you appear to be offering to the funder as an asset, a way of helping him fulfill his own purposes, will not become a liability by turning into a drain on his resources.

A sample Why statement: Noting the recent rise in the popularity of jogging, the National Institute of Allergies and Disease Control (NIADC) decides to distribute a Request for Proposal calling for research that will help provide a cure for athlete's foot.

One of the many respondents, the Laboratory for Superscience Studies (LSS), is primarily engaged in conducting basic research in molecular biology. Applications to the solution of health problems are a little removed from LSS's main emphasis. However, LSS is nearing completion of a major study on protean molecules and is running out of money. It wants very much to continue its investigations, since its researchers are close to achieving a major breakthrough in understanding the protean molecule, but they are not sure they can successfully shift to a related field just to get a grant. The NIADC Request for Proposal looks very good to them; it raises the possibility that they might be able to design a project that links what NIADC wants to have done with what LSS wants to do in a way that would violate neither the NIADC requirements nor the basic LSS orientation. But doing this calls for a deft sales approach.

Here is the argument that LSS constructs:

GENERAL PROBLEMS

Athlete's foot (ringworm) is a common problem long thought to be an insignificant health hazard. However, its incidence has risen dramatically in recent years. According to a longitudinal study conducted by Lam and Horowitz (1977), whereas a decade ago only about 1 million Americans were afflicted with the problem, today the figure is closer to 60 million.

The fungus strikes without discrimination as to age or sex, but it is especially prominent in men aged 16 to 45. Lam and Horowitz estimate that this group constitutes about three-quarters of the affected population. Its incidence in this group is significantly correlated with the presence of hyperhydrosis, or excessive perspiration in the hands and feet.

Although the disease is usually not considered a serious health hazard, it can develop to quite painful stages and, if untreated, can require hospitalization. The scaling and itching of even moderate cases of athlete's foot can be highly uncomfortable. From an epidemiological point of view, the presence of the disease in about one out of every four Americans constitutes an epidemic and qualifies the disorder for serious attention by the medical and research community.

METHOD

Conventional preventive and environmentally oriented approaches to treating athlete's foot are inadequate. Foot baths, powders, creams, specially ventilated footwear, ultraviolet light, and the wearing of chemically treated socks all share a common failing: They attempt to treat the problem dermatologically, once the disease has developed detectable symptoms. No serious attempt to delineate the early biological evolution of the ringworm fungus has yet been undertaken, although a great deal of closely related work in the area of the molecular substratum underlying its growth has been accomplished in recent years. Exploring the possibility of a fundamental biomedical solution that will inoculate individuals against the appearance of the disease in the first place now seems entirely feasible, but only rigorous laboratory investigations will demonstrate the validity of this approach. Once the phases that a ringworm fungus must pass through in order to achieve viability in a host organism are identified, follow-up studies on the application of these findings will stand a better chance of determining how best to block the process in the first place, whether through improved dermatological swabs or through ingestion of a chemical antagonist. It may even be possible to eradicate the ringworm fungus entirely, but this admittedly remote option clearly would require further exploration of ancillary environmental impacts.

TYPICAL CASE

The most promising context for test investigation of the biomedical substratum to athlete's foot would seem to be the protean molecule, since its behavior is entirely characteristic of the ringworm fungus constellation, but exhibits none of the idiosyncratic patterns common to other molecular ringworm constituents.

LITERATURE REVIEW

Although no work whatsoever, to our knowledge, has yet appeared on the ringworm molecular structure as a discrete entity, there are related studies in the literature on protean characteristics.[1]

As well as the longitudinal study cited previously, Lam and Horowitz have extensively described their intubated molecular investigations at the University of Swarthington.[2] In addition, an extensive body of protean molecule literature is cited in the

[1]See Stiller, 1969a, 1969b; Halmholtz, 1954; and NIADC, 1972.
[2]*Proceedings on the ADS,* 1973.

bibliography of LSS's most recent report on peptide molecule loading (see Appendix A).

SELF-CREDENTIALS

LSS is a world-renowned leader in the field of molecular research, particularly that focusing on the protean element. In addition to serving as the sponsor of the ADS for the past five years, Dr. Edward Vesicle, director of LSS and proposed principal investigator, is an internationally respected authority on invasive fungi lesions. Dr. Vesicle's seventeenth monograph[3] on symbiotic transferences in the subarachnoid segment has just been published.

The LSS labs are equipped with the most recent scalar emanators and computer scan refractors. No other facility in the world can duplicate the LSS capability for this project.

The What Section: The Goal

This section presents your intended change. What will your project do? What will the funder's money purchase? And, especially, what difference will your project make in the world?

To focus your thoughts on this section, try this exercise. Take a sheet of paper and fold it in half lengthwise. Keeping it folded, write *What Is* at the top of the left side of the page and under it list the major characteristics of the problem area and the client group, as they now exist. An example drawn from the Center for Independent Living profile of Chapter II might look like this:

WHAT IS

1. Low mobility of handicapped.
2. Tendency of service agencies to "warehouse" severely handicapped individuals.
3. Severely limited educational and job opportunities.
4. Little or no influence on political processes affecting handicapped lives.

[3]Herald Press, 1978.

Then turn the page over, label the right side *What Will Be,* and describe the changes that your project will have brought about by its final day. It may be that you have only one central goal in mind. Or, more likely, there will be a number of possible goals, ranging from the specific to the highly abstract, from the trivial and obvious to the global and nebulous. List them all.

A hypothetical *What Will Be* list based on the CIL story might look like this:

WHAT WILL BE

1. All handicapped people will be able to enjoy maximum mobility.
2. Barriers between the mainstream culture and the handicapped will be removed or minimized.
3. The Center for Independent Living will have a physical facility of its own.
4. The Center will be financially self-sufficient, through fees and the sale and repair of powered wheelchairs.
5. Public consciousness about the handicapped will have to be raised.
6. Curb cuts will have been made in all city streets.
7. Bathrooms will be designed to accommodate the handicapped.
8. Public buildings will be made accessible to the handicapped with ramps, wider aisles, and wider doors, among other things.
9. Greater amounts of tax money will be allocated to helping advance handicapped well-being.
10. More unemployed persons will be subsidized to train for jobs as aides to the handicapped.

If you have trouble envisioning in detail the effects that your project will bring about, sometimes a fantasy helps visualize these potential changes more vividly. Imagine that you have available a magical helicopter with a time button. On the first day of the project, you get in it, you push the time button, and you zoom forward to the last day of the funding period. Then you just hover over the project site and the community around it, and you look around, identifying all the different changes that your project has been responsible for. You observe different physical circumstances, different attitudes, different procedures, different ways of behaving, different topics of conversation, different ways to accomplish things. All this can help expand your list of goals.

Once you have a representative number of items in the goals list —say between five and ten—the next step is to go back and winnow out the two extremes, the superficial and the grandiose, and concentrate on those in the middle range, those that are ambitious but feasible. Also, as you go through your first goals list, you will probably notice interrelationships among items, that some seem to be logically subordinate to others. For instance, in the CIL example above, the first two goals are almost the same—"All handicapped people will be able to enjoy maximum mobility" and "Barriers between the mainstream culture and the handicapped will be removed or minimized" are almost identical; the second states the first in negative terms. Furthermore, in that same list, items 6, 7, and 8 are really just a series of specific objectives that need to be accomplished if the first two broad goals are to be achieved. Also, item 9, "Greater amounts of tax money will be allocated to helping advance handicapped well-being," is more of a statement of means, of one method by which the major goals of greater mobility and assimilation are to be achieved.

So you have to become critical about what is a broad goal and what is a more specific and limited objective, a concrete milestone along the way to achieving more abstract purposes. You also have to distinguish clearly between ends and means, between where you want to go and how you want to get there.

Next try to narrow your first list down to one central, overarching goal. It should encompass all the dimensions of your project and yet be specific enough so that a funder can immediately grasp what it is you are after. Cast it in formal terms the first time around and then rewrite it more casually for submission to less formal funders. If possible, write it in the form of a two-part sentence, containing a first clause that sums up *what* you want to do, followed by a secondary clause that conveys *how* you intend to accomplish it, in general terms.

Again, the CIL example of such a goal statement might start out something like this:

> The goal of CIL is to promote greater opportunities for participation in mainstream American culture for all types of handicapped individuals, by assertively demonstrating to the American public that even the most severely handicapped individuals are entirely capable of leading autonomous and productive lives if given equal, competitive access to governmental, educational, and employment resources.

This version may be a bit too grand. Preferably, your goal will mesh smoothly with the funder's own mission but will not compete with its scope or scale.

The critical issues that a funder would almost certainly want clarified somewhere in the proposal following this CIL goal statement would be: What specifically does "promote greater opportunities" mean in terms of measuring the feasibility and likely success of the project? What would constitute an assertive demonstration of handicapped autonomy and productivity? Honing the first try at a goal statement down a bit to a more manageable level would yield this second version:

> CIL intends, by operating a community resource and advocacy center staffed by quadraplegics and paraplegics, to show that even severely handicapped Americans need not be excluded from equal participation in all facets of American life simply because of physical disability.

This is a goal that both grantee and funder can live with and be realistically optimistic about achieving. It tells what you want to do and how you want to approach it. It does not threaten a funder with global overtones. More detail about the nature of the demonstration and how it was to be effectively disseminated would have to be forthcoming in the remainder of the proposal, but the basic statement of the concept is sound: not too small, not too large . . . but just about right.

The How Section: The Plan

This section, usually called the Project Description, is the heart of the proposal. Here you show your funder exactly how you plan to get from the first day to the last day of the actual operation of the project, the point at which your intended changes should have materialized in three-dimensional reality.

Objectives

The first thing to do is a little surveying. Map out the major steps that will take you from Day One to Project Termination, the last day of the funding cycle. These major steps, which are actually subgoals, are like the intermediate base camps on a mountain-climbing expedition. They are conventionally called Objectives or Milestones.

The best way to map these out is chronologically. What do you need first, to get the project underway? Second? Third? Typically, a project will have at least six to eight major chronological milestones. The first might be something like Project Organization; the second, Planning; the third, Field-Testing; the fourth, Pilot Implementation; the fifth, Operation; the sixth, Evaluation; the seventh, Future Funding or Phase-Out; and the eighth, Dissemination of Results.

Some of these steps may not turn out to be strictly sequential. Operation, for example, would probably overlap with Evaluation, Phase-Out, and Dissemination. Dissemination might begin while Phase-Out was being wrapped up. But for the purposes of presentation in the Project Description, simply focus on the starting date for each milestone and maintain the chronological sequentiality of this section.

Activities

Once you have identified the major milestones, your next step is to break them down even further into specific activities. Project Organization, the first major milestone, might logically subdivide into: (1.1) Coordination with sponsor, (1.2) Coordination with collaborating agencies, (1.3) Purchase of materials, (1.4) Rental and alteration of space, (1.5) Hiring of staff, and (1.6) Staff orientation. At this point, it will help to begin charting these sections of the Project Description in a parallel format, like that shown on page 186. The more closely parallel you can make your plan in the How section of your proposal, the more clearly you will be able to visualize the sequence of the project's operation and the more likely it is that you will be able to convince your funder that you are thoroughly familiar with what you are doing. Remember, however, that the Project Description is a *plan,* not a cast-inbronze contract. There is a tentative element about it, and your funder will almost always suggest changes in it. Furthermore, the very implementation of the project will inevitably bring you face-to-face with contingencies that will also force further modification and improvisation. So, treat the Project Description as a generally accurate but provisional document. Do not get trapped into non-negotiable positions of absolute commitment to fulfilling its every detail before the project has even started.

In your division of objectives into activities, be as detailed as possible. Plot every individual step that has to be taken, short of reducing the plan to an absurdly obsessive level. The more significant detail you can bring to it, the more competent you will appear in the funder's eyes.

Documentation

The next step in the Project Description is Documentation, your plan to establish a paper trail so that all your activities can be traced in tangible form and eventually evaluated. For instance, if you plan to hire a coordinator, then you should note in this column that you will be opening a personnel file for him or her. And, if you then plan to put the coordinator to work setting up contacts with other agencies in your service delivery system, you will want to have some formal record of the coordinator's activities, perhaps in the form of agreements between your agency and another. The point is that all your activities must be trackable.

Schedule

The documentation section of the Project Description is followed by construction of the timeline, an approximate schedule showing how long you think it will take you to reach each milestone. Novice grantseekers characteristically tend to underestimate the amount of time that these major steps will take. If you do not feel experienced enough to make sound judgments about these estimations, get some expert advice from a consultant, someone who has been directly involved in planning and implementing a social service project. Or, if your funder offers any kind of technical assistance, do the best you can to work these times out on your own, and then explore the possibility of getting further assistance in defining them more accurately with your funder's help.

Budget by Objectives

Finally, you get to the meaty part of the Project Description, the budget. How much is it going to cost you to get to each milestone? What percentage of your budget will have been spent by the time you are one-third of the way through the funding period? Half-way through? Three-quarters?

Having broken your budget down by objectives in this way will make it that much simpler to then go back and aggregate your anticipated expenses for each of the typical categories in a conventional line-item budget. Budgets for social service projects typically subdivide into two major categories: expenses for personnel, which often accounts for 75 to 80 percent of the total project cost; and everything else. A standard line-item budget will include these categories:

- Personnel
  - Wages and salaries
  - Fringe benefits
  - Consultants and contract services
- Non-personnel
  - Space costs
  - Rent, lease, or purchase of equipment
  - Consumable supplies
  - Travel
    - Local
    - Out-of-town
  - Telephone
  - Purchase of services (i.e., computer time, printing, publication costs)
  - Other (i.e., postage, subscriptions, library acquisitions, insurance, professional dues, etc.)
  - Indirect costs

For each of these categories, show how much of your total budget will be coming from local and other sources. Include donated services and other "in-kind" contributions. These demonstrate to the funder that your project enjoys the committed support of the community, and that the funder is not being expected to shoulder its costs all by himself.

Most funders have pre-established budget guidelines for you to follow, so check with them on this point before preparing this section. Generally, you can expect government grantors to require more extensive budget breakouts and justification for line items than foundations. In any event, check on allowable direct cost categories, indirect cost percentages, whether or not the funder will expect you to submit a standardized budget form, whether a percentage of your budget request *must* come from local sources (i.e., from "matching funds") and if so, how much. Also find out what adjustments, if any, can be made to the budget once the project is underway. Try to research budgets for projects similar to yours so that you can make your salary and other cost figures competitive. Finally, do not pad your budget or starve it. Neither over- nor under-estimating the costs of a project is ever a good tactic. Most funders are already far too sensitive to project costs to be taken in. A sample Project Description is shown on page 186.

Evaluation Design

A good proposal includes a separate section on evaluation, outlining the process that will be used to judge the project's degree of success in actually causing change. Evaluation designs serve a dual purpose: First, they provide a system of feedback, more or less continuously, so that a project can take in-progress readings on its impact as it moves along and can thus redirect its activities, if necessary, so as to more fully realize its objectives. Second, the evaluation system sets forth the basis for judging its success in achieving its goals once the funding period is over. Ideally, each purpose serves the common function of building in a learning process by which you and your funder can benefit from your mistakes.

If you have separated out your Whys, Whats, and Hows, and already spelled out how you are going to document your activities, a good basic evaluation design is easy to write. Essentially, the design simply states what you are going to evalu-

PROJECT DESCRIPTION: A BILINGUAL GRADE SCHOOL PROGRAM

Objectives	Activities	Documentation	Schedule	Budget by Objectives	Percent of Budget Expense
1. By 9/1/78, the organizational structure of the project will have been established and the initial planning completed.	1.1 Hire coordinator 1.2 Select site 1.3 Acquire supplies and materials 1.4 Recruit and hire staff 1.5 Establish project policies 1.6 Develop liaison with related projects 1.7 In-service staff workshops on test development 1.8 Establish community advisory committee	1.1 Personnel file 1.2 Lease 1.3 Invoice 1.4 Ad copy/Interview schedule sheet/personnel files 1.5 Policy memo 1.6 Contact record 1.7 Workshop memo, schedule/sample tests 1.8 Invitations to serve	1. Completion of all Objective 1 activities within first three months of project operation	$37,500	25

ate and how you are going to go about doing it. Divide it into these five parts:

1. Overview

What changes are you trying to bring about through the operation of your project? State them. Will there be any special problems involved in determining whether these changes have taken place due to your project? State them too. Do time, money, or other limiting factors restrict what can be evaluated? Say so.

2. Data

Refer to your documentation plan and summarize the kinds of raw materials you are going to use as a base for your judgments (e.g., tests, sign-in sheets, monitoring forms, monthly turnover charts, board minutes, director's reports, tapes, photos, etc.). Will these documents tell you all you need to know? Will you have to supplement them with data from other sources or subjective reports?

3. Data Collection Procedures

How are you going to collect your evaluation data? How often? Where will it be stored? Who will take care of it? How will it be managed? Will a secretary take care of it? Will it need a separate filing system?

4. Analysis

How are you going to make judgments once the information has been collected? Who will do the analysis? How often?

5. Dissemination

What will you do with the results of the analysis? How, when, and to whom will it be distributed?

Embellishments: The Title Page, the Abstract, and the Future Funding Plan

Once you have completed the three major components of the proposal, the Why, What, and How sections, you are in a good position then to go back and tack on a couple of additional elements, which, though of secondary importance, are still valuable.

Title Page/Cover Letter

The title itself should be as short but as descriptive of the project as possible. Include the name of your organization, along with a contact person's name, address, and phone number; the name of the funder to whom you are submitting the proposal; the inclusive dates of the proposed project; the total amount of money you are requesting; and signatures of any members of your organization who must sign-off on proposal submissions.

Government funders usually have a standard title page form for applicants to use. If you are applying to a private-sector philanthropist, your proposal itself will tend to be shorter and more informal, and your cover letter will probably convey a more personal touch.

The Abstract

The abstract is a highly condensed overview of the entire proposal, touching pithily (no more than 300 words; about 1 page of typescript) on the problem area you are addressing, the solution you are proposing, your objectives, evaluation procedures, dissemination plans, and the total cost. It distills the essence of each major proposal section and serves it up neat.

There are two functions to an abstract: (1) the psychological function of forcing yourself to specify your ideas in concrete terms, which in turn brings them down to earth and makes them feasible, and (2) the sales function of giving the funder concise answers to all his immediate questions, forestalling his natural tendency to go directly to the budget and use its bottom line as the sole criterion for deciding whether to go ahead and read through your proposal in detail or to push it back to the bottom of the heap. A sample abstract is shown on page 196.

Future Funding Plan

Unfortunately, you can't ever rest in the grants world. You have to use what you didn't have before to try to get what you are going to need next. Even at the proposal stage, you have to consider what you intend to do once the funds from one source run out, to assuage your prospective funder's inevitable fears that you are going to be dependent on it forever and ever.

Options for future funding that grant-supported projects can pursue once the first funding cycle draws to a close fall into six major categories:

1. You can seek a continuation grant from the same funder, that is, support to keep on doing what you have been doing, somewhat refined and improved because you now have much more experience with doing it well. If you know before you ever apply to a funder in the first place that you may want to come back to it later for a continuation grant, you can structure your first proposal so that it makes that contingency explicit: If the first funding period is successful, it will be regarded as a trial run, a pilot period, and it is understood by both you and the funder that you will reapply for a second grant at its close.

2. You can also go to another grantor, one who is interested in supporting the area you work in, and preferably one who offers long-term "hard" funding. A good way to make this transition is to explain to your first funder that your long-term goal is to move into a more secure funding network, and that you want to use its grants to pay for the project's shakedown cruise so that you can gain enough credibility to attract more secure support. The first funder is then in the position of acting as a catalyst. It pays your start-up costs and gets you off the ground and into a position where you can bring other resources to bear on your project goals. Most grantors enjoy this role of bringing a new and promising idea into the light and then passing it on to more secure funding sources. Other than working your way into the United Way's good graces, this option usually means lobbying to shift local, state, or federal budget priorities, or those of your sponsor, so as to incorporate your project into their long-term plans.

3. You can move toward contracts. Once you know you have a service to provide and skill in doing so, it usually is not hard to

reorient your funding search toward contracts rather than grants. This is the process followed by Joan Cooney in the evolution of Children's Television Workshop, described in Chapter II.

4. You can carry Step 3 a bit further and actually begin to explore nongrant sources of income for your project, such as offering your services to your clients for a fee. Naturally, your ability to achieve this kind of self-sufficiency depends on the nature of your market. Is there sufficient demand for what you do? Or will your project create that demand? What kind of competition is there? What fee level will your clients tolerate? Would they continue to seek and use your services if you charged for them?

Another type of nongrant income is the annual fund-raising program, which attempts to mobilize reliable past donors as well as tap new prospects. In most cases, taking this course means learning something about direct mail solicitation and how to effectively bargain with print and electronic media. Some nonprofit organizations, such as museums, meet a substantial part of their operating costs each year through membership and educational programs. Others hold special events, like fairs or dinners.

5. You can change the basic nature of the project. Typically, the experience of the first year of operation opens up insights into how your efforts could be redirected so as to more appropriately meet old and new needs. You may see opportunities for spin-off projects, new satellites created by your orbit. Or you may want to move away from providing direct services and into more emphasis on disseminating what you have already learned and on training others to take over service delivery. Projects evolve as they operate, and the gradations of their growth can be arranged along a continuum.

6. You can plan to phase out. As we stated earlier, some foundation executives predict an imminent rise in the number of ad hoc, short-term projects intentionally designed to have only a brief lifespan but whose repercussions continue after the project itself dissolves. Once these projects end, the need is not to perpetuate them but to see that their lessons are well disseminated so that others can make use of what was discovered in the process.

The underlying point is that no organization is a fixed entity. As you enter and move through the granting process, into contracts, fees for service, memberships, and outright development of commercial markets, the nature of your organization will also inevitably change. If you understand this principle and plan for it, you can stay on top of the grant cycle, anticipate the next steps, and grow. If you do not understand it, you can get stuck in a mentality common among grantseekers, one that sees the end of each funding cycle as nothing more than a dreadful hurdle, when the tedious need to search for new money to continue to do what they have been doing arises yet once more. A chart that describes how one hypothetical grantee made a creative transition from one grant to another is included on the following page.

ONCE THE FUNDING DECISION HAS BEEN MADE

If you have been successful and have gotten the grant, congratulations. Immediately put a thank-you note in the mail to the grantor, something along the lines of the example shown on page 195.

Note that the example asks for a list of similar projects funded by the same grantor in the past. By making this request, you can extend your potential contact with the service delivery system and develop the basis for a coalition of service providers in your field.

It is unfortunately far more likely that your first efforts to get a grant will fail. But it is important to try to learn as much as you can from your failure before reworking the proposal and looking for another prospect. Be sure that you have exhausted all feedback channels and appeal opportunities with the current funder first. As soon as you receive your letter of rejection, send a formal request asking for more detailed reasons for the turn-down. (A sample is shown on page 194.)

SAMPLE FORMATS

In the previous chapter we emphasized the importance of having a grasp of the *principles* of proposal writing and then writing an abstract or concept paper that describes your project. The next step is to tailor your proposal to an individual funding source, altering the structure to fit into the format suggested by a particular funder.

HOW ONE GRANT CAN LEAD INTO ANOTHER

Feasibility Study	Seed Grant	Basic Research Grant	Applied Research Grant	Demonstration Grant	Spinoffs	Contracts	Market Development	Planning Grants	Training and Dissemination
Example: To study whether wind can be tapped as an energy source in the Midwest	To pay start-up cost of windmill	To study the attributes of wind power	To test the hypothesis that wind power is potentially cheaper than	To light the streets of Chicago's Loop by wind power	Spinoff Grants: To light the billboards along the Loop as well	To subcontract to utility company to provide ongoing services	To residential wind generators and lobby to remove public subsidy of nonwind utilities	To recommend how utility policies could be changed to remove subsidies on nonwind forms of electricity	To train wind energy technicians for depressed rural areas with high wind velocity

In the next few pages we have included examples of written communications between grantors and grantees: letters and an actual successful proposal, submitted by the Palo Alto (California) Adolescent Services Corporation to the San Mateo Foundation, which was profiled in Chapter III. It was written in part by its Executive Director, Ms. Cheri Miller, who is unusually deft at tailoring her projects to public and private funding sources.

While reading the sample proposal, note the matter-of-fact discussion in the cover letter showing the organization's concerns about the uncertainty of funding from CETA and the fact of the simultaneous submission of this proposal to other local funders. In the section labeled "The Problem—Background" (page 204) note the emphasis on locally developed statistics to verify the need for the program. Note that in this case the goal was written generally, but the objectives are quite specific. In keeping with proposals to community foundations, the method ("How") section is not detailed, since it is assumed that the funder will have ongoing contact with the grantee during the project's implementation. The original proposal contained several important appended materials which have been omitted here for the sake of brevity.

SAMPLE LETTER OF INTENT TO SUBMIT A PROPOSAL

December 15, 1978

Ms. Nancy Brewer
Program Officer
Women's Educational Equity Act
Office of Education
400 Maryland Ave. S.W., Room 3121
Washington, D.C. 20202

Dear Ms. Brewer:

I understand that the Women's Education Equity Act administers funds in the area of career development for postsecondary students. I am interested in implementing a project called New Careers for Women.

I would appreciate your reviewing the enclosed concept paper for that project, which is now in the planning stages. I feel that the project fits perfectly within the intention of the legislation of the Act.

I welcome your comments regarding the project's design. I particularly would like to get your suggestions of what women's groups we should be contacting and possibly affiliating with. If you believe we are eligible, please send all necessary forms. If you believe we are ineligible, please explain why and refer me to other funders with the Office of Education or elsewhere.

Very truly yours,

Karen Jones
Executive Director
Middletown Y.W.C.A.

SAMPLE LETTER OF RESPONSE TO A REJECTION BY A GOVERNMENT FUNDER[4]

February 1, 1979

RE: Project 31417A

Ms. Nancy Brewer
Program Officer
Women's Educational Equity Act
Office of Education
400 Maryland Ave., S.W., Room 3121
Washington, D.C. 20202

Dear Ms. Brewer:

I received with disappointment your letter informing me that our New Careers for Women project was not approved for funding.

The reasons you gave for the disapproval of the application were quite general. Would you please provide us with the *specific* reasons for its rejection.

Could I submit an amended application in the near future? Do you have suggestions of other possible sources of support?

[4]According to the Freedom of Information Act, an individual has the *right* to know the specific reasons for the disapproval.

Thank you for your consideration.

Sincerely yours,

Karen Jones
Executive Director
Middletown Y.W.C.A.

SAMPLE THANK-YOU FOR THE GRANT LETTER AND A REQUEST FOR LISTS OF OTHERS FUNDED

April 30, 1979

Ms. Elinor G. Barber
Program Officer
Ford Foundation
320 East 43rd Street
New York, New York 10017

Dear Ms. Barber:

We wish to acknowledge your letter of April 15, 1979, informing us of the award of $75,000 to support the Nuclear Proliferation Study project by our organization.

Please accept our gratitude and appreciation for this grant. Be assured that it will be administered in accordance with Ford Foundation policies. Further, we wish to establish an ongoing communications with you to assure that our study becomes part of your program in International Affairs and that it has a maximum amount of impact on your own policies in this area.

We wish also to be in touch with, and possibly to form, collaborative relationships with others involved with similar projects. I would appreciate your sending the names and addresses of those presently funded through your division.

Thank you for your help.

Sincerely yours,

Henry Harrison
Executive Director
Peace Initiatives, Inc.

SAMPLE ABSTRACT OR CONCEPT PAPER

"Making Waves in the Mainstream"

Matrix of Change proposes to the Carnegie Corporation the first year funding of a Western regional states' conference on special education called "Making Waves in the Mainstream."

Now is the crucial time for the funding of this conference, since a vast number of local school districts throughout the nation in the Fall of 1978 began implementing special education programs under federally mandated legislation known as PL 94-142 for ages 3 to 18. By 1980 ages 3 to 21 will be covered under this law.

The new law impinges on public schools at a critical time when they are faced with financial burdens of declining enrollments, reduced tax bases, inflation, an overabundance of older faculty at the upper end of the salary schedule, and collective bargaining. It also makes new demands at a time when schools are criticized for failing to provide "normal" children with adequate educational experiences. The new mainstreaming could be seen as simply another stress factor bringing the system close to bankruptcy and adding to the adversary atmosphere that presently pervades public schools. However, along with the stresses come new possibilities. In fact, there are many influences (legal, political, economic, educational, and moral) that suggest that the mainstreaming effort could lead toward individualization of instruction for *all* children; it could create a new understanding of how all children learn; and it could force all concerned groups to take responsibility for bringing these changes about without simply "throwing new money" at the problem. The proposed conference will create an open-ended forum for examining all the diverse factors that must be integrated for this latent potential of the mainstreaming effort to be realized. It will be structured to provoke the underlying issues, stimulate debate, and begin steps toward providing education with a new source of leadership. Classroom teachers, special education teachers, administrators, school board members, specialists in educational and other settings, and parents will attend a conference in the Spring of 1979 with a program that encompasses major themes derived from economic, political, educational, legal, and moral influences on mainstreaming. The sum of $12,700.00 is requested for this purpose.

The setting for the proposed conference is the San Francisco Bay Area. A total of 800 to 1200 participants are expected, as well as a series of distinguished speakers and workshop leaders. The outcomes of the conference are expected to be (1) a list of specific recommendations for meeting the intention of PL 94-142, (2) the formation of action groups to implement these recommendations, (3) a book distributed to educators and ancillary professions chronicling the edited proceedings of the conference, (4) a quarterly newsletter for information exchange, and (5) a plan for the dispersion and dissemination of the results of this conference to other organizations working in the same field.

SAMPLE PROPOSAL TO A FOUNDATION

March 21, 1977

Mr. Bill Somerville
Executive Director
San Mateo Foundation
1204 Burlingame Avenue
Burlingame, California 94010

Dear Mr. Somerville:

Enclosed is our revised proposal for a group home. The request is for an 8-month period, June 1, 1977, to January 31, 1978. We intend to run the program on board and care fees after that date.

The time-line is shown on the budget summary, page 4. That summary also contains two "bottom line" figures. We will need $26,998 if we do not receive the CETA grant for the program developer/administrator. If we *do* receive the grant, we will need $19,333. We will not know the decision on our CETA request until late May.

The great news arrived the other day that our IRS 501(c)(3) status was approved! A copy of that letter is attached to the proposal.

Also attached are letters from local officials indicating the need for the program. One from Gloria Ambersini, of the County Department of Social Services, has gone astray in the mail. We will send it on as soon as it arrives.

A copy of the agreement between the Corporation and James Stewart, who has agreed to buy the house and rent it to us, is also attached. He will be happy to discuss this further with you, and can be reached at his home (1550 Middlefield Road, Palo Alto, 327-0905) or at his law office (11 W. St. John St., San Jose, 286-9700).

We are gathering other support, too. At our annual meeting March 16, the president of the Palo Alto Jaycees announced that they would provide manpower for renovation and maintenance of the group home.

Meetings are being arranged with representatives and board members of the Rosenberg, Hewlett, Packard, Hancock, and Klein Foundations. Our proposals will be submitted to each of these foundations. It is our hope that, of the six foundations receiving the proposal, at least five will be willing to provide one-fifth of the needed funding each.

We appreciate your consideration of this proposal. If you have any questions, please phone me (327-1968) or Mary Cottrell (326-4887).

Sincerely,

Lois Smith,
President

(continued)

Palo Alto Adolescent Services Corporation
Funding Proposal

CONTENTS

	Page
Abstract	000
Budget/Funding Needs	000
Balance Sheet	000
Background of the Problem	000
Goals	000
Objectives	000
Target Group	000
Methodology	000
Group home population	000
Placement/Intake	000
Postplacement counseling and evaluation	000
Utilizing community resources	000
Support and cooperation	000
House policies	000
Staff	000
Program developer or administrator	000
Houseparent (4)	000
Social workers, counselors, and screeners (part-time positions)	000
Future Funding Expectations	000
Unit Cost of Program Services	000

Appendix

Minutes of PAASC Board Meeting, March 9, 1977, approving group home proposal.

Internal Revenue Service federal tax-exempt letter.

Copy of letter from Family Service Association concerning services they will provide.

Copy of letter from Palo Alto Jaycees concerning services they will provide.

(continued)

Copies of letters concerning need for a group home from:
- Philip Bliss, Palo Alto Unified School District.
- Captain Gary Tatum, Palo Alto Police Department.
- Gloria Ambersini, Santa Clara County Department of Social Services.
- Dr. Newman Walker, Palo Alto Unified School District

Copy of contractual agreement between PAASC Board and an individual offering to purchase the facility.

(continued)

Palo Alto Adolescent Services Corporation Funding Proposal

ABSTRACT

There are very few alternative living situations for adolescents in Palo Alto. Counselors, social workers, and public agencies are frequently forced to place status offenders, or other adolescents who need homes, in another part of the county. The Palo Alto Adolescent Services Corporation believes that providing living space and other services to teenagers within Palo Alto will allow them to maintain their links with school, friends, and community while at the same time they can receive help and learn to deal with problems at school and with parents.

The primary goal is diversionary, to help the adolescents before they become seriously involved with the juvenile justice system. We propose a six-bed, co-ed group home which will prepare adolescents for return to better relationships at home and provide longer-term shelter for those who cannot return to their homes. Adolescents will receive evaluation and counseling as well as other services coordinated by the Corporation in the areas of education, vocational training, employment, health, and recreation.

The group home situation will provide peer support and will allow the young persons to mature and take some control over their lives while they still enjoy the advantage of adult support and supervision.

The Family Service Association of the Mid-Peninsula will be directly involved in providing group counseling, houseparent training, family counseling at a reduced rate, and individual therapy for group home residents as needed.

Staff for the group home will include a Project Director/Administrator, houseparents, part-time counselors and houseparent trainers, evaluators, and the assistance of the PAASC Coordinator in obtaining services for residents from other community agencies and programs.

(continued)

PALO ALTO ADOLESCENT SERVICES CORPORATION
BUDGET/FUNDING NEEDS

	CAPITAL	OPERATING COSTS								TOTALS	
		Preliminary				Start of Operation				Without	With
	COSTS	June	July	Aug.	Sept	Oct.	Nov.	Dec.	Jan.	CETA Funds	CETA Funds
One-Time Costs											
Furniture*	$5,000										
Renovation*	5,000										
Phone installation	50										
Contract services (early intensive training for staff)†						240				240	240
Total Capital Costs	$10,050										
On-Going Costs											
Salary: developer/administrator		1,000	1,000	1,000	1,000	1,000	1,000	1,000	1,000	8,000	1,335
Fringe benefits		150	150	150	150	150	150	150	150	1,200	200
Salary: houseparents						1,600	1,600	1,600	1,600	6,400	6,400
Fringe benefits						240	240	240	240	960	960
Contract services: social worker (group leader)†							108	108	108	324	324
Workshops for staff and volunteers†							24	24	24	72	72
Individual therapy†							84	84	84	252	252
Space:											
Rent		800	800	800	800	800	800	800	800	6,400	6,400
Utilities		80	80	80	80	80	80	80	80	640	640
Phone				20	20	20	20	20	20	120	120
Insurance		85	85	85	85	85	85	85	85	680	680
Maintenance					50	50	50	50	50	250	250

Miscellaneous:										
Food for staff					165	165	165	165	660	660
Auto mileage	100	100	100	100	100	100	100	100	800	800
Total operating costs	$2,215	$2,215	$2,235	$2,285	$4,530	$4,506	$4,506	$4,506	$26,998	$19,333

*Furniture costs ($5,000) will be donated by a private donor, and renovation will be provided by P. A. Jaycees (see letter from Palo Alto Jaycees in the Appendix).

†These costs reflect the actual cost to PAASC; counseling services in the amount of $4,816 will be provided by the Family Service Association (see letter from Family Service Association in the Appendix).

Note on Operating Costs (Budget/Funding Needs): The following costs will be incurred once there are residents in the home. These costs will be funded by board and care fees from public agencies and will also cover rent, salaries, utilities, and so forth, after the home is occupied.

Recreation	$150
Automobile	200
Food	500
Clothing	100
School supplies	80
Administrative overhead	25
Total	$1,055 per month

Palo Alto Adolescent Services Corporation
Balance Sheet

December 31, 1976

ASSETS

Cash—checking and savings	$1,603.79
Petty cash	30.98
	$1,634.77
Surplus	$1,634.77

Operating Statement

July 1 to December 31, 1976

Income

Donations	$1,015.00
Fund raising	1,422.11
Membership	227.00
	$2,664.11

Expenses

Rent	$75.00
Supplies	264.52
Telephone	298.07
Professional fees	10.00
Postage	336.57
Publications	21.74
Insurance	12.95
Licenses	5.00
Brochure	98.36
	$1,122.21
Operating profit	$1,541.90

THE PROBLEM—BACKGROUND

Many Palo Alto adolescents need housing other than the family home for a variety of reasons: alcoholic parents, broken homes, families in severe crisis, and the conflicts of adolescence that can cause severe problems between parents and children. Some of these adolescents become what is legally termed *status offenders* [truant, beyond parental control, incorrigible]. Others, through no fault of their own, are in need of alternative living situations. In Palo Alto, police and social service agencies frequently have no choice but to remove these young persons from their community, friends, churches, and schools and place them in a group or foster home in a different part of the county. There are few foster homes in Palo Alto that will accept teenagers, and only one group home (for girls and boys needing intensive therapy, ages 13 to 15).

To address these problems, the Palo Alto Human Relations Commission, the Palo Alto PTA Council, representatives from churches, social service agencies, the school district, the Palo Alto Police Department, and concerned professional and community people banded together to form the *Task Force for Alternative Housing.* This group later incorporated and became the *Palo Alto Adolescent Services Corporation* (PAASC).

The passage of Assembly Bill 3121 has made it impossible for those young persons who are status offenders to be placed in Juvenile Hall. Foster homes and group homes are in short supply in Santa Clara County. Public and private agencies frequently have no choice but to return these young people to an unhealthy family situation.

Emergency Treatment Center and Alum Rock Center have been designated by Santa Clara County as being the placement agencies for status offenders in the county. Emergency Treatment Center (the agency which receives most of the North County referrals) presented the following statistics to the Child and Adolescent Commission on March 3, 1977:

Total requests for placement:	28
Placement in group or foster homes:	8

In researching the needs of adolescents in Palo Alto, PAASC has heard the following accounts:

A high-school student was living in the attic of his school because he had no other place to go.

A sixteen-year-old girl turned herself in to Juvenile Hall because her family situation was too painful to endure.

A fourteen-year-old boy's parents are extremely restrictive because of the anxiety caused by an older brother's delinquent behavior. Police have been called when the brother physically abuses him.

Although Palo Alto is commonly perceived as an upper-middle-class, high-income community, the "Community Analysis" prepared by Economic and Social Opportunities, Inc. (the designated antipoverty agency in the county) presented to the City Council in January of 1976 reveals the following facts:

Only seven areas (out of 15) in Santa Clara County have a higher high-school dropout rate.
One quarter of the Palo Alto census tracts has a higher than county average of persons living below the poverty level.
Many areas of Palo Alto have a higher than county average high-school dropout rate.
In one area of Palo Alto, juvenile referrals are greater than the county average.

These particular census tracts also have a higher than county average of single-parent families and families in which both parents work.

In order to validate PAASC's perception of the need for alternative housing for young people in Palo Alto, a random survey of Palo Alto School District students and parents was taken in 1975. Responses from 279 adolescents showed that:

Ten percent had run away from home.
Eight percent would like to live in a group home.
Six-and-a-half percent would prefer a foster home to their present situation.

Out of 154 responses from parents, these results were obtained:

Eleven-and-a-half percent said one or more of their children had left home because of a personal or family problem.
Eight percent expressed interest in a group home for their adolescent child.
Twelve percent felt the need to place their child in a foster home.

The appendix contains letters that emphasize the need for alternative housing for adolescents. They are from: Gloria Ambersini, Santa Clara County Department of Social Services; Philip Bliss, Special Problems Counselor, Palo Alto Unified School District; Captain Gary Tatum, Palo Alto Police Department; and Dr. Newman Walker, Superintendent of Schools, Palo Alto Unified School District.

GOALS

The Palo Alto Adolescent Services Corporation is primarily concerned with diverting adolescents from involvement with the juvenile justice system. We wish to see that help is available to them before they have become so psychologically damaged as to need special treatment and care. The adolescent will have the opportunity to live in a nurturing environment in a group home until the family home becomes stable enough for his or her return. Return to the family home will be an important goal.

OBJECTIVES

1. To place 20 adolescents in a group home in the first year of operation.
2. To provide ongoing counseling and evaluation for 20 adolescents.
3. To facilitate provisions of education, employment, vocational training, health care, and recreational opportunities through available resources in the community.
4. To graduate 14 adolescents from the program to the following:
   (a) Their original home.
   (b) Other healthy living situations in the community.

TARGET GROUP

In order not to diminish the effectiveness of the PAASC program by attempting to address too broad a target group, PAASC intends to focus its services on:

1. Those adolescents living in Palo Alto or attending school in Palo Alto (8,484 adolescents between the ages of 10 and 18).*
2. Those between the ages of 13 and 18.
3. Those not having severe emotional, physical, or drug-related problems requiring special treatment. (We do not intend to deal with psychotic or severely disturbed adolescents or with those needing on-site medical care requiring special equipment or medical personnel.)
4. Those who do not have such serious juvenile records as to endanger other adolescents in the program.

METHODOLOGY

Many young persons need a complete change in living situations. Their relationships with their families have deteriorated to an extent that they find it difficult to adjust to another family situation, even in the best of foster homes. The PAASC program will offer them an opportunity to grow independently, with the support of their peers and houseparents who care. Living with other young people with similar problems and

*1975 Census. Adolescents from other areas may be admitted on a space-available basis.

sharing their experiences in group counseling sessions will help them cope with the experiences they have had in the family home.

Group Home Population

The home will be designed to accommodate six boys and girls and resident house parents.

The Palo Alto Adolescent Services Corporation has consulted with many group-home operators and program designers and, without exception, they have recommended a co-ed facility for the following reasons:

1. A co-ed group offers the opportunity to learn responsible behavior in an environment that reflects the realities of the society to which they will return.
2. A one-sex group tends to produce exaggerated masculine and feminine behavior.
3. Residents very quickly start to assume a brother-sister relationship.
4. Residents learn how two people of opposite sex should treat one another in a home atmosphere (a model frequently lacking in the home situation).
5. Residents attend school as a family and become supportive of one another.
6. A mixed group produces a better atmosphere for homework; a one-sex group has difficulty in settling down.
7. Male staff is reluctant to work in an all-female group home because of the possibility of being accused of inappropriate behavior (far less likely to happen in a home where attention is not focused on one male).

The corporation recognizes that a co-ed group home requires special consideration in administration, supervision, and selection of the facility.

Placement/Intake

Referrals will be made by the Juvenile Probation Department, the Department of Social Services, the Palo Alto Police Department, community social service agencies, the schools, and by individual families requesting placement.

Those adolescents referred by Santa Clara County Department of Social Services will have received an intake evaluation by the department before being referred to PAASC.

Young persons referred by agencies not having a capacity for evaluation or by their families will receive a professional intake evaluation (by counselors, houseparents, and professionally qualified volunteers). After a consultation with the young person (who must be willing to be placed in the group home) and parents, and a review of records (school, juvenile justice, health, etc.), a determination will be made as to how the adolescent will fit into the group home. If it is decided that the adolescent should remain in the family home or would not fit into the PAASC home, we shall refer the adolescent and the family to an appropriate counseling service or another placement agency.

Postplacement Counseling and Evaluation

Each adolescent entering the program will be involved in group counseling and will receive individual counseling when needed. A continuous evaluation of the young person's personal growth and benefits from the program will be undertaken.

Those families requesting counseling will be integrated into the total program. Emphasis will be placed upon assisting families in developing a healthy, nurturing home situation for their children.

Utilizing Community Resources

The PAASC Administrator will work with schools, vocational training programs, employment services, and health and recreational facilities to coordinate their services with the PAASC program. Emphasis will be placed on encouraging each individual resident to take advantage of services in the community that would assist the youth in his or her personal growth.

Support and Cooperation

Family Service Association of the Mid-Peninsula, a PAASC Agency Affiliate, has agreed to provide the following services for the PAASC group home. (The costs for these services are reflected in the budget.) These services include:

1. Group and individual therapy for adolescents in the group home.
2. Early intensive training for houseparents and volunteers.
3. Workshops for houseparents and volunteers.
4. Ongoing staff development and renewal.

Other PAASC Agency Affiliates that have indicated a desire to become part of the PAASC program when the need arises are:

1. Youth Clinic Association, Stanford University.
2. Foothill Council of Campfire Girls.
3. Palo Alto Information and Referral Service.

4. Volunteer Bureau–Voluntary Action Center.
5. New Ways to Work—Youth Employment Service.
6. Learning House, Inc. (an intensive-therapy group home for preadolescents.
7. Stanford Counseling Institute.
8. Youth Advisory Council, City of Palo Alto.
9. Emergency Treatment Center.
10. Various individuals* have committed themselves to the following services:
    (a) Assisting in renovation of the group home.
    (b) Collecting furniture for the group home.
    (c) Fund raising.
    (d) Typing.
    (e) Providing recreational opportunities for group home residents.
    (f) Special tutoring.

House Policies

Residents will be encouraged to make their own personal decisions within the limitations of the policies established by the group home. The adolescents will be expected to assume responsibilities within the group home commensurate with their maturity and demonstrated responsible behavior.

House policies will be established with the following considerations in mind:

1. Residents' relationship with one another and with the staff.
2. Realistic goal setting by each individual resident with the expectation of fulfillment.
3. Establishing guidelines concerning inappropriate behavior (drug abuse, sexual activity, violence, curfew violations, truancy, criminal behavior, and any other activity that might have a negative effect on other residents or the program).

STAFF

The PAASC group home requires a paid staff consisting of a Program Developer/Administrator, live-in houseparents, and several part-time social workers to train houseparents and volunteers and to work with residents in individual- and group-counseling sessions, and to evaluate the program and the progress made by each young person in the program.

*Names available on request.

POSITION TITLE 1: Program Developer/Administrator.

PURPOSE OF POSITION: To establish group home, to act as Chief Administrator of the program.

SALARY: $1,000 per month plus 15 percent fringe benefits.

DUTIES TO BE PERFORMED:

First Three Months of Employment. Locate home,* oversee renovation and furnishing, obtain a state license, assist in hiring houseparents, assist in houseparent training, design treatment program (in coordination with houseparents and part-time counselors), and, in general, to develop the program.

Duties After Home Is Established. Act as Chief Administrator of program, serve on Placement/Intake Committee, be responsible for hiring and firing group home staff, supervise and participate in counseling sessions, continue to be responsible for licensing and legal procedures, maintain working relationship with the Department of Social Services and other placement agencies, develop and implement volunteer services for the group home (volunteers to provide special tutoring, instruction in arts and crafts, special recreational opportunities, etc.), supervise and participate in counseling sessions, and develop and be responsible for financial procedures.

QUALIFICATIONS: An M.A. in clinical psychology or the equivalent, verified experience with a group home and with adolescents.

POSITION TITLE 2: Houseparent (4).

PURPOSE OF POSITION: Manage group home for six adolescents.

*The PAASC Board of Directors and an individual have entered into a contractual agreement in which this person will buy a house of our choice and rent it to the Corporation for a reasonable rate. Copy of agreement is in the appendix.

SALARY: $1,600 per month (for 4)* plus 15 percent fringe benefits and room and board while on duty.

DUTIES TO BE PERFORMED:

Basic operation of home and program:

1. Provide care, guidance, and discipline to create maximum benefits to each individual and the group well-being.
2. Create a homelike atmosphere in which young people have the opportunity to maximize their potential.
3. Plan and oversee necessary household cleaning and maintenance by residents, volunteers, and hired assistants.
4. Plan wholesome and appetizing meals for residents and staff and oversee the preparation and serving.
5. Assist the Program Developer/Administrator in designing appropriate intake and/or screening procedures, treatment programs, and evaluation mechanisms.
6. Participate in group counseling sessions.

QUALIFICATIONS: Significant group-home experience and/or counseling experience.

OTHER POSITIONS: Social Workers, Counselors, and Screeners (part-time positions).

PURPOSE OF POSITIONS: To train, counsel, screen applicants, and evaluate program and progress of adolescents.

SALARY: Variable, according to agency providing service.

DUTIES TO BE PERFORMED:

1. Train houseparents and volunteers.
2. Counsel adolescents, both individually and in groups in the group home.
3. Evaluate program and progress each adolescent in the program is making.
4. Take part in intake screening.

*Staffing patterns will be established when hiring is done. It may be full-time houseparents with salary plus room and board, who will be relieved by part-time houseparents every other weekend and one day per week; or, two sets of houseparents who will serve alternate three-and-a-half days each week and will be provided room and board while on duty.

FUTURE FUNDING EXPECTATIONS

The Palo Alto Adolescent Services Corporation anticipates that after the initial start-up costs and three months operating time, the program will be supported from the following sources:

1. Santa Clara County public agencies will pay the costs of many of the group home residents.
2. Those adolescents not eligible for county funding will be funded on an "ability to pay" scale.
3. PAASC fund-raising activities will supply partial funding for private placement and for unoccupied beds.

UNIT COST OF PROGRAM SERVICES

The cost of the program compares favorably with similar programs in Santa Clara County.

1. The monthly cost for housing an adolescent in the group home ($926.93) is lower than many comparable facilities ($750 to $1,000*).
2. The cost of maintaining the adolescent in the PAASC program is far, far less than maintaining a young person in the juvenile justice system, taking into consideration law enforcement and court costs, juvenile probation expenses, housing at "The Ranch" (currently $1,400 per month), and many other related expenses.
3. The only other group home in Palo Alto, Sunporch, has a monthly cost per adolescent of $1,060. Their program would not deal with the same target population as PAASC's.
4. The Skylark program in San Mateo County has an average cost (varies from month to month) per adolescent of $386. However, there is no provision in the budget for counseling, houseparent training, relief houseparents, and houseparents' salaries. The Palo Alto Adolescent Services Corporation believes that well-trained houseparents, an effective counseling program, and adequate staffing are necessary components for a group home situation in which the goal is to graduate a fully functional young person from the program.

*Figures obtained from Santa Clara County Juvenile Probation Department and the Department of Social Services.

* * *

FURTHER READING

Developing Skills in Proposal Writing, Mary Hall, Office of Federal Relations, Oregon State System of Higher Education, September 1971. (Order from Continuing Education Publications, P.O. Box 1491, Portland, Oregon 97207.)

This is the best available manual on the conventional proposal format. Well-written and highly understandable, it covers proposal preparation from A to Z. It is primarily focused on preparing proposals to federal agencies for the funding of service projects, not research grants, but much of what Ms. Hall has to say applies to any proposal.

Terms are defined, models and examples given, and steps laid out in easy-to-follow order. A classic, this manual covers the grant idea, the funding source, needs assessment, objectives, procedures, evaluation, dissemination, and personnel and budget preparation.

"A Guide to Needs Assessment in Community Education," U.S. Department of Health, Education, and Welfare, Order No. 017-080-01609-5, Superintendent of Documents, U.S. Government Printing Office, Washington, D.C. 20402, 1976.

For 55 cents, you can obtain a copy of this simple, clear discussion of what a needs assessment (a Why statement) is and how to go about conducting one. Since this is a critical step in writing any proposal, you need information like this. Only thirty pages long, it covers the rationale for needs assessments; the process of performing them; what to watch out for; how to use Census Bureau data; where to get other kinds of information; and how to define terms, survey local service agencies, hold public hearings, conduct interviews, measure needs, set priorities, and state objectives.

The Grass Roots Fundraising Book, Joan Flanagan, Swallow Press, Chicago, 1977. (Available for $5.25 from the National Office, The Youth Project, 1000 Wisconsin Avenue, N.W., Washington, D.C. 20007.)

This is a new and extremely good source of material on fund raising. It covers an exceptionally wide range of fund-raising activities—sales, memberships, special events, suppers, raffles, auctions, bazaars, parties, dances, books, luncheons, theatre parties, fairs, carnivals, concerts, dinners, mock casinos, premiers, telethons, marathons, tournaments, dues, bingo, direct mail, neighborhood canvassing, newsletters, and guest speakers—in a thorough, readable way, as well as touching on the basics, like how to handle tax and legal matters.

VI

Current Trends and Future Possibilities

Grantspeople, because they are grantspeople, must face a future of uncertainty. No monthly trek to the Post Office for the pension check. No security after twenty years of service. No unions to fight to maintain your position when the walls around your project crumble. You cannot ask an employer not to fire Dear Old Jane when the grant runs out. You can indeed count on the eventual termination of your project. But what of the next one—will it always be possible to jump from one to the other? Will there always be a grants sector? What will happen to it in our time of economic crisis? What do we know about the future of this business?

Our research has impressed us with the fact that impermanence and open-endedness pervade granting from top to bottom. Although it has high risks proportional to its high rewards, undeniable trends exist that could be expected to continue. In this chapter we briefly examine general trends and then speculate on the future of several major areas of granting, with an eye toward uncovering new hot spots or at least areas where our intuition tells us we are getting warm.

GENERAL TRENDS

1. Increased Importance

Grants will occupy an increasingly important role in our society. The argument goes like this: As we march through the 1980s, there will be more and more *public* problems—conflicts that must be solved not privately but by governmental policymakers. These policymakers will choose grants increasingly over the alternative routes available to them because grants are less expensive and time-consuming, and frequently more effective than the government's departmental efforts to solve these same problems.

Nongrant governmental solutions can regulate and stimulate but have trouble when they must instigate a new approach. For example, the government's regulatory agencies can only put limits on an industry's profit or tie it up in a morass of environmental impact statements. By awarding grants to develop appropriate technologies, however, the businessman can discover ways to apply his profit-making urges to the creation of industries that do not harm the environment.

It is likely that more such conflicts will develop and be resolved in the grants sector. After all, we are living on "spaceship earth" in the "era of limits." In the last century we could have pursued our self-interest blithely without always bumping into someone else pursuing his self-interest. Today we can no longer avoid knocking into each other. In more and more ways the self-motivated activity of one is apt to infringe on the pursuits of another. It is likely that grants will continue to be called upon as a way of managing such conflict or of resolving the conflict through public investment in new knowledge that renders the basis of the old conflict obsolete.

2. The End of Growth

At the same time that grants become more and more important, the overall volume of the grants economy will probably level off and may even decline.

However, a decline in appropriations would not necessarily reduce the number of overall new grants awarded, or even the total amount of money up for grabs. It remains to be seen whether the nation's mood of fiscal conservatism will result in a restriction on new, experimental funding in preference for refunding the Old Guard or whether it will provoke a "cut out the fat" mentality, forcing the defunding of some of the ineffective grantees who until now have been funded year after year. In the second possibility, more money would be available each year for new projects. In either case new grant awards will probably be more numerous, smaller, and less likely to be refunded.

The tax revolt that swept America in 1978 and 1979 had the effect of reducing overall governmental income and putting a lid on expenditures. The impact on the grants system was that policymakers began to regard existing grants as more precious. Grantees became more competitive. While advocates of public problem solving predicted catastrophe, some of the actual effects of the new restrictive mood were hopeful for new grantseekers. What happened follows:

Fewer large grants. Federal funders tended to eliminate large construction grants and focus on small grants for special projects, many of which were highly experimental.

More accountability. Reduced expenditures reintroduced a fervor among policysetters to make existing grantees more accountable for their effectiveness—many grantees were defunded, which opened up new money for new programs.

Planning for self-sufficiency. There was a stronger emphasis on funding those projects that had the greatest chance of self-sufficiency after only one grant period as well as those that consolidated existing services; therefore, those grantspersons who were capable of designing projects effectively had an advantage over the old timers who tended to focus on bricks and mortar alone.

Some new money. While there are few new initiatives in the antipoverty area, some new and experimental funding programs (such as the appropriate technology program of DOE in Chapter III) continue to emerge, indicating that experimental programs were no longer considered frivolous indulgences during periods of crisis. Such programs suggested that new ideas, funneled through Research and Development mechanisms, are more necessary than ever before. Since high-risk grants are also small, but with high payoffs, it is likely that they will continue to be allocated.

Public outcry. United Ways are an example of the kind of funding agencies currently under attack from consumer and public-interest groups for their "monopolistic practices." Critics such as Robert Bothwell of the National Committee on Philanthropic Responsibility claim that United Ways perpetuate an inner circle of grantees who rely on the subsidy rather than develop sound business practices. Furthermore, they argue that the new advocacy groups representing disenfranchized minorities are excluded. In the face of such criticism many United Ways are already shifting to the practices of the community foundations, opening themselves to grantees, infusing themselves with "management support," and in some cases sending their grantees on their way after as few as three years.

FUNDING FOR THE ARTS

In recent years about $2 billion in grants per year has been contributed to the arts, an amount that is growing rapidly and will probably continue to expand. Private foundations are still the main contributor, but government support has kept pace in recent years. In fact, arts is the only field of funding where government has not overwhelmed the private sector.

The hot new area for the arts is corporate philanthropy. In 1972, the arts received only 4 percent of the average business dollar contributed. Four years later they were getting 12 percent while the overall level of corporate granting had nearly doubled. This is a very quick sixfold increase in absolute dollars.[1] It can be attributed to a new recognition by corporations that the arts are an ideal form of tax deduction, have great public relations value, encourage tourism, and provide cultural fringe benefits for employees.

Perhaps the most fundamental impact on arts by government in the past decade has been the creation of a network of arts councils at state, local, and regional levels, stimulated through National

[1]According to the Cultural Resources Director of the National Endowment for the Arts, May 1978.

Endowment for the Arts (NEA) matching grants. In the coming decade these councils can be expected to generate new sources of funds to develop the arts scene locally. It could be that the hotel-tax model used by the San Francisco Arts Commission may be more generally applied. This method imposes a 1 percent tax on the tourist industry, which goes to arts groups who apply to the Commission. Other cities will work out a United Way-type approach to arts funding. In any case, the success of arts councils will depend on their lobbying efforts with budget-minded state legislatures and negotiations with groups like Chambers of Commerce. The NEA funding is already so visible, so beseiged by existing grantees, that it cannot be expected to fund many new projects.

In 1977 to 1978, NEA had a great idea. Realizing that it could not command the funding required to respond to the needs of all American artists, its staff went across town to encourage nonarts government agencies, like the Comprehensive Employment and Training Administration (CETA), the Community Development Administration (CDA), and the Economic Development Administration (EDA) to open up their programs[2] to artists, who, after all, were a hidden class of the unemployed. In fact, in recent years, more money has gone to artists from these economically oriented programs than from NEA itself. To get the money, artists have had to redesign their services for new audiences, such as the elderly and the handicapped, and they have collaborated heavily with city and county Parks and Recreation Departments, libraries, and museums.

Arts funders at all government levels can be expected to strengthen their funding of management assistance (bookkeeping, fund raising, marketing, copyright law, loan getting) rather than emphasize support for projects per se. Such assistance is their way of bolstering the business mentality of arts administrators (if not artists) so that more groups can eventually become independent with on-going grant support.

[2]"Opening up their programs" has frequently required as a precondition that these agencies adopt "cultural policies" to explain their position on arts-related activities.

Revamping Public Media

Public media—that is, public broadcasting and radio—will go through rapid transformations in the next few years, with the result that governmental funding will probably increase threefold. What is more, the whole system will change. Much more of the money, at least 25 percent, will go for programming and program development rather than for administrative expenses, which now eat up huge chunks of these grants.

By changing the funding system, government will also attempt to get the public media out of their present mess. The problems of the past stem from the fact that America has not produced much in the way of good programming (the British continue to exceed us in the quality of adult shows); nor has our public broadcasting been sufficiently experimental, since we have become obsessed by the need to attract a broad membership base, which favors the continuation of proven shows.

Our public TV system has also been criticized for being overly dependent on the corporate underwriting of individual programs, a new form of advertising for donors like Mobil Oil and Exxon that exercise extensive control over public broadcasting, which in a way makes public broadcasting all too similar to the big corporation-dominated private networks.

The new system will seek more public participation and experimentation in programming by the 270 public broadcasting stations. There will also be more of an attempt to involve local filmmakers in the production facilities of their PBS affiliates. These problems have all been assessed and pondered by the Carnegie Commission on the Future of Public Broadcasting, which recommends new policy to the government. The new order will inevitably streamline the system's governing bodies, perhaps eliminating the overlapping functions of the Public Broadcasting Service, the Corporation for Public Broadcasting, National Public Radio, and the industry's various associations.

One big question is whether the panic of local stations over how to cover their operating expenses during inflationary periods is going to override the broader need to tap into the creative impulses of local filmmakers.

The Ford Foundation has been the largest private funder of the current system. Having originally concentrated on building up the largest PBS stations (in New York and Los Angeles), it may now shift to the development of local talent in smaller cities, although the main initiative for that effort will probably come from local industry.

Future Projects

What kinds of arts projects will be funded next? Unless you are on the guest list of the trustees of the Mellon Foundation, forget the construction grant and rent a room at the YMCA. Make your arts proposal into a special project for a specific kind of audience. You might choose to follow the example of one woman puppeteer in Richland, Virginia, who kept getting rejection slips from funders until she decided to design puppets for paraplegic children, who could only move limited parts of their bodies. So she made puppets for the toes, puppets for the head, and puppets for the little finger. She got the grant and now teaches school teachers how to do the same.

Talk about your project as social rehabilitation or cultural revitalization, as a way of motivating people or building a sense of community identity, as part of a summer recreation program or a way to teach basic skills painlessly.

If you can, team up with arts groups that are already funded. Bring your touring program into rural areas that are "culturally deprived." Build in a training component to your performance program so that the local people can learn to do it themselves. If you are an individual artist and do not like the idea of forming an organization, use the local arts commission, the Parks and Recreation Department, or the local museum or library as your sponsor.

FUNDING FOR EDUCATION

In education, the real question is, now that the federal government has gotten so heavily invested in the field, what are they going to do about it? Since 1968 the U.S. Office of Education has pumped about $6 billion per year into education while private giving amounts to only $3 billion when you "total in" all sorts of private contributors. Most private giving goes to higher education, although the private share of higher education budgets has dropped from 60 to 10 percent in the past century, while the government has increased its share by an inverse proportion.

The rationale for federal involvement in the educational system (which is supposed to be financed by states and localities) is that it is a federal responsibility to provide "equal educational opportunity" by giving a boost to low-achieving students, giving them an equal chance to catch up with high achievers. Despite all the billions, the federal government has failed to do this: There is no evidence that increased federal funding produces increased long-term learning. Heretofore, the Department of Health, Education, and Welfare has relied on two approaches: (1) sponsoring research into new ways to learn and teach through the National Institute of Education, and (2) linking the research to educational projects supported by the 100 or so funding programs of the Office of Education. Almost all federal funding goes to pay for special projects that are housed in public school districts, but private schools and other private nonprofit agencies can get some of this money by writing themselves into a proposal submitted by a Local Education Agency (LEA) or by applying for a few special programs for which they are directly eligible.[3]

In the last few years, state-level departments of education have played an increasing role in directing federal money, some of which is matched with state funds. The states draw up plans for each major area of their concern, such as special education or bilingual education, and then allocate their funds as a way of implementing their plans. The educational coordinating councils of states have review power (which sometimes means veto power) over any educational project financed by a federal grant. Of special importance are the state coordinating councils of higher education, which have acquired steadily increasing power over the funding system for state universities and colleges.

Community Colleges have been rather neglected in the federal

[3]There could be a change in the offing. If we adopt a voucher system, which would be tied to the student rather than to the school, private and public school students would be treated equally. In that case, private schools would benefit greatly.

funding network. But CETA may change that. It is likely that community colleges will become more sophisticated in their efforts to develop vocational training projects that fit into the planning being done by local CETA agencies, making the colleges into more of an integral part of the effort to eliminate unemployment in a particular region.

Basic Educational Opportunity Grants will continue to be the basic tool for student loans in higher education, despite public outcry at the ineffectiveness of BEOG's staff in getting the loans repaid. New loan programs will benefit middle-income as well as lower-income students. Graduate assistantships and traineeships have already been drastically reduced, but they will continue to reappear in subject areas, such as geoscience, in which the government wants to encourage the output of more Ph.D's.

As in the other fields, construction money for education will be all but eliminated.

On the private side, the big growth area is corporate donations for education. In 1947, educational institutions received 14 percent of the corporate dollar. By 1970 they were getting 38 percent. At the same time the overall amount of corporate granting has skyrocketed. Some corporations are now considering grants to education as a manpower investment. They are creating new kinds of partnerships with colleges and universities and backing up financial aid with technical assistance.

Projects for the Future

Inventive linkages will arise between education and jobs, between art and education, between public schools and vocational schools, between school districts and general efforts at community development, between university-sponsored research and industrial product development. The hidden logic behind all these linkages is simple: How can we overcome the hardening of the categories that now plagues our institutions, bypass the bureaucracies, and solve educational problems as quickly and cheaply as possible?

FUNDING FOR SOCIAL REHABILITATION

This is the hardest field to define or even to name. We used to think of it as a part of "welfare" and assume that it was a matter of providing payment to those who could not make it on their own. That notion has now been discarded because it has been discovered that if you treat a group of people as dependent, they will soon become dependent. Instead of helping them, you inadvertently build barriers between them and "regular" people. The new trend is to call the field "rehabilitation," which has to do with promoting the self-reliance of all sorts of stigmatized groups, whether they happen to be poor, under stress, or just isolated. This field also involves changing conventional attitudes and procedures so that they will accommodate all kinds of people.

Rehabilitation funding is intended for the mentally ill, the retarded, the physically impaired, the blind, the deaf, people who are unemployable for one reason or another, criminals and ex-cons, addicts and ex-addicts, people who are senile, runaways, and alcoholics, plus a few other more specialized minorities. The funding programs are under the broader categories of criminal justice (including juvenile justice and corrections), mental health, drug abuse, employment and training, vocational rehabilitation for the handicapped, aging, special education, and of course, social services.

Within HEW there are two divisions that deal with rehabilitation. One has the oh-good-grief title of Office of Human Development Services, which fits into the crevice in the organizational chart between the Division of Education and the Public Health Service. The OHDS administers funding programs for rehabilitating the aged, handicapped, runaways, and other groups. They have "research and demonstration" money that they give out directly in Washington, but most is disbursed out of the ten regional offices or directly to the states, which fund according to plans drawn up by the state commissions. Again the new emphasis is not to fund construction but to provide training and technical assistance to the existing sheltered workshops and treatment centers. There is also new funding aimed at streamlining the current rehabilitation system. The funding level of OHDS can be expected to keep pace with inflation for the next few years.

The other key area of HEW that is hidden within the Public Health Service has the lyrical acronym of ADAMHA (Alcohol, Drug Abuse, and Mental Health Administration. Until 1974 one of ADAMHA's concerns was building networks of treatment facilities and halfway houses. Recently, the management of that program has been turned over to the states, which now receive the biggest share of ADAMHA dollars. However, funders in Washington are still looking for interesting new ideas for rehabilitation that could be converted into demonstration projects. These projects must be designed so that the entire rehabilitation community can learn and benefit from them.

About 100 big foundations are active in rehabilitation funding. All but 15 have recently backed down from providing construction money and are following the lead of the federal government in providing training and program development money.

In school districts, money is available for "mainstreaming," which in this case means bringing students out of special education and into the regular classroom, where teachers must have new curricula or new methods for instructing them.

Funding for the deaf and blind will have more of a community focus, that is, it will be aimed at reinforcing a sense of identity and the means of self-help within the visually and hearing impaired communities. The emphasis will be on reducing the isolation of these groups through media services (new library services, telephones for the deaf, etc.), which enable them to become employed.

One uncertain area in the rehabilitation scene is the future of sheltered workshops. These industrial training centers are run by churches, service organizations like the Salvation Army, other private nonprofits, or the government. The workshops provide job training for the severely retarded, usually in mechanical tasks. The approach runs counter to the philosophy of "deinstitutionalization" espoused in other parts of the rehabilitation system. While applauding their good intentions, many rehabilitation critics accuse some of these workshops of a lack of professionalism and of a tendency to isolate their clients. There will be new funding aimed at making these operations more competitive with industry and thereby freer of governmental subsidy. There will also probably be new forms of corporate grants for sheltered workshops that have much to gain from a close, nonadversary relationship to local businesses.

In the area of criminal justice, the public funding system is dominated by the Law Enforcement Assistance Administration, whose future is uncertain. The funds are controlled by local anti-crime councils that earmark grants according to their own plans and priorities. Frankly, most of that money goes to the government rather than to private nonprofit groups working in the areas of prevention or rehabilitation.

FUNDING FOR SCIENCE AND TECHNOLOGY RESEARCH

Science funding is almost the same as research funding since science drives the research and development machinery in this country. The idea is that a government investment in laboratory research can pay off greatly in new defense technology, new medical discoveries, new forms and uses of energy, new kinds of space exploration, better agricultural products, and stimulate production in lagging industries. Of those major applications, energy and biomedical research are the big new growth areas. Just as Sputnik created a granting system for space, the oil crisis created a sudden billion-dollar boost in government-supported energy research. Widespread cancer and heart ailments keep the dollars flowing to the biologists. New fields like aquaculture and disaster prevention are getting new grant programs.

In 1979 the federal government spent nearly 30 billion for science research, with the National Institutes of Health, the National Science Foundation, The Department of Energy, NASA, and the Department of Agriculture leading the pack. (We exclude the Defense Department for this study since its money does not go into the nonprofit sector, by and large, which is the focus of this discussion). Most of this money is available through contracts rather than grants. But because it is a competitive system involving nonprofit recipients it functions like a granting system.

Most science grants are gobbled up by the 100 major universities that already have well-equipped laboratories and well-known researchers. But a substantial number go to nonprofit research institutes. Some of the money never leaves government pockets, since it is used by government laboratories, or government-owned facilities operated by profit-making concerns.

There are trouble signs ahead for the university arm of this research system. For one thing, universities themselves are having difficulty providing their share of costs for the research effort. Enrollments are declining; inflation is forcing up operating costs; and old laboratory equipment is breaking down or becoming obsolete. The cost of doing the paperwork required to manage federal grants has passed the $2 billion mark. The universities have responded to these dismal facts by raising their indirect cost charges, sometimes to the point that grantors and principal investigators have been driven away.

There are other problems, too. State governments are wary of the research function of universities, since it tends to shift academia away from teaching as a primary concern. Research and teaching should complement each other, they maintain, but they have grown increasingly separate. Furthermore, granting has brought conflict between researchers and central administrators who ask the Ph.D.'s to do their own proposal writing and manage some of the paperwork that follows the grant.

Although the grants issue is creating divisiveness within universities, grantmakers themselves are sometimes turning away from universities in favor of research institutes. Furthermore, the "mission" agencies (those government funding agencies interested in supporting specific developments) are receiving larger allocations from the United States budget than the university-oriented agencies, such as the National Science Foundation. Some funders are also criticizing the wide gap between "basic" research (open-ended, exploratory) and "applied" research (linking discoveries to new services or products), which they claim is created by the isolation of universities from the business world. Many complain of the conservatism in the research establishment of the elite universities that is reinforced in part by the peer review system.[4] Furthermore, the fact that many have adopted a policy of "no new

[4]Peer review is a system for judging proposals, in which those people who are already established in a field, often themselves in universities, comment on new proposals.

tenures," due to their financial crunch, has meant that younger researchers with new ideas are not entering the system in great numbers.

Despite these problems the public's need for Research and Development increases. For that reason the entire system may well keep pace with inflation in the next few years.

Small universities and state colleges may decide that it is not worth the "paper shuffle" to get into research. If they do become involved in research, they may focus on developing their particular research specialties rather than seek to establish a track record in all departments of science and technology. The other possibility is that locally oriented institutions will develop research projects that respond to the economic development and manpower needs of their regions.

There will be more attempts to tap the creativity and intelligence of the "mad inventor" types who are outside the formal Research and Development system. More and more seed grants will be made available to these individuals through small-scale technology programs and private foundations. In some cases private foundations will continue to pool their efforts in the research area, perhaps using the New York-based Research Corporation as the receiving agency as they have done in the past.

There will be more attempts to relate research to the development of clean, labor-intensive, low-technology (i.e., not requiring vast capital outlays) industries in geographical areas that are economically depressed.

As in other areas, corporate philanthropy may play a larger role in universities, since academia is overcoming its antibusiness tendencies (after suffering a ten-year headache from filling out all those federal forms). For their part, corporations are identifying the new rewards entailed in strengthening ties with university-based research. For example, the Monsanto Corporation recently gave $23 million to Harvard Medical Center, and in return got a guarantee that Harvard would hand over proprietary rights to any inventions resulting from its research. Harvard would not have entertained such a proposition a few years ago, but today it makes sense for universities to do some of the Research and Development that would otherwise be done in industrial labs.

It seems likely that in the future much applied research will be directed toward developing products for mass production and refining the service delivery systems, rather than toward large-scale, complex, centralized technologies, as was true in the past.

FUNDING FOR RELIGIOUS GROUPS

Churches and government never used to work together to solve social problems. For one thing, government agencies would not grant funds for sectarian organizations, since they assume religious grants would not necessarily advance the general public interest. Churches, for their part, did not really feel excluded—they were involved with their own spiritual matters. They certainly did not want to risk governmental control over any of their activities.

In the 1960s and 1970s things began to change. The government discovered that churches were an enormous untapped resource. Imagine it: Churches have most everything the government needs to implement its social programs effectively. They enjoy the strong support of the communities they serve. They are everywhere: downtown, in the neighborhoods, and all over rural areas, even the most depressed or isolated. They are linked by state councils of churches and by national and even worldwide associations. They have strong communication networks (such as newsletters) that can be quickly mobilized. They already have spacious facilities, lots of meeting rooms that are underused on weekdays. Their summer camps also often remain dormant through the school year. They have lots of volunteer power; it does not cost them a lot to get a lot done, particularly in rural areas. Church leadership is the same as, or closely associated with, local business and political leadership through Chambers of Commerce, Rotary Clubs, and so on. Churches often have the kind of altruistic spirit necessary to implement a program that attempts to transcend prevailing conditions.

Those facts make churches into the kind of grass-roots resource that a government planner cannot afford to ignore. And indeed they have not been bypassed. Particularly in the 1970s, all sorts of new ties have been woven between church and state, and there are likely to be many more. Liberal Protestant, Christian, and

Jewish denominations have gotten involved with community development granting in a big way, not through the churches themselves but through sponsorship of nonprofit agencies. For example, the Reverend Leon Sullivan founded Philadelphia's Zion Nonprofit Charitable Trust after a frustrating effort to organize consumer boycotts of businesses that refused to employ minorities. His strategy was to create minority-oriented businesses himself. The Zion Trust obtained Ford Foundation and government grants that enabled the development of shopping centers, health centers, and large-scale inner city housing projects. Soon Zion's budget exceeded $50 million a year. Similarly, the Reverend Jesse Jackson formed Operations PUSH and EXCEL in Chicago, national organizations that won HEW grants for subjects that focused on strengthening the basic skills of blacks in junior and senior high schools.

Churches have been highly active in HUD's efforts to create neighborhood councils to receive funds from the Community Development Block Grant program.

Many churches became sponsors of Head Start programs for HEW, and some have received funds from the Office of Aging and other government programs for senior citizens. Many minority churches in the inner city became sponsors of low-income housing projects, programs that severely tested the churches' abilities to manage the incredible reporting requirements imposed by HUD. Frequently, churches got together with Parks and Recreation Departments to develop neighborhood parks located on church-owned land.

Religious schools have been largely excluded from federal funding, but that too is changing. Recent court cases have made them eligible for more of the Office of Education's 100 grant programs, particularly for scholarships. Some private schools have teamed up with school districts as "support services," helping the public schools link the schools with the community. Many churches receive government grants for their sheltered workshops and other facilities for the handicapped.

The grantee role of religious organizations moved to a whole new level when churches and ecumenical associations became the primary recipients of funds that financed the Indo-Chinese Resettlement Program after the Vietnam war. This program actually put churches in the role of implementing national policy, a role that may well expand in the future.

Private philanthropy to churches has, of course, come largely from individual church members. A few large foundations give to religions, but most of them give only to one particular sect. A few give across denominations. Most of this giving is for church-sponsored higher education. In almost all of the small private foundations that support churches, regular staff members are lacking, which means that it is hard to contact them, and once you do, they are liable to have earmarked their funds for specific church groups.

There will be more efforts by grantors to bring churches into regional planning efforts in the general field of human services. Attempts will be made by funders to tap into the churches' volunteer capacity and into the network of facilities that many churches operate. Rural churches will be considered a particularly important part of any effort to revitalize rural areas. Churches can be expected to participate more actively in collaborative efforts with YMCA and YWCA as well as other general-purpose community development organizations.

FUNDING FOR HEALTH CARE

It has always been quite difficult for the government to know how to establish a uniform funding process for health services. In the early 1970s it mostly gave out grants directly from Washington, which created a big mess because there was no coordination of efforts at the local level. Services were often duplicated. Then it tried relying on federal regional offices to conduct planning and liaison with state governments. Soon it found that effort overwhelming and decided to create regional units within each state called Health Systems Agencies (HSAs) that are charged with the responsibility of finding out what the health care system in each area is and what its needs are. They must also determine what the future of these regional health systems ought to be.

The HSAs will write all this information into plans, to be approved by state Health Coordinating Councils, whose members are for the most part gubernatorial appointees composed of a cross section of health care providers and consumers. Once the plans are approved, the HSAs would become the funders for most of the Public Health Service's granting programs. The PHS at that point would merely funnel the money directly to the HSAs and then make sure everything was going according to the rules and regulations.

Right now most of the HSAs are still in the planning stage, and there are a lot of kinks in the system to be worked out. But the key point is that in the future, federal public health care funding will be locally controlled. That means that if you have a great new idea for holistic health or home-based care of the elderly, you will have to introduce it as a way of complementing the existing health care in your region. Rather than talk about your project as an alternative to hospital-based care, you should present it as an extension of the hospitals.

Some federal grant programs outside the reach of the HSAs will remain, but they too will still have to pass through the review of the health care coordinating councils.

New funding areas for the future will include various schemes to prevent bad health or solve it without drugs or surgery; ways to broaden the roles for medical technicians, nurses, and health paraprofessionals; and the means to return to home-based care for some patients (such as the terminally ill). There will be many new programs in health education, with a strong consumer emphasis. Holistic health has become a granting field that emphasizes new methods for diagnosis and treatment of illnesses that are based on psychogenic causes.

Another new area of health granting will be one that links the results of biomedical research and demonstration projects to the health care system. Still other funding will focus on the connection between urban and rural health systems, or between public and private facilities.

Many private foundations have moved out of the general health care field following government expansion in this area during the 1970s. Some have moved into areas of experimentation with health practices in an effort to demonstrate to the local hospitals that new methods are worth further publicly supported investigation. Other foundations are busy trying to find gaps in the government-financed system in an effort to determine where to place their grants for maximum effect.

FUNDING FOR URBAN AND RURAL DEVELOPMENT

This field has been the most frustrating of all, perhaps because its mission is greater than all the others. It must undo the cycle of vicious problems affecting minority youth and halt the deterioration of depressed rural areas.

Following the Civil Rights Act of 1964, the funding for urban areas emphasized self-help activities within minority communities and support for the resurgence of entrepreneurism within the inner city. The Great Society produced a series of minority advocacy programs such as the Office of Economic Opportunity with its Community Action Agencies and the Model Cities Program. These agencies all emphasized a blend of economic assistance, adult education, and social service programs. This generalist, antipoverty approach suffered from bad management and some very naïve notions about self-help. By the mid-1970s these organizations were supplanted by the better-funded, more systematic, planned procedures of CETA, the Community Development Block Grant, and Economic Development Administration, and certain offices of the Small Business Administration. The old programs continue to survive largely because existing grantees formed themselves into associations that successfully pressured Congress to at least maintain current levels of funding.

Comprehensive Employment and Training Administration

Since 1973, CETA has been the most influential and sizable of all urban development programs. From CETA's point of view its mission is to get jobs for the unemployed and make the unemployed more employable through various types of training.

In CETA's case "training" has been stretched to include everything from schooling to on-the-job training and apprenticeships. CETA hires workers for a year, and then the following year may place them in a local government slot, an industrial job, or in a private nonprofit agency. Even though it was not intended as a public works bill, CETA has been considered a godsend by local government and private nonprofit organizations that have used it as a way of subsidizing their own operations. Many nonprofit organizations have become unwittingly dependent on CETA to pay staff salaries, to the extent that losing CETA slots has meant bankruptcy. Groups receiving CETA support rarely plan for the day when the funding will be discontinued.

The continuation of any one CETA grant from year to year is uncertain, but the continuation of the grant program until at least 1982 is assured. However, the actual year-to-year allocations will be hotly debated.

The new CETA emphasizes on-the-job training by private employers, who can conceivably hire their CETA worker at the end of the grant. It also emphasizes the development of nontraditional jobs rather than preparation for those jobs within the existing economic structure. The program will offer many new grants to test out various methods of job development as well as new ways to "transition" existing CETA workers out of subsidized employment. It will also experiment with vocational counseling for new groups or workers who rarely have been treated as a separate category (see our Displaced Homemaker case study in Chapter 2).

Since CETA prime sponsors and state agencies assess needs for both new jobs and new training within their geographical jurisdiction, they are introducing planning for the first time into the various components of local employment and training systems. Future grants will undoubtedly be influenced by the outcomes of these plans, resulting in grants that effectively link up the various vocational education services of school districts, community colleges, vocational training centers, adult schools, industries, unions, and public and private nonprofit organizations. Each of these groups is bound to come to CETA with proposals that seek to legitimate itself as an essential, specialized element of local efforts to eradicate unemployment.

Prime sponsors are governed by local elected officials who make final decisions on grants. That fact alone means that the planner's approach of linking needs assessment to funding strategies may not go far, since the elected officials must respond to competing interest groups and even use the funding as a form of patronage to political allies.

Community Development Block Grants

This is the biggest of the block grants and the one with the broadest scope. It includes $9 billion that has been given since

1974 to local governments, leaving to the cities a certain amount of discretion over how to use the money. In many cases the grants became a tug of war between downtown interests who wanted to use them for large capital improvements and neighborhood groups who wanted to use them for local physical improvements or human services. In many cities, this struggle resulted in the emergence of vocal neighborhood groups who have used their block grant funds to mobilize other grants and finally to become active in such areas as housing, manpower, and crime control. These groups are expected to play a role in implementation of national urban policy.

FUNDING FOR ECONOMIC DEVELOPMENT

Government-sponsored efforts to develop the inner city have been of two kinds: either construction or physical improvements; or development of small businesses through loans, technical assistance, and training oriented toward minority entrepreneurism. The biggest of these programs, under HUD sponsorship, are low-income housing projects for the poor, the handicapped, and the elderly. These programs have been so fraught with difficulties that in one program a majority of grants, though awarded, could not be implemented.

A more recent approach to physical improvement has been to offer low-interest loans to homeowners willing to renovate inner city homes. While this has proved successful in some cities, it has had the effect of driving up property values and rents, often depriving poor urban residents of affordable housing.

Another approach has been sponsored by the Small Business Administration through its Office of Minority Business Enterprise (OMBE). This office funnels money through community development corporations (CDCs) serving a specific geographical area. These programs promote managerial expertise, economic development, and employment opportunities in deteriorating inner-city areas. Community Development Corporations have experimented with all sorts of ways to attract industry to undeveloped areas: organizing cooperatives and credit unions, encouraging local banks to give loans to minority small businesses, and brokering funds from other government programs into the inner city. The Ford Foundation was so impressed with some CDC programs that it created a consortium of foundations called the Cooperative Assistance Fund that pooled its money into a loan program to support CDC-generated projects. Foundations have also played a role in supporting Small Business Administration efforts by providing emergency rescue for small businesses that have been established with governmental support.

The results of these investments have been impressive, in some ways. There has been a large increase in the number of adequately capitalized minority businesses, but there is little evidence that the success of new ethnic entrepreneurs has reduced the hardcore minority unemployed.

FUNDING FOR OTHER AREAS OF URBAN DEVELOPMENT

Libraries, museums, parks, zoos and other local governmental services have been hard hit by a combination of inflation and declining revenues from property taxes. In some cases their crises have kept them from putting up the matching share required to get federal grants. It has also forced them to shift their grantgetting away from specialized issues and attractive new projects in the direction of pleas to foundation and government grantors to help subsidize ongoing operations. The most fundable future projects will most likely be those that consolidate or streamline existing services (such as the installation of computer services in libraries) or programs that offer the resources of urban facilities to an overall community development effort, such as library media services that link up with city-sponsored recreation programs, or a museum program for the deaf that is part of an HEW-sponsored special education program for a school district, or a summer zoo project that fits into a YMCA program for juvenile delinquents.

FUNDING FOR RURAL ISSUES

Until recently, the closest approach to a rural granting system was the USDA's Agricultural Extension Service, which combined research projects conducted in government laboratories with educational programs in state university systems and public information programs that extend into towns and villages. By the late 1960s the federal role had broadened its focus on nonagricultural human problems that were beginning to appear in small towns. For example, in many areas, mechanized agriculture created high unemployment among agricultural laborers, some of whom eventually left for the cities. Many rural areas have stagnated when new forms of transportation or industrial development undermined their economic bases.

Since passage of the Rural Development Act, new money has been poured into areas that are officially "depressed," including big grants from Housing and Urban Development and the Economic Development Administration. The results are not promising, since most of these grants actually created new problems. Some towns with budgets of less than $10,000 were suddenly administering $500,000 housing projects. Most did not have the necessary administrative skills. Other grants benefited only a small group who knew the ways of the city bureaucrats but did not know how to design projects in such a way that they augmented local economic development efforts. Many of these grants raised expectations about developments and new forms of citizen participation that simply did not materialize. The net effect was to solidify the feeling of passivity and helplessness that seems to be growing in rural America.

Another effect has been to alter the political structure of rural areas. The unquestioned leaders in days past were county commissioners, representatives of farmers, and other landowners. Alongside the commissioners, mayors and town managers did not really have much power. Many county commissioners have tended to view human service programs with bewilderment, partly because they were so unlike the roads-and-bridges approach to problem solving with which they were familiar. Furthermore, the money seemed more tied to statistics and to towns than to the land. In many cases town managers as well as the social planners who staff county offices or local Councils of Government (COGs) have had a better understanding of the grants system and principles of social design, and their grants have challenged the political harmony of the landed leadership and introduced accountability into rural political life for the first time.

Out of all this confusion and turmoil, the government is getting feedback and redesigning its programs along new lines. Here are some trends:

1. The Agricultural Extension Service, with its emphasis on public information, self-help, and conservation, has already been extended to the new field of energy. Each state will soon have its own Energy Extension Service, which will give grants to develop new energy sources in rural areas as well as stimulate public participation in the policy-making process. The Extension model may also be used for the same purpose in new areas if the experiment proves useful.

2. There will be an even greater emphasis on regional planning to guide the rural granting system. Rather than fund city by city, town by town, the government will consider how to use grants to develop a region as a unit. These regions are based not so much on political boundaries as on geographic and demographic commonalities. Most have already been formed into COGs, comprising a dues-paying consortium of city and town governments. These COGs have staff members who will develop and ratify plans and then fund according to them. The COGs also have a big role in qualifying a rural area for receiving a share of government funds through gathering statistics and writing proposals. So the rural COGs fulfill a kind of brokering function. They concentrate most of a region's skills in grantsmanship. They will frequently act as pass-through agencies, sponsoring projects until a private nonprofit agency is capable of getting its own IRS approval as a legitimate tax-exempt nonprofit agency.

3. There is sure to be more collaboration between the various traditional social sectors in rural communities: County commissioners will be getting together with mayors who will be chatting with school boards, PTAs, church groups, Chambers of Commerce, weekly newspaper publishers, Rotary groups, Lions, Kiwanis, Elks, Eagles, and Oddfellows as well as their female counterparts. Rather than remain isolated from these Old Guard forces in every small town, the granting system will undoubtedly infiltrate them, causing a great deal more infighting in the short run, but perhaps a lot more cooperation in the long run. One effect will

be that all these groups might get redefined as partners in an effort to develop a rural area.

4. There will be more inventive schemes funded for developing new and appropriate industries in rural areas whose economic base is being undermined. For example, projects will be funded that strengthen deteriorating industries or develop new ones, such as a local energy industry, which tap local skills and needs.

FUNDING FOR INTERNATIONAL ISSUES

It used to be that international granting was a pretty cut-and-dried process. There were rich nations and there were poor nations. When the affluent nations gave to the disadvantaged, they tended to have two very distinct motivations: cynical or naïve.

The cynical part was that the foreign "aid" was often a matter of buying political and military support from foreign countries and of providing a market for our defense industries and outmoded or surplus products. After all, most U.S. foreign aid was administered out of the State Department, which was fundamentally concerned with advancing American interests abroad. In 1970, just over $3 billion was given in foreign aid by the government.[5]

The naïve part was "overseas charity," conducted by church groups and service organizations, which has generally responded to the outbreak of well-publicized world disasters by providing direct relief. But the charity approach rarely included ongoing attempts to solve the problems that created poverty in the first place. In 1970, total private giving of this sort equaled about $350 million and has held steady since.[6]

Today the international granting picture is more complex and sophisticated, since several new approaches seek to go beyond the cynical and naïve approaches of the past. Here are trends, which are already prevalent or soon to come:

1. *New kinds of collaboration between countries.* It is no longer a cut-and-dried case that some nations have arrived and others have not,

[5] *Giving USA,* p. 7.
[6] Ibid.

a two-part model that lends itself to paternalistic ties between rich and poor. Some nations (like the Arab nations) have money, but their people by and large lack the skills or technological capacity to enter the "developed world." Other countries (like the United States and Britain) have a dwindling supply of money but they have advanced technological development, not just because they have accumulated capital but also because they have a finely tuned system for producing knowledge and then applying it in ways that stimulate industrial production. Still other countries (like China) have scanty money and skills but a lot of untapped physical and human resources to offer to worldwide development efforts. And, of course, still other countries seem to have nothing but problems.

The current state of the world has led to suggestions for pooling efforts in new ways. Perhaps that is why after the 1973 energy crisis, which left both the United States and Japan highly dependent on expensive imported oil, Japan suggested that the two countries each contribute $500 million to sponsor joint Research and Development in alternative energy exploration. Of course, not all countries are in as favorable a bargaining position as Japan. Led by China with its new policy of modernization, many countries are now redefining or broadening their old ideologically tinged versions of their self-interest so that they are open to designing proposals that link up money, skills, energy, and materials in new ways. The United States is finally understanding that its real strength is not just money or products but its abundant resource of knowledge that it can grant in exchange for materials that are in short supply.

2. *Science is the key.* In 1978, the president's science advisor, Frank Press, proposed the creation of a mammoth Foundation for Development that would provide funds for international granting along the lines of the National Science Foundation.

The notion that science is the key to international granting was based on these points:

a. The scientific community was the only group broad enough to transcend ideological and religious boundaries between cultures.
b. Science could promote the production and transfer of knowledge and products in each country so that the wealth of a

country would not be limited to its existing resources and skills. Science could in effect increase the size of the economic pie, eliminating the need (at least for now) for changing the way the same pie is cut.

c. Scientific projects could be designed to link the indigenous universities to the development problems in their own regions, when possible. Nonprofit, nongovernmental research institutes could be established in areas where universities are not workable.

The limitation of science as a force for international granting is that the science lobby, in this country and elsewhere, is not powerful enough to press the governments to invest huge sums in international development. One agency, the United Nations University, was endowed by Japan a few years ago with $100 million which it hoped would be matched by the United States and other countries, for the specific purpose of linking the world's universities to the world's regional problems. But the United States did not contribute to this fund. A new possibility is that the science lobby in the United States (the American Association for the Advancement of Science, the National Academy of Science, and the university-based associations) may team up with the "holy lobby" of religious associations, like the World Council of Churches and its Catholic and Jewish counterparts, to press for new congressional allocations.

3. *Doing it cheaply: not capital but technical assistance.* Many authorities on international granting, such as E. F. Schumacher, suggest that the fundamental problem is to support small-scale entrepreneurial efforts, particularly in rural villages. When new kinds of large-scale technology displace local industries, the cities fail to create enough jobs to handle the influx of workers from stagnating towns. He claims that grantors ought to be concerned, not with the expensive transfer of large-scale technologies but with the creation of jobs and small-scale enterprises. This grass-roots activity requires bringing into countries new forms of technical assistance. This sounds like the Peace Corps' approach. What is needed, in Schumacher's view, is funding substantial enough to revitalize 2 million villages. This is the approach being taken by scores of nongovernmental organizations, nearly 5,000 of them, who are now seeking to provide that kind of assistance, often working with

regional associations of government units. It is also the approach being funded increasingly by many of the 125 internationally oriented foundations that are based in this country and by new private foundations in other countries.

4. *New coalitions of international private foundations and corporations.* In 1978 an informal group of donors called the Consultative Group on International Agricultural Research agreed to pledge $88 million that year and to continue donating in the long term to a group of at least eleven research institutes strategically placed worldwide to support applied research on food production in the developing world. It was the result of over thirty years of background work, largely by the Rockefeller and Ford Foundations, that involved painstaking negotiations with the leaders of world associations, the World Bank, and foreign governments, and years of experimentation with grain research by the Rockefeller and Ford Foundations. Finally, there was enough private and public support to launch the full-scale program with the built-in support of all groups necessary for its success.

The same coalitions, some including multinational corporations, have been or are being carefully crafted through public and private negotiations that result in new avenues of funding for population control, transportation and water supply, communications, cultural exchanges, and arms control. Sometimes, these consortia agree to set up an independent organization to receive and pass on the grants to other institutions.

FROM TRENDS TO RESOURCES

The description of trends in the preceding pages provides a map of the kinds of funding prevalent in the 1980s. In order to take advantage of them, you will need more specialized and current information. There are a great number and variety of resources describing new trends in all areas of granting. The information is specialized both by interest areas, such as arts or science funding, and also by geographical region. Partly because it changes so quickly, we have not included a resource guide with this chapter. For up-to-date resources in any of the areas of granting, write to Grantspeople, Inc., (1027 Twenty-third Avenue East, Seattle,

Wash. 98112). For $12 we will provide you with an up-to-date, fifty-four-page Grants Resource Guide covering both government and foundation funding. The price also includes a six-month update to the guide.

VII

Grantspeak: Learning the Language of Grants

Much of the skill required in working effectively with funders depends on being able to put your thoughts into their words and to relate your concepts to those of not only the funder, but also of your clients and your sponsor. The novice grantsperson can be intimidated by the language he encounters in the strange world of grants. At times, it seems to be about as far as you can possibly get from plain, blunt English—more like a series of abstract noises (that begin and end nowhere) and relate to nothing concrete at all.

But that is not really true. The problem is that it tries to communicate too much. Grantspeak is an attempt to simplify a barrage of information. Like any other shorthand method, it tends to favor the initiated, which means that you need a quick course in shorthand yourself to catch up on the Old Boys who are already in the know. This we have tried to provide in the glossary that follows.

To develop your fluency in this strange tongue, the major thing you have to do is get your attitude straight. Of course, you would like to have the grantor extend himself into your territory, to adopt your ways of perceiving the world. No such luck. Since you are trying to sell him on your ability to help accomplish his mission for the fewest possible dollars, you must be able to speak his language if you want to close the deal.

More than anything else, this requires patience. Try to pick up clues to the funder's world from his literature. If you show that you can work in his frame of reference, he will be that much more inclined to hear what you have to say. It's like being able to remember someone's name.

Eventually, as you grow more familiar with using these terms and phrases, you will find yourself resenting them less. You will find that, as with any specialized jargon, they provide a convenient, occasionally vivid way of summarizing the complex processes, points of view, and underlying principles that characterize the complex grants world.

Accountability. Growing concern about the extent of human needs and the limitations of the financial resources available to meet them has placed increasing emphasis on keeping careful accounting of where grant money goes, how it is spent, and whether it seems to have had an effect on the problem it was intended to help resolve. The result has been increasingly stringent auditing and accounting requirements by grantors and more sophisticated evaluation designs written into proposals by grantees.

Action grant. A grant made to explore an issue or to provide a service in a real-life setting. Usually distinguished from research grants, made for work to be conducted in a laboratory setting.

A-95 clearinghouse. A mechanism requiring a range of local and state-level officials and service providers to look over and comment on applications being made to any of over 200 federal funding programs. This preliminary review—an early warning system—assures that proposed projects conform to Equal Opportunity and environmental protection legislation and, most important, that they do not duplicate other federally funded projects already in existence.

Applied research. Research undertaken in order to attempt to resolve human problems, rather than simply to add to the sum of human knowledge. See also *Basic research.*

Approval/Disapproval time. The length of time that it takes a funder to review proposals and to make decisions on them. The time can range anywhere from a few days to several months.

Authorization. The legislation that establishes a basis for the inception of a government granting program.

Basic research. Research oriented toward simply expanding knowledge, rather than directed at solving a specific problem. The research that led to theories of nuclear fission was basic; building an atomic bomb was *Applied research.*

Begging or stealing. The two most common pathologies in the grants culture. Prospective grantspeople—at least those who do not understand the intrinsic logic of the grants system—invariably believe that anything that smacks so strongly of the free lunch must arise either from the funder's pity or stupidity, and that they should try to act accordingly.

Behavioral objectives. Your project is designed to try to get its clients to do something different (e.g., drink less alcohol). Behavioral objectives are usually stated in such a way that they can be measured both before and after the project's operation. See also *Procedural objectives.*

Bequest. A sum of money made available for a foundation's use upon the donor's death. See also *Endowment.*

Bid list. The fast track in contract, and, to a lesser extent, grant circles. Those on a bid list are invited by the funder to respond to an RFP or to apply for a grant. The advantage to getting your name on bid lists is that you may learn of certain funding opportunities much sooner than other potential applicants do, which gives you more time to work on your proposal.

Block grant. Federal grants made under very broad, general subject areas, for example, Community Development. Decisions about the ultimate allocation of these funds are left to the discretion, within limits, of local or regional authorities. Block grants are usually contrasted with *Categorical grants.*

Boilerplate. Sections of any document, especially a proposal, that have been used and reused so often that they have become standardized elements that change very little if at all with each new use. Résumés used in Personnel sections of proposals are a good example of boilerplate copy. To some degree, general boilerplate sections on what your organization is and how it operates are very useful because they save you the time and expense of redoing them for every new proposal submission.

Categorical grant. A federal grant made under narrow, specific program guidelines that carefully spell out such matters as eligibility requirements, program time frames, and intended beneficiaries. Much less discretion about the distribution of categorical grants is left to local or state authorities than is common under *Block grant.*

Challenge grant. More commonly known as a *Matching grant.* Challenge grants are offered by a funder with the express stipulation that the prospective grantee organization must locate another funder who will share a percentage (usually ranging from 10 to 50 percent) of the project costs. Federal grant programs use this provision to assure the participation of local resources in grant programs.

Channeling. Also know as *Conduiting,* channeling occurs when an intermediary organization accepts funds from one grantor and passes them directly on to a predesignated grantee. Typically, the intermediary has tax-exempt status, better credibility, and more visibility than the grantee, which might have difficulty qualifying for the funds if it applied to the funder directly. See also *Sponsor.*

Client. The individual or group who ultimately receives the services that the grant is intended to support.

COG. Council of Government. COGs are regional, voluntary associations of local governments that attempt to promote better communication with state and federal officials, to plan for a region's development, and work for better delivery of services. They often serve as the areawide *A-95 clearinghouse,* and may also play a direct and active role in helping groups obtain grants.

Conceiver. The person with the initial inspiration for the grant project. The conceiver is essential to the success of the grants search and the application process, since he or she provides the project's central concept and can help bridge the inevitable gaps in communication that develop among the funder, the sponsor, the project's staff, community groups, and other elements in the *Service delivery system.*

Conceiver's disease. The chief symptom of this illness is an uninterrupted stream of ingenious grant project possibilities, none of which ever get implemented.

Conceptual dexterity. An important asset in the grants search is the ability to translate your ideas into the set of mental reference points that are familiar to your funder, sponsor, or clients. It means being able to think like they do, to speak their language.

Conduiting. Synonymous with *Channeling.* The United Way is a classic example of a conduiting organization. The use of an intermediary may be initiated by the grantee or by the funder. Private foundations sometimes work out arrangements with tax-exempt public charities (e.g., community foundations) so that they can make grants to groups that are not yet tax exempt. The participation of the public charity or community foundation allows the private foundation to avoid the burdensome *Expenditure responsibility* that was imposed on all private foundations by the 1969 Tax Reform Act. If they are set up carefully and are agreed to in writing by all the parties involved, these arrangements are perfectly legal. See also *Pass-through agency.*

Contingency funding. Support offered with a catch—you have to comply with certain requirements before you can qualify for the money. For example, all federal funding above a certain minimal level is contingent on compliance with Equal Opportunity and environmental protection laws.

Contract. Basically, a tool used to purchase goods or services. The funder identifies a need, outlines the program, and then solicits bids from interested and qualified organizations. The difference between a contract and a *Grant* is not always cut and dried, but it is safe to say that a funder plays a much more active, generative, and initiatory role in contracting. Most contracting is done by government agencies, departments, and institutes; very little is done by foundations.

CON. Contract Opportunity Notice. A CON is a public notice issued by a funder, usually a government agency, stating that it wishes to procure a service. The CON describes the needed service and invites interested groups to submit statements describing their qualifications and past experience in the pertinent field. The CON is perhaps best thought of as the preamble to the *RFP,* in that the description of the needed service is usually quite general and the requested qualification statements are only intended to weed out prospective contractors who are less qualified for the job. Frequently, a CON is issued even before the specific tasks to be performed by the contractor have been very well defined. On the other hand, RFPs usually identify the objectives, methods, and tasks in some detail as well as indicate the type of personnel to be included in the project staff and the general funding range available for the performance of the job.

Cost-benefit. Actually, this is a complex concept, and its economic and social ramifications are abstract and detailed. At its simplest, it connotes a concern for getting the most and best service for the least cost, but this obviously can be a difficult matter to judge. If a project is considered to have juggled quality, cost, and quantity well, it is deemed "cost-effective."

Defunding. A bureaucratic euphemism meaning "You've lost your money . . . the auditors gave you an F."

Deinstitutionalization. The subject of a new trend in granting. It refers to the activity of transferring dependents out of state-supported institutions where they are forever stigmatized as outsiders, and into the mainstream. See *Mainstreaming.*

Data analysis. What you do with the information you have collected in order to make sense of it.

Data collection procedures. Systems established, usually at the start of a project, to keep track of project operations so that its *Effectiveness* and *Efficiency* can later be analyzed.

Demonstration grant. A grant made to set up an innovative project that will function as a model and which, if successful, will be duplicated in other locations and other fields by different grantees. Demonstration grants usually stress the importance of wide dissemination of the project results through careful evaluation and reports, conferences, articles, videotapes, opening the project site up to visitors, and so forth.

Direct costs. The specific, identifiable costs of operating a grant-supported project. Usually broken down into categories in the budget, such as Personnel, Travel, Equipment Purchase and Lease, Consumable Supplies, Rent, and so forth. See also *Indirect costs.*

Discretionary funds. Grants that are allocated according to a funder's judgment rather than according to a pre-established guideline or set of criteria.

Dissemination. The act of seeing that the results of the project are made widely avilable so that others may learn from it. Because information networks among grantees, among funders, and between these two groups are very informal and fragmented, this is still one of the weaker areas of the grants world. Typical modes of dissemination include reports, journal articles, addresses at conferences, newsletters, service directories, press releases, and so forth.

Documentation/Record-keeping. The paper trail that any project generates in keeping track of its staff, clients, services, and budget. Documentation is the raw material used to evaluate the success of a project, or, if success was not attained, to determine what actually happened.

"Doing your homework." Means seeing to it that you have looked into the available resources to gather as much basic information as you can before you approach a funder. You come across as being much more believable if you have already devoted the time required to visit libraries, read some annual reports, make some calls, and talk to people in the field. Similar to the concept of "paying your dues."

Donor control. Something of an issue in the foundation world. One camp believes that donors should have relatively little to say about where their money goes, since they tend to indulge their biases and give very idiosyncratically. (See also *Vanity funding.*) This party points to the example of community foundations and argues that decisions about the distribution of grant funds should be made by a committee composed of representatives of the community, who, it is claimed, have a better grasp of the community's needs than the donor usually does. The opposing point of view is that donors who in the past have kept careful control over the eventual allocations of their gifts have neither a worse nor a better record for making good grants than any other group does. In fact, say advocates of donor control, the donor frequently is much more willing to risk his or her funds on genuinely innovative grant projects.

Edsel's Law of Grants. "When the Ford Motor Company produced an Edsel, lack of market response quickly forced them to stop manufacturing it. But when the Ford Foundation funds an Edsel of a grant idea, there's nothing to prevent them from continuing to make the same kind of grant for years and years and years." (Kenneth E. Boulding)

Effectiveness. Does it work? Does it have any effect?

Efficiency. How well does it operate? Are its procedures and methods smooth, or do they involve a lot of wasted motion and duplication of effort?

Endowment. The sum of money that is made available to a foundation by a donor and is then invested so as to provide funds out of which grants are made, taxes paid, operating expenses met, and so forth.

Evaluation. The process of comparing what a project set out to do with what it actually accomplished. Evaluations are undertaken for the sake of learning what happened in the hope that grantmaking, service delivery, and project management techniques can be improved. Evaluations used to be performed rather informally and discursively, but in the last decade or so have become something of a technical art.

Exemplary project. A funder may designate one project as an example of how others should be run. Usually, this means that other practitioners in the same field become very interested in finding out as much as they can about the project so that they can refine their own funding strategies. See also *Model/Demonstration project.*

Expenditure responsibility. Because the IRS wants to insure that the foundation concept is not abused by affluent individuals who might be tempted to turn it into a tax dodge, it has imposed some fairly stringent restrictions on private foundations in guidelines promulgated under the 1969 and subsequent Tax Reform Acts. One of these makes a funder legally liable if its grants, which are of course supposed to be made for philanthropic purposes, are instead made for private gain or for more than a small amount of political lobbying. Specifically, the IRS has taken the position that private foundations should only make grants to groups that either already have tax-exempt status or could qualify for it if they applied. Otherwise, states the IRS, foundations have to assume the responsibility of seeing that the expenditures are made for suitable charitable, religious, or educational purposes, and not for private gain or political activities. This involves fairly extensive and time-consuming financial and program reporting. Few private foundations have the staff resources to handle this responsibility.

This restriction does not apply to community foundations, which are by definition tax-exempt, so inventive private foundations have been known to work out arrangements with cooperative community foundations who are willing to assume enough of a role in making the grant so that even if it goes to a group without a tax-exemption, no expenditure responsibility is incurred by the private foundation.

Expenditure responsibility is one of the most compelling reasons why a new grantseeking group needs to hook up with a credible sponsor, preferably one with tax-exempt status. It is more difficult to get most private foundations to listen to you if you are not tax-exempt.

Formative/Process evaluation. Determining whether the methods and techniques—the "how" of a project's operations—worked as they were intended to.

Formula grant. A grant that apportions funds among localities solely on the basis of such factors as population, the number of people living below the poverty level, the tax "effort," urbanization, and so forth. This is the other end of the spectrum from competitive grants, the more common form. Theoretically, to get a piece of a formal grant, you just have to apply and to demonstrate that your project area falls within eligibility guidelines. But in effect, since there is never enough money to meet community needs adequately, even the "application" process can be quite competitive. *Revenue sharing* is the predominant federal formula grant.

Foundation. A foundation is in essence: (1) an *Endowment,* contributed by a donor, which is invested so as to realize an income from which grants are made; and (2) a board or committee that reviews proposals and decides where the money will be placed. There are two general categories of foundation: public and private. Private foundations can be further subdivided into these types: general purpose, special purpose, family, and operating. Public foundations are synonymous with community foundations.

Funder. Any person, institution, or agency that makes grants. Usually subdivided into three major categories: government, foundations, and corporations.

Funding cycle. The pattern of announcement, proposal review, and grantee notification that characterizes any funder. Government agencies frequently operate according to firmly established deadlines, and their funding cycles tend to be structured around those deadlines. Foundations may also make grants at set intervals, or they may be continuously involved in review and notification functions, that is, they may operate under a funding cycle that is essentially continuous.

Funding period. The length of time that the grant covers: most often one year, with a possibility of renewal. Rarely more than three years.

Giving pattern. The overall configuration of the kind of projects that the funder has supported in the past, where they are located, how much money they have received, and what kind of organizations have conceived, sponsored, and managed them. Knowing a funder's past record of granting is the best way to predict the likelihood of its approving your own grant application.

Goal. The broad, general, all-inclusive social change that the grant is intended to foster and the project is designed to help achieve. How the world would be different if the project succeeded in completely realizing your vision. Sometimes differentiated from *Objective.*

GPO. Stands for the Government Printing Office, which issues mountains of documents daily, many of which are of great pertinence to grantseekers. Most are available at very reasonable prices. The *Catalogue of Federal Domestic Assistance, The Federal Register,* the *Government Manual,* and a host of others are good basic references for government grants work. You can order by mail directly from the Superintendent of Documents,

Government Printing Office, Washington, D.C., 20402, or if you live near one of the ten federal regional headquarters, you can check with the local GPO outlet to see if they have what you want on hand. Also, the agency authoring the publication may be able to provide you with copies of it.

Grant. A one-way, voluntary transfer of money or other economic goods or services from a *Funder* to a *Grantee,* made in order to support the philanthropic activities outlined by the grantee in the *Proposal.* Grants are distinguished from other market activities, including contracts, in three ways: (1) the funder gets nothing of economic value back in return for making the grant; (2) grants are made only for philanthropic purposes, broadly defined as alleviating dependency or enriching cultural opportunities; and (3) it is the grantee who initiates the transaction and defines the uses to which the grant funds will be put. Most grants are awarded on the basis of selection from among competing proposals.

Grantee. The group, or, rarely, individual, that receives the grant from the funder and uses it to realize the goal of social change by creating and establishing the project outlined in the grant proposal.

Grants-in-Aid. A synonym for *Grant.*

Grantsmanship. The knack of knowing where the money is and how to get at it. The term is often used with the same pejorative connotation as "gamesmanship," when it implies that grants are awarded less on merit than on the ability of the applicant to manipulate the funder.

Grants officer. The individual in a government agency who is responsible for direct administration of a grant program. Usually, your most productive contact during the actual *Funding period* of a government grant will be with the grants officer.

Grantspeople. The essential catalyst in the grants system. Grantspeople are those individuals who, sparked by a vision of change, shoulder the enormous task of researching funders; pulling together proposals; surveying related *Service delivery systems;* mediating between client, community, and further perspectives; and inspiring others to get involved in the project.

Grantseeker. Grantspeople before they get funded.

Green match. See *Hard match.*

Grievance procedure. It is a little-known fact that federal granting programs have established grievance procedures for applicants who are turned down. Foundations will also usually try to give you additional feedback on your declined proposal if you request it tactfully. Do not file grievances whimsically or vindictively—use them to learn in more detail just what it was that did not work in your approach, or use them to argue, if you are in a position to prove it, that those who did receive the grants are less qualified or capable than you are, to prove that the funder's granting pattern shows a clear bias in favor of one group or type of grantee.

Guidelines. A funder's statement of its goals, priorities, eligibility criteria, and application procedures, or those of one of its programs. Guidelines will either tell you how to write your proposal or they will include forms to use that, when filled out, will constitute your proposal.

Hard match. Money, rather than facilities or services. See also *Matching; Soft match.*

Hard money. Dependable, long-term sources of funding. There are few, if any, permanent sources of funding. Money at its hardest comes from government budgets or from the budgets of large, powerful fund-raising agencies, such as the United Way, and these sources are subject to sudden shifts in priorities as well. One form of hard money is dependable money from fees. Another form is tax revenues. But in times of inflation and tax cuts, even these reliable hard sources can go soft.

Homo bureaucraticus. The human being as a creature of routine, motivated primarily by security and characterized by conformance to the ritualistic manipulation of paper, which is customarily defended as necessary and rational, though it may appear obscure to the observer. Homo bureaucraticus is the agent of the budget as a social planning tool.

Homo economicus. The predecessor, along with *Homo bureaucraticus,* of the grantsperson, *Homo grantus.* Homo economicus represents the human being as an egocentric animal, motivated by self-interest and the pursuit of profit. Homo economicus tends to accept the values determined by the marketplace as those of primary importance in life.

Homo grantus. The human as a socially responsible being willing to hustle to fulfill visions of social change. The nonprofit entrepreneur.

Human services. In order to distinguish funding programs that concentrate on providing certain kinds of services to people from those that, for example, support research or construction projects, government organizations have in the last few years begun to lump all of their social service activities under the heading "human services," or "human care services." The category is very broad, of course, but some typical kinds of actual services provided under this heading may include child-care referral systems, nutritional counseling for the elderly, battered women's refuges, equal opportunity advocates, and so on.

Impact. Effect, result.

Implemented. Actually put into practice or operation.

Indirect costs. A budget category that is intended to cover those general administrative costs of operating a project that are hard to assign to specific project functions. Typically, these costs include building rent and maintenance, depreciation, general local travel, and so forth. Indirect costs are usually calculated as a flat percentage of either the budget as a whole or the personnel category alone. In negotiations with a *Sponsor,* indirect costs can become a complex issue. Also known as *Overhead.*

Information overload. It is possible to know too much. For example, it can be paralyzing to learn that only one out of every twenty proposals submitted to a child-care funding program got past the first review stage. Also, although there is a surfeit of information in some areas of the grants world, such as on how to write proposals, there is a deficit in others. If you pay attention only to what is already known, you will not learn much.

In-kind. Describes contributions other than money, usually services, facilities, or equipment. See also *Matching.*

Intervention. A common rationale for some kinds of grants projects. Intervention means stepping into a developing problem to prevent it from getting progressively worse.

Joint funding. It is not uncommon for grant projects to be supported by more than one funder, each of whom may either provide support for one self-contained component of the overall project or who may contribute to a common pool of grant funds. The joint-funding strategy can be initiated by the grantmaker or by the grantseeker. On the federal side, joint funding that spans various governmental departments is handled under the Joint Funding Simplification Act, through the activity of the Federal Regional Councils. See also *Matching.*

"Laundering federal money." The act, which usually occurs at the state government level but which may also take place at local or regional levels, of redefining and refining the priorities of a federal funding program so as to align it more closely with state and local priorities.

LEA. Local Education Agency.

LEAA. Law Enforcement Assistance Administration (part of the Department of Justice).

Letter of intent/inquiry. Your first contact with a prospective funder often takes this form rather than a phone call. You briefly state your intention to apply for its funds and give a very brief idea of the nature of your planned project. This usually means that the funder will send pertinent guidelines and other information back to you, and will also probably open a file on you.

Letter of support. Written statements attached to the back of proposals. They are provided by organizations and individuals who endorse your project's efforts and who are considered credible in the eyes of the funder. The best letters of support are much more than mere testimonials; they actually spell out in just what ways the established group is willing to help you out.

Leveraging. Using one grant to get another. Also known as dominoing and *Pyramiding.*

Mainstreaming. Bringing a disadvantaged client group out of its excluded status and back into the central current of socioeconomic events. Originally meant as the process of shifting children out of special education classes and into the regular classroom, the term has now acquired broader connotations and is liberally used to refer to the reintegration of any group that has traditionally been set apart from society, for whatever reasons. See *Deinstitutionalization.*

Matching. Many federal and a few foundation grant programs require that applicants obtain a portion—usually anywhere from 10 to 50 percent of their total request—from other sources, to show that there is wide local support for the intended project. Putting together viable matching packages is a highly sophisticated art.

Model/Demonstration project. A project that obtains funding with the express intention of being established so as to prove an untried idea, set an example, and make the result available to others in the same or related fields.

MSO. Management Support Organization.

Multipocketed budgeting. Obtaining support for your project from a wide variety of sources, each of which may either offer support for a distinct component of the project or *Unrestricted funds* for you to use as you see fit.

Narrative. The explanatory prose portion of a proposal that supplements the application form in many federal grant programs.

Needs assessment. This is perhaps the most critical component of the proposal, the section that answers the question, "Why is this project needed?" It should provide a rationale, hopefully a persuasive one, for the funder's consideration. Good needs assessments not only point out what the needs are, and why remedies for them are needed, but they also back up these assertions with the judicious use of quantitative data.

Nonprofit corporation. This is the predominant organizational form of grant recipients. Nonprofit corporations, like other corporations, must have officers, a board of directors, and a set of by-laws, but they do not pay dividends from profits or invested capital. In most states, the Attorney General regulates the formation and activities of nonprofit corporations. Creating the nonprofit corporation is usually the first step in seeking tax-exempt status.

Objectives. The proposal's *Goals* must be translated into specific, quantified targets or levels of achievement in order to provide a set of criteria by which the success or failure of the project can be judged. Objectives set forth desired changes in terms of numbers of clients, the level of activity or skill, and deadlines.

Old Boys' network. There is usually an insiders' circle, in any field, of people who have known one another for years and can thus communicate among themselves quickly, informally, and efficiently. Such networks can be used in a good way, to reinforce more elaborate formal procedures, to spread news rapidly, or to cut through unnecessarily cumbersome procedures. However, they can also be used in a negative way, as happens when outsiders are tacitly but effectively excluded from serious grant competitions for very biased or personal reasons.

OMB circulars. Instructions, guidelines, and directions, issued to all federal grantmaking programs by the Office of Management and Budget, the supervisor of federal granting activities and source of the *Catalogue of Federal Domestic Assistance.* Since the objective of most OMB circulars is to set standards for federal grantmakers, it is to your advantage to keep track of what they have to say.

Overhead. See *Indirect costs.*

Packaging. The art of presenting the basic elements of your proposal in such a way as to respond most appropriately to the varying priorities, goals, and guidelines of different funders.

Pass-through agency. Another name for *Conduiting* and *Channeling* agencies. A pass-through organization is an intermediary that accepts funds from one source and distributes them to another. State government departments and agencies play a prominent pass-through role in reallocating federal grant funds, particularly under block programs. Foundations also may perform this function for donors who have very well-defined ideas about where they want their money to go.

Payout requirement. The 30,000 private foundations in the country are legally required to make grants each year in an amount equal to the net return on their investments or 6 percent of the total value of those investments, whichever is larger.

Peer review. Critical reading of a proposal or contract by reputable practitioners and others conversant with the field it addresses, who are in a position to judge the competence of the applicant. See also *Technical review.*

Philanthropoid. A denizen of the grants culture. According to John M. Russell, author of *Giving and Taking: Across the Foundation Desk*[1] and long-time executive director of the Markel Foundation, this term was first coined by Frederick P. Veppel, ex-president of the Carnegie Corporation. See also *Homo grantus.*

Preliminary proposal. A brief, early draft of the proposal itself that is used to elicit feedback from the prospective funder so that the proposal may be more closely tailored to funder expenditures. Also known as a discussion paper, preproposal, or preapplication.

Pro bono publico. Relatively few law firms are devoted exclusively to serving the common good, but a large number are willing to donate some time to working for a good philanthropic cause. If you need legal

[1]Teachers' College Press, Teachers' College, Columbia University, New York and London, 1977.

services and are not in a position to pay for them, check around and see if you can interest an attorney in donating some time.

Procedural objectives. Your project will cause a process to change (e.g., simplify welfare intake procedures). See also *Behavioral objectives.*

Profile of funder. This is one of the later stages in the grants search, which occurs once you have identified your project idea, made it a fundable one, and worked out a general sense of which areas of the funding world would be most appropriate for you to approach.

Proposal. The written application for the grant funds. It serves five purposes: description, selling, planning, contracting, and evaluating. Types of proposals range from the informal, discursive letter to voluminous and complex application forms. The standard elements of most proposals are designed to explain why the project is needed, who is going to do it, and how much it will cost. Components can include a cover letter, abstract, introduction, literature review, needs assessment, goals, objectives, method, tasks, budget, personnel, evaluation design, future funding plans, dissemination, and letters of support.

Provider. The agency or corporation that actually dispenses the services supported by the grant to the *Client* group.

Public interest. This term, which has come into common use in the last decade or so, denotes a certain type of firm, such as law office or an accountant, that would ordinarily be found operating in the private sector, usually as a profit-making organization, but which is devoted to serving public issues and low-income clients. See also *Pro bono publico.*

Public sector. All the groups, agencies, departments, and other organizations that are supported by tax money and that exist to provide governmental and other public services. In the grants culture, the public sector comprises federal, state, and local government, community foundations; and all nonprofit, tax-exempt organizations supported by tax dollars and providing public services.

Pyramiding. See *Leveraging.*

Revenue sharing. This is essentially a massive formula grant program that the Department of the Treasury has been operating since 1972. Money collected from individual income taxes is returned to local municipalities for redistribution as local authorities determine, within broad limits.

RFP. Stands for Request for Proposal. This is the public notice that is issued by a funder who wishes to procure a service from a contractor. Federal RFPs are generally quite detailed, outlining the tasks to be performed and the kind of expertise the funder believes will be necessary to perform them.

Risk capital. It is a common practice for business ventures to devote some percentage of their profits to exploring risky options. Most of these turn out to be blind alleys, but the rare one that proves feasible can be a gold mine. The same principle should apply to public service organizations, which often can afford to indulge in experimentation only if they get a grant.

Rules and Regulations. Once authorizing legislation for a federal grant program has been passed by Congress, the actual details of its operation are set forth in the *Federal Register* under the heading Rules and Regulations. Since these are what the funder must follow in making its grants, it helps to know them yourself so that you can understand what the funder legally can and cannot do.

Sacrifice trap. A characteristic neurosis of grantsmakers favoring the Old Boys who get funded year after year. It refers to the tendency of grantors to refund their grantees, because if they do not, they would feel that they made a mistake in giving the grant in the first place.

SEA. State Educational Agency.

Seed grant. An endangered species. At one time, it was more common for funders to make small initial grants to encourage promising groups and projects. Seed grants could be used to mount a campaign for larger grants to bring the project through the difficult first phases of operation. Now they are getting very rare.

Serendipity effect of grants. An unanticipated positive result. Grant projects rarely wind up having done exactly what they set out to do. Whatever they produce on the plus side that is unexpected is due to the serendipity effect. (The term was coined by Ruth Chance, ex-director of the San Francisco Rosenberg Foundation.) See also *Spinoff projects.*

Service delivery system. The network of organizations with a past or current record of attempting to address the problem toward which your project is directed. You need to make certain that your intended services complement or enhance those already in existence, since funders are understandably reluctant to support a duplication of effort.

Set-aside. Grant funds earmarked in advance for specific groups, or even specific single recipients, usually as a result of effective lobbying. One result of set-asides is to limit competition and to increase legislative influence over grant allocations.

Sign-off. An authorized representative of your sponsor (or fiscal agent) will have to put his or her signature on a variety of documents for them to be approved by the funder, especially if it is a government agency. In the case, for example, of a request to waive a fiscal reporting requirement, the sponsor's sign-off indicates that it is in agreement with your request; this reassures the funder that you are not playing fast and loose with the money. Often something of a *pro forma* activity.

Site visit. It is not uncommon for a funder to want to visit the actual project facilities, to chat with the staff, take a look around, and generally get the feel of the applicant's organization. The site visit may be the last step in the application process before notification of the funding decision itself, in which case receiving such a visit is a good sign that you are a strong contender for the money, or it may be part of the evaluation phase at the end of the grant.

Social entrepreneur. Anyone who brings to public service the same drive, hustle, and nose for an emerging area of need that has traditionally characterized success in the commercial world.

Soft match. Service, facilities, equipment—in short, anything but money. See *Hard match; Matching.*

Soft money. Insecure funding. Usually available for no more than a year.

Spinoff disease. Constantly thinking of new variations or additions that might logically evolve from your project, instead of getting down to work and improving the one you have.

Spinoff projects. In attempting to respond to identified needs, grant projects often unearth new, previously unrecognized needs, and thus generate the rationale for new projects, which in their implementation share the resources developed in the initial grant project.

Sponsor. An agency or institution that undertakes to assist and support a grantee by offering it credibility and perhaps also services or space, but not money. The role of the sponsor is a much more active one than is performed by *Channeling* or *Pass-through agencies.* Also known as fiscal agent.

Street-level bureaucrats. Most government legislation is enacted without adequate appreciation for the complexity of actually making it work, of implementing it. What this means is that nuances in the law actually get defined according to the discretion of those who represent it most directly to the public, and these individuals become street-level bureaucrats. For instance, civil and criminal laws are selectively enforced by peace officers, who make constant decisions about how to exercise their considerable power over members of the public. Street-level bureaucrats can be helpful, in that they have the power to overlook or bypass unnecessary formalities. But they can also be detrimental if they exercise their discretion only so as to make their jobs easier or more manageable.

Summative/Product evaluation. Determining whether the intended results—the "what" of the project—occurred.

Support services. Those functions in an organization that exist to help other, primary functions do whatever it is that the organization is designed to do. For example, in an engineering office, support services might include a technical library, drafting, accounting, report preparation, and so forth.

Target population. The intended beneficiaries of a grant-supported service project. Also known as client population. A service project may have both direct and indirect beneficiaries.

Tax-exempt. A cherished status, something of a seal of approval, bestowed by the IRS and the individual states on organizations that have adequately demonstrated their charitable, educational, religious, scientific, or literary nature, By far the largest part, but not all, of tax-exempt organizations are *Nonprofit corporations.* Others include trusts and benevolent associations.

Technical assistance. Information and training services provided by the funder to grant applicants that improve the quality of proposed projects as well as broaden the range of people who have access to the funder's grant programs. TA, as it is most commonly known, can range from simply mailing out rules and regulations to applicants to much more active roles, such as actually taking a hand in the proposal writing process, or even seeking out promising grant candidates and helping them to apply. Technical assistance from one funder can frequently be used to help you get a grant from another funder. If they cannot get you money, they can at least tell you how to get it from someone else.

Technical review. Critical reading of a proposal or contract by specialists within its content area, to determine its congruence with the state of the art. See also *Peer review.*

"Three years and out." At one time the rule of thumb for the duration of foundation grant support was no more than three years, after which —if you were lucky—you were taken over by United Way. These days, three years is probably an overgenerous estimation of the normal length of a grant; one year, maybe two, has become the standard, and United Ways are absorbing fewer and fewer lapsing grants.

The "as-if" principle. Chutzpah. No one knows everything about grants, so do not let your ignorance slow you down—behave as if you know what you are doing and soon you will.

The myth of expertise. Experts are those who know every crack and grain in every brick of the intellectual castle they inhabit, but who are often oblivious to the countryside outside its walls.

The myth of objectivity. The notion that there is a "real" world that exists independent of our perceptions of it and is unaffected by our attitudes toward it. This is occasionally a pleasant and handy notion but not when it prevents you from accepting your own experiences as valid.

Tragedy of the commons. Vacant lots fill up with garbage because they belong to nobody and anybody. On a larger scale, the sea is being polluted and fisheries depleted for the same reason. Seeking ways to avoid the tragedy of the commons is becoming the rationale for an increasing number of grant projects.

Unexpended funds. What is left in a funder's grantmaking budget as the year draws to a close. There is usually increasing pressure to disburse these funds before a new funding cycle begins. This pressure may result in a last minute giveaway of the funds (also known as a "fourth-quarter throwaway").

Unrestricted funds. Grants made without prior stipulations as to their use, to be spent as the grantee sees fit. See also *Discretionary funds.*

Unsolicited applications. Although most government funding programs operate according to firm deadlines, disseminated in Program Announcements and in the *Catalogue of Federal Domestic Assistance,* some do not, and neither do most foundation and corporate grantors—submissions to these funding programs are called unsolicited applications.

Vanity funding. Funding motivated by a desire to gratify the funder's ego and dramatize his or her existence rather than by genuine altruism.

Appendix A

Foundation Center Libraries

Foundation Center National Libraries

The Foundation Center
888 Seventh Avenue
New York, New York 10019

The Foundation Center
1001 Connecticut Avenue, N.W.
Washington, D.C. 20036

Foundation Center Field Offices

The Foundation Center—San Francisco
312 Sutter Street
San Francisco, California 94108

The Foundation Center—Cleveland
Kent H. Smith Library
739 National City Bank Building
629 Euclid Avenue
Cleveland, Ohio 44114

National Cooperating Collection

Donors Forum of Chicago
208 South LaSalle Street
Chicago, Illinois 60604

Regional Cooperating Collections

Alabama

Birmingham Public Library
2020 Seventh Avenue, North
Birmingham 35203

Auburn University at Montgomery Library
Montgomery 36117

Alaska

University of Alaska, Anchorage Library
3211 Providence Drive
Anchorage 99504

Arizona

Tucson Public Library
Main Library
200 S. Sixth Avenue
Tucson 85701

Little Rock Public Library
Reference Department
700 Louisana Street
Little Rock 72201

California

University Research Library
Reference Department
University of California
Los Angeles 90024

San Diego Public Library
820 E. Street
San Diego 92101

Colorado

Denver Public Library
Sociology Division
1357 Broadway
Denver 80203

Connecticut

Hartford Public Library
Reference Department
500 Main Street
Hartford 06103

District of Columbia. See Maryland.

Florida

Jacksonville Public Library
Business, Science, and Industry Department
122 North Ocean Street
Jacksonville 32202

Miami-Dade Public Library
Florida Collection
1 Biscayne Boulevard
Miami 33132

Georgia

(Also covers Alabama, Florida, South Carolina, and Tennessee.)

Atlanta Public Library
126 Carnegie Way, N.W.
Atlanta 30303

Hawaii

Thomas Hale Hamilton Library
University of Hawaii
Humanities and Social Sciences Division
2550 The Mall
Honolulu 96822

Idaho

Caldwell Public Library
1010 Dearborn Street
Caldwell 83605

Illinois

Sangamon State University Library
Shepherd Road
Springfield 62708

Indiana

Indianapolis-Marion County Public Library
40 East Saint Clair Street
Indianapolis 46204

Iowa

Des Moines Public Library
100 Locust Street
Des Moines 50309

Kansas

Topeka Public Library
Adult Services Department
1515 West Tenth Street
Topeka 66604

Kentucky

Louisville Free Public Library
Fourth and York Streets
Louisville 40203

Louisiana

New Orleans Public Library
Business and Science Division
219 Loyola Avenue
New Orleans 70140

Maine

University of Maine at Portland-Godham
Center for Research and Advanced Study
246 Deering Avenue
Portland 04102

Maryland

(Also covers District of Columbia.)

Enoch Pratt Free Library
Social Science and History Department
400 Cathedral Street
Baltimore 21201

Massachusetts

Associated Foundation of Greater Boston
294 Washington Street, Suite 501
Boston 02108

Boston Public Library
Copley Square
Boston 02117

Michigan

Henry Ford Centennial Library
15301 Michigan Avenue
Dearborn 48126

Purdy Library
Wayne State University
Detroit 48202

Grand Rapids Public Library
Sociology and Education Department
Library Plaza
Grand Rapids 49502

Minnesota

(Also covers North and South Dakota.)

Minneapolis Public Library
Sociology Department
300 Nicollet Mall
Minneapolis 55401

Mississippi

Jackson Metropolitan Library
301 North State Street
Jackson 39201

Missouri

(Also covers Kansas.)

Kansas City Public Library
311 East Twelfth Street
Kansas City 64106

The Danforth Foundation Library
222 South Central Avenue
St. Louis 63105

Springfield-Greene County Library
397 East Central Street
Springfield 65801

Montana

Eastern Montana College Library
Reference Department
Billings 59101

Nebraska

W. Dale Clark Library
Social Sciences Department
215 South Fifteenth Street
Omaha 68102

New Hampshire

The New Hampshire Charitable Fund
1 South Street
Concord 03301

New Jersey

New Jersey State Library
Reference Section
185 West State Street
Trenton 08625

New Mexico

New Mexico State Library
300 Don Gaspar Street
Santa Fe 87501

New York

New York State Library
State Education Department
Education Building
Albany 12224

Buffalo and Erie County Public Library
Lafayette Square
Buffalo 14203

Levittown Public Library
Reference Department
1 Bluegrass Lane
Levittown 11756

Rochester Public Library
Business and Social Sciences Division
115 South Avenue
Rochester 14604

North Carolina

William R. Perkins Library
Duke University
Durham 27706

North Dakota. See Minnesota

Oklahoma

Oklahoma City Community Foundation
1300 North Broadway
Oklahoma City 73103

Tulsa City–County Library System
400 Civic Center
Tulsa 74103

Oregon

Library Association of Portland
Education and Psychology Department
801 S.W. Tenth Avenue
Portland 97205

Pennsylvania

(Also covers Delaware.)

The Free Library of Philadelphia
Logan Square
Philadelphia 19103

Hillman Library
University of Pittsburgh
Pittsburgh 15213

Rhode Island

Providence Public Library
Reference Department
150 Empire Street
Providence 02903

South Dakota. See Minnesota

Washington

Seattle Public Library
1000 Fourth Avenue
Seattle 98104

Spokane Public Library
Reference Department
West 906 Main Avenue
Spokane 99201

West Virginia

Kanawha County Public Library
123 Capitol Street
Charleston 25301

Wisconsin

(Also covers Illinois.)

Marquette University Memorial Library
1415 West Wisconsin Avenue
Milwaukee 53233

Wyoming

Laramie County Community College Library
1400 East College Drive
Cheyenne 82001

Puerto Rico

(Covers selected foundations.)

Consumer Education and Service Center
Department of Consumer Affairs
Minillas Central Government Building North
Santurce 00908

Mexico

(Covers selected foundations.)

Biblioteca Benjamin Franklin
Londres 16
Mexico City 6, D.F.

Appendix B

Regional Foundation Associations

ASSOCIATIONS OF GRANTMAKERS*

REGIONAL	<u>Principal Contact</u>
Conference of Southwest Foundations P.O. Box 8832 Corpus Christi, Texas 78412	Mrs. Maud W. Keeling Executive Secretary
Southeastern Council of Foundations 134 Peachtree Street, N.W. Atlanta, Georgia 30303	Mr. Robert Hull Executive Director
STATE	
Association of Ohio Foundations Columbus Foundation 17 South High Street Columbus, Ohio 43215	Ms. Leeda Marting
Cleveland Foundation Resources 700 National City Bank Building Cleveland, Ohio 44114	Mr. Homer C. Wadsworth President

*From *The Handbook of Community Foundations,* Council on Foundations, Inc., 888 Seventh Avenue, New York, New York 10019, 1977, pp. 18–21.

Kansas City Association of Trusts and Foundations
406 Board of Trade Building
127 West Tenth Street
Kansas City, Missouri 64105
Mr. Charles E. Curran
President

Los Angeles Inter-Foundation Center
Westwood Center
1100 Glendon No. 1414
Los Angeles, California 90024
Mr. Joe G. Dempsey
Executive Director

Metropolitan Association for Philanthropy
607 North Grand Boulevard
St. Louis, Missouri 63103
Mr. R. D. Dunlop
Executive Director

Minneapolis Foundation
(Foundation Services)
400 Foshay Tower
821 Marquette Avenue
Minneapolis, Minnesota 55402
Mr. Jerry V. Catt
Associate Director

Pacific Northwest Grantmakers Forum
Medina Foundation
1616 Norton Building
Seattle, Washington 98104
Mr. Gregory P. Barlow
Executive Director

Urban Dynamics/Inner City Fund
111 East Wacker Drive
Chicago, Illinois 60601
Mr. Kenneth A. Vaughn
Executive Director

LUNCHEON GROUPS

Association of Colorado Foundations
c/o The Denver Foundation
209 Sixteenth Street
Denver, Colorado 80203

Council of Michigan Foundations
18 North Fifth Street
Grand Haven, Michigan 49417
Ms. Dorothy A. Johnson
Executive Secretary

The Foundation Forum of Southeastern Wisconsin
Milwaukee Foundation
161 West Wisconsin Avenue
Suite 5146
Milwaukee, Wisconsin 53203

Mr. David M. G. Huntington
Director

Minnesota Council on Foundations
821 Marquette Avenue
Minneapolis, Minnesota 55402

Ms. Judith Healey
Executive Director

New Hampshire Charitable Fund and Affiliated Trusts
1 South Street
Concord, New Hampshire 03301

Mrs. Jean L. Hennessey
Executive Director

CITY

Associated Foundation of Greater Boston
1 Boston Place, Suite 948
Boston, Massachusetts 02108

Ms. Janet C. Taylor
Executive Director

Clearinghouse for Midcontinent Foundations
Post Office Box 8102
Kansas City, Missouri 64112

Dr. Linda H. Talbott
Executive Director

Co-ordinating Council for Foundations, Inc.
36 Woodland Street
Hartford, Connecticut 06105

Mr. Robert S. Merriman
Executive Director

Donors' Forum of Chicago
208 South LaSalle, Room 840
Chicago, Illinois 60604

Ms. Eleanor P. Petersen
President

Central Florida Foundations Luncheon Group
Edyth Bush Charitable Foundation, Inc.
5800 Diplomat Circle Building, No. 105
Orlando, Florida 32810

Mr. David R. Roberts
President

Columbus Area Funding Group Columbus Foundation 17 South High Street Columbus, Ohio 43215	Ms. Leeda Marting
District of Columbia Luncheon Group Eugene and Agnes E. Myer Foundation The OFC Building, Suite 1212 1730 Rhode Island Avenue, N.W. Washington, D.C. 20036	Mr. James L. Kunen President
Foundation Executives' Luncheon Group 1150 Union Street San Francisco, California 94109	Mrs. Ruth Chance
Foundation Luncheon Group The Fund for the City of New York 342 Madison Avenue New York, N.Y. 10017	Mr. Gregory R. Farrell Executive Director
Rochester Foundation Group c/o Rochester Area Foundation 315 Alexander Street, Room 205 Rochester, New York 14604	
Winston-Salem Luncheon Group The Winston-Salem Foundation 2230 Wachovia Building Winston-Salem, North Carolina 27101	Mr. Sebastian C. Sommer Executive Director

Index

About Foundations: How to Find the Facts You Need to Get a Grant (Foundation Center), 95
Abstracts, 188, 196–197, 259
Accountability, 217, 245
Action grants, 245
Active Corps of Executives (ACE), 128
Activities, 182–183
Affirmative action, 78
Agency for International Development (AID), 62
Agricultural Extension Service, 236–238
Agriculture, Department of, 125, 226
Alcohol, Drug Abuse, and Mental Health Administration (ADAMHA), 225
Alliance for Displaced Homemakers, 51
American Association for the Advancement of Science, 241
American Association on Aging, 52
A-95 clearinghouse review, 132–133, 138, 245
Annual fund-raising program, 190
Applied research, 192, 227–229, 245, 246
Appropriate Energy Technology (AET) program, 117–121, 217
Approval/Disapproval time, 245
Arts, funding for, 86, 218–221
"As-if" principle, 263
Associated Foundations of Greater Boston, 141–142
Association for the Study of Grants Economics, 15
Associations of grantmakers, 274–277
Authorization, 245
Authorization Act of the Department of Energy (DOE), 116

Background section of proposals, 173–178
Basic Educational Opportunity Grants, 223
Basic research, 192, 227, 246
Battelle Institute, 59
Begging, 72–73, 154, 246
Behavioral objectives, 246
Believability, 147–168
kinds of, 149–153
Benevolent associations, 262
Bequests, 102, 108, 246
Bid lists, 246
Bio-Gas, Inc., 3

Block grants, 113–114, 230, 233, 234–236, 246, 258
Boilerplate section of proposal, 246
Bothwell, Robert, 218
Boulding, Kenneth E., 15–16, 26–27, 250
Brookings Institution, 145–146
Brown, Jerry, 11, 51, 112
Bruyn, Henry, 42, 43
Bryant, Anita, 11
Budget by objectives, 184–185
Business enterprise, 16–17

California Department of Corrections, 4
Capitalism, 16, 65
Carnegie Commission on the Future of Public Broadcasting, 220
Carnegie Foundation, 37, 38
Carter, Jimmy, 4, 34, 52, 61, 116–117
Catalogue of Federal Domestic Assistance (CFDA), 121–122, 124, 125, 131, 252, 258, 263
Categorical grants, 112–113, 246–247
Category Trap, 134–137
Center for Homosexual Education, Evaluation, and Research (CHEER), 3
Center for Independent Living (CIL), 45–48, 178–181
CETA. *See* Comprehensive Employment and Training Act
Challenge grants. *See* Matching grants
Chambers of commerce, 84, 219
Chance, Ruth, 89–90, 260
Channeling, 247–248, 258, 261
Chester, Tom, 117, 120
Children's Television Workshop (CTW), 37–41, 164, 190
Church, Frank, 56
Civil Rights Act of 1964, 233
Civil rights movement, 68, 77
Client, 247, 259
Coalition building, 161–168
COGs. *See* Councils of Government (COGs)
Commerce Business Daily (CBD), 116, 124, 129
Commissions on the Status of Women, 52
Community Action Agency, 139, 233
Community colleges, 222–223
Community Development Administration (CDA), 219
Community development block grants, 230, 233, 234–236
Community foundations, 100–110, 251
  compared to private foundations and fund-raising groups, 101–102
  growth of, 101
  profile of, 103–109
  researching, 109–110
Community support, 152, 153, 161
Comprehensive Employment and Training Act (CETA), 4, 5, 48–52, 135, 136, 139, 141, 219, 223, 233–234
Conceivers, 247
Conceiver's disease, 247
Concept papers, 196–197
Conceptual dexterity, 247
Conduiting, 247–248, 258, 261
Conference Board, Inc., 84
Construction projects, 86
Consultative Group on International Agricultural Research, 242
Consumer protection, 157–160
Contingency funding, 248
Continuation grants, 189
Contract Opportunity Notice (CON), 115–116, 158, 248
Contracts, 115–116, 128–130, 189–190, 192, 248, 253
Cooney, Joan Ganz, 36–41, 67, 164, 190
Cooney, Timothy, 36
Cooperative Assistance Fund, 236
Corporate Foundation Directory (ed. Brodsky), 85
Corporate funding, 8, 23, 25, 26, 75–85
  arts and, 218
  education and, 78, 80, 223
  giving levels, 75–78
  in-kind donations, 77–78, 82
  profile of, 79–83
  researching, 83–85
  science and, 228
Corporate Philanthropic Public Service Activities (Conference Board, Inc.), 84
Corporation for Public Broadcasting, 220

Cost-benefit, 39, 68, 248
Council on Foundations, 97, 102
Councils of Governments (COGs), 132–133, 237, 238, 247
Cover letters, 188, 259
Credibility, 139, 147–148
Crisis intervention, 111
Curriculum, university, 12–14

Data analysis, 249
Data collection procedures, 249
Decentralization, 113
Defense, Department of, 53, 226
Defunding, 249
Deinstitutionalization, 225, 249
Demonstration grants, 192, 249
Dependency syndrome, 27, 42
Designated grants, 103
Developing Skills in Proposal Writing (Hall), 214
DIALOG Information Retrieval Service, 100
Direct cash contributions, 25
Direct costs, 249
Direct mail solicitation, 190
Discretionary funds, 249
Discussion papers, 83–84, 258
Displaced homemakers movement, 51–53, 234
Dissemination, 192, 249, 259
Documentation/record keeping, 183, 249
Doing your homework, 147–148, 249–250
Dominoing, 256
Donor-advised grants, 103
Donor control, 250
Dun & Bradstreet's Reference Book of Corporate Management, 84

Econometrics, 16
Economic development, funding for, 235–236
Economic Development Administration (EDA), 219, 233, 237
Economy of Love and Fear, The: A Preface to Grants Economics (Boulding), 7*n*
Edsel's law of grants, 26–27, 250
Educational funding, 78, 80, 86, 221–223
Effectiveness, 250
Efficiency, 250
Electric Company, The 40
Endowments, 102, 250
Energy, Department of (DOE), 53, 54, 58, 59, 61–63, 116–121, 217, 226
Energy issue, 53–63, 240
Energy Research and Development Administration (ERDA), 59, 60
Entrepreneurism, 64–67
Environmentalists, 53, 62
Equal Rights Amendment, 11
Evaluation, 185, 187, 250, 259
Exemplary project, 250–251
Expenditure responsibility, 92, 149, 248, 251
Expertise, myth of, 263
Exxon Corporation, 220

Face sheet, 94
Family foundations, 87
Feasibility study, 192
Federal Advisory Commission on Intergovernmental Relations, 131
Federal Assistance Program Retrieval System (FAPRS), 125–128
Federal government funding, 7*n*, 9, 10, 110–133; stimulating private industry through, 18–19
  A-95 review, 132–133, 138, 245
  arts and, 218–219
  block grants, 113–114, 230, 233, 234–236, 246, 258
  categorical grants, 112–113, 246–247
  compared to foundation funding, 85–86
  contracts, 115–116, 128–130, 189–190, 192, 248, 253
  decentralization, 113
  displaced homemakers movement, 51–53
  education and, 86, 221–223
  profile of, 116–121
  rehabilitation and, 41–48, 224–226
  research and development, 18–19, 22, 226–229, 240–241
  researching, 121–131
  revenue sharing, 113–114, 252, 259
  solar research, 55–56, 58–63
  stimulating production, 126, 226
Federal Regional Councils (FRCs), 130–131, 256
Federal Register, 122, 124, 138, 252, 260

Fees for service, 190
Feminists versus profamily issue, 11–12
Filer, John H., 144
Filer Commission (Commission on Public Needs and Private Philanthropy), 75, 76, 78, 81, 85, 144–145
Filmmaking, 4–5
Fiscal agents. *See* Sponsors
Flanagan, Joan, 214
Ford, Gerald, 60
Ford Foundation, 38, 41, 141, 155–156, 220–221, 230, 236, 242
Foreign aid, 239
Forestry, 4
Formative/Process evaluation, 251
Formula block grants, 113
Formula grants, 113, 251–252
Fortune magazine, 84–85
Foundation Center, 95–100, 135
  libraries, 99–100, 265–273
Foundation Center National Data Book, The (Foundation Center), 96
Foundation Center Source Book Profiles (Foundation Center), 96
Foundation Directory, The (Foundation Center), 92, 95–96
Foundation for Development, 240
Foundation Grants Index, The (Foundation Center), 97–99
Foundation Grants to Individuals (Foundation Center), 96
Foundation News, 97
Foundations. *See* Community foundations; Private foundations
Foundations Under Fire (ed. Reeves), 143–144
Fourth-quarter throwaway, 263
Franchise Tax Board, 149
Freedom of Information Act, 67
Free enterprise, 16–18
Funding cycle, 252
Funding duplication, 107
Funding period, 252
Future funding plan, 189–191, 259

Gardner, John, 21
Gay advocacy groups, 3
General purpose foundations, 87
General Revenue Sharing (GRS), 113–114
General systems theory, 15
Giving in America: Toward a Stronger Voluntary Sector (Filer Commission), 144–145
Giving patterns, 75–78, 252
Goals section of proposals, 178–181, 252, 257, 259
Golden Fleece awards, 26
Government funding. *See* Federal government funding
Government Manual, 252
Government Printing Office (GPO), 252–253
Government regulation, 17–18
Grants: How to Find Out About Them and What to Do Next (White), 143
Grants Magazine, Journal of Sponsored Research, 32*n*
Grantsmanship, 253
Grantsmanship Center, 101
"Grantsmanship Center News, The," 143
Grants office, 253
Grantspeople, 30–69, 253
  case studies, 36–63
  as entrepreneur, 64–67
  flexibility of, 67–69
  ideal, 36–63
  typical, 33–35
Grantspeople, Inc., 143
Grass Roots Fundraising Book, The (Flanagan), 214
Great Society, 9, 233
Green match, 253
Grievance procedures, 68, 254
Guidelines, 254
"Guide to Needs Assessment in Community Education, A" (HEW), 214

Hall, Mary, 214
Handicapped, 41–48, 163, 178–181, 224–226
Hard match, 254
Hard money, 21, 189, 254
Hart, Gary, 55, 56, 60
Harvard Medical Center, 228
Head Start, 112, 123, 230
Health, Education, and Welfare, Department of (HEW), 3, 107, 111, 141, 214, 222, 224–225, 230
  Office of Education, 2, 38–40, 44, 221, 230
  Public Health Service, 5, 224, 232

Health (*cont'd*)
  Rehabilitation Services Administration, 43, 45, 46
Health care, funding for, 231–232
Health Coordinating Councils, 231
Health Systems Agencies (HSAs), 231–232
Hessler, John, 42–47, 67
Homo bureaucraticus, 29, 254
Homo economicus, 28, 254
Homo grantus, 29, 63, 66, 68–69, 254
Horizontal contacts, 140
Housing and Urban Development, Department of (HUD), 34, 35, 47, 141, 230, 235, 237
Human services, 255
Humphrey, Hubert, 56, 59

Impact, 255
Independent living, concept of, 45–48
Indiana, University of, 156
Indirect costs, 154–156, 255, 258
Indo-Chinese Resettlement Program, 230–231
Information overload, 255
In-kind donations, 77–78, 82, 255
Internal Revenue Service (IRS), 23, 25, 75, 92, 101, 102, 149, 251, 262
International issues, funding for, 239–242
International Women's Year Conference (1977), 11
Intervention, 255
Invisible hand theory, 16–17

Jackson, Jesse, 230
Jobs for Older Women, 50
Joint funding, 140, 255
Joint Funding Simplification Act, 255–256
Justice, Department of, 81
  Law Enforcement Assistance Administration, 33, 90, 226, 256

Kennedy, Edward M., 56
Keynes, John Maynard, 15

Labor, Department of, 48, 52, 136
Laboratory for Superscience Studies (LSS), 175–178
Lamm, Richard, 54–55, 56
Laugh-In, 38
"Laundering federal money," 256
Law Enforcement Assistance Administration (LEAA), 33, 90, 226, 256
Letters of agreement, 159–160
Letters of intent/inquiry, 256
Letters of rejection, 191
Letters of support, 152, 153, 161, 256, 259
Leveraging, 256
Liberalism, 65
Living gifts, 108
Lobbying, 68
Local Education Agency (LEA), 222, 256
Local government funding, 10, 131–133

McAllister, Bard, 142
Mainstreaming, 256
Management Support Organization (MSO), 257
Market development, 192
Mass production, 66
Matching grants, 38, 91, 104, 219, 247, 256
May, John, 72–73, 74
Mead, Margaret, 37
Media, 36–41, 164, 190
Medical Data Systems, 3
Medical service delivery system, 88
Mellon Foundation, 221
Midwest Research Institute (MRI), 59, 60
Migrant farmworker issues, 88, 90, 94–95
Milestones, 182
Miller, Cheri, 193
Mills, Wilbur, 144
"Mission" agencies, 227
Mr. Rogers, 37
Misuse of funds, 27–28
Mobil Oil Corporation, 40, 220
Model Cities Program, 233
Model/demonstration project, 256–257
Monopolies, 17, 27, 66
Monsanto Corporation, 228
Morrisett, Lloyd, 36, 37
Muckraking, 68
Multiple proposal submissions, 94
Multipocketed budgeting, 257

Narrative section of proposals, 257
National Academy of Science, 241
National Aeronautics and Space Administration (NASA), 55, 156–157, 226
National Center for Atmospheric Research, 156–157
National Chamber Foundation, 84
National Council on Aging, 52
National Endowment for the Arts (NEA), 136, 218–219
National Institute of Allergies and Disease Control (NIADC), 175–177
National Institute of Education, 222
National Institute of Mental Health (NIMH), 141
National Institutes of Health (NIH), 226
National Public Radio, 220
National Science Foundation, 55, 226, 227, 240
National Technical Information Service, 131
Needs assessment, 173–178, 257
Neo-Marxism, 65
Networks of contacts, 68
New Federalism, 113
Nixon, Richard M., 34
Nonprofit corporation, 257, 262
Nuclear energy, 53, 61–62

Objectives section of proposals, 182, 257
Objectivity, myth of, 263
Office of Aging, 230
Office of Economic Opportunity, 233
Office of Education, 2, 38–40, 44, 221, 230
Office of Human Development, 123
Office of Human Development Services, 224
Office of Management and the Budget (OMB), 25, 125, 132, 257–258
Office of Minority Business Enterprise (OMBE), 235
Office of Technology Assessment, 56
Old-Boys' Network syndrome, 27, 139, 257, 260
Older Americans Act, 50
O'Neal, Tip, 59
Operation EXCEL, 230
Operation PUSH, 230
Otis, Web, 117, 120
Overhead, 154–156, 255, 258

Packaging. *See* Proposals
Palo Alto Adolescent Services Corporation, 193, 197–213
Pass-through agencies, 258, 261
Paternalism, 42
Patman, Wright, 144
Payout requirement, 258
Peace Corps, 241
Peachman, Joseph A., 145–146
Peer review, 227, 258
People's Development Corporation, 3–4
Philanthropoid, 258
Physically Disabled Students Program (PDSP), University of California, 44–47
Pitch, 173–178
Piton Foundation, 141
Plan section of proposal, 181–185
Planning grants, 192
Poetry Playhouse, 2–3
Preapplication, 258
Preliminary proposal, 258
Preproposal, 258
Prescreening, 94
Press, Frank, 240
Princeton University, 77
Private foundations, 8, 25, 26, 85–100, 251, 252
  compared to community foundations, 101–102
  compared to government funding, 85–86
  educational funding, 86
  family, 87
  general purpose, 87
  health care funding, 232
  profile of, 87–95
  range of giving, 8–9
  researching, 95–100
  special purpose, 87
Problem Statement, 173–178
Pro bono publico, 258–259
Procedural objectives, 259
Profile of funder, 259
Profit motive, 22
Project Description, 181–185, 186

Proposals, 2, 94, 105, 169–214, 258, 259
abstracts, 188, 196–197, 259
believability and, 148–153
cover letters, 188, 259
evaluation designs, 185, 187, 259
functions of, 170–172
future funding plans, 189–191, 259
goals, 178–181, 252, 257, 259
pitch, 173–178
plan, 181–185
sample formats, 191, 193–213
title page, 188
Provider, 259
Proxmire, William, 26
Public Broadcasting Service, 220
Public foundations. *See* Community foundations
Public Health Service, 5, 224, 232
Public information, 68
Public interest, 259
Public media, 220–221
Public sector, 259
Public television, 36–41, 164, 190
Pyramiding, 256, 259

Rappaport, Paul, 54, 61
Rasé, Hank, 54–63, 67, 164
Rationale of proposals, 173–178
Reagan, Ronald, 47
Redistribution to the Rich and the Poor; The Grants Economics of Income Redistribution (ed. Boulding and Pfaff), 9*n*
Reeves, Thomas C., 143–144
Reference works, 84
Regional foundation associations, 110, 274–277
Regional planning, 133
Registry of Charitable Trusts, 100
Regulatory agencies, 17, 18, 216
Rehabilitation funding, 41–48, 224–226
Rehabilitation Services Administration (RSA), 43, 45, 46
Religious groups, funding for, 229–231
Request for Proposal (RFP), 116, 140, 248, 260
Research and development, 18–19, 22, 226–229, 240–241
Research Papers (Filer Commission), 145
Response to rejections, 191, 194–195
Revenue sharing, 113–114, 252, 259
Review process, 138
Risk capital, 68, 260
Roberts, Edward, 42–44
Robert Wood Johnson Foundation, 87
Rochester University, 156
Rockefeller, John D., I, 20
Rockefeller, John D., II, 20
Rockefeller, John D., III, 19–20, 144
Rockefeller Foundation, 87, 242
Rosenberg Foundation, 87–95
Rudney, Gabriel, 76
Rules and regulations, 260
Rural Development Act, 237
Russell, John M., 258

Sacrifice Trap, 27, 260
Sample proposal formats, 191, 193–213
San Francisco Arts Commission, 219
San Francisco Foundation, 92
San Mateo Foundation, 103–109, 193
Schlaffly, Phyllis, 11
Schoen, Sterling, 156
Schumacher, E. F., 241
Schumpeter, Joseph, 64–66
Science funding, 226–229, 240–241
Screening, for San Mateo Foundation, 105
Seed grants, 192, 228, 260
Self-sufficiency, 217
Senior Corps of Retired Executives (SCORE), 128
Serendipity effect of grants, 89, 260
Service delivery systems (SDSs), 133, 162–168, 191, 247, 260
Sesame Street, 36–41
Sesame Street Magazine, 40
Set-aside, 261
Setting National Priorities: The 1978 Budget (ed. Peachman), 145–146
Sheltered workshops, 225
Shields, Laurie, 51–52
Shultz, George, 144
Sign-off, 261
Simon, William, 144
Site visit, 261
Sloan Foundation, 141, 156
Small Business Administration (SBA), 128–130, 141, 233, 235, 236
Smith, Adam, 16

Social entrepreneur, 261
Social investment, 68
Social rehabilitation, funding for, 41–48, 224–226
Social Security Administration, 111
Sociology, 13
Soft match, 261
Soft money, 21, 261
Solar energy, 53–63, 94–95, 164
Solar Energy Research Institute (SERI), 53–63
Somerville, Bill, 103–109
Sommers, Tish, 49–52, 67, 164
Spinoff disease, 261
Spin-off projects, 190, 192, 261
Sponsors, 151, 255, 261
  alternatives to finding, 156–157
  consumer protection and, 157–160
  finding, 153–156
Standard & Poor's Register of Corporations, Directors, and Executives, 84
Standard Oil of New Jersey, 77
State, Department of, 239
State and Local Fiscal Assistance Act of 1972, 113
State Educational Agency (SEA), 260
State government funding, 10, 131–133, 258
Stealing, 73, 246
Street-level bureaucrats, 262
Student loans, 86
Submission dates, 31
Sugarman, Norman, 101, 102
Sullivan, Leon, 230
Summative/product evaluation, 262
Support services, 262

Target population, 262
Tax-exempt status, 92, 101, 149, 153, 251, 257, 262
Tax Reform Act, 79, 248, 251
Technical assistance (TA), 137–143, 153, 262–263
Technical review, 263
Technology funding, 226–229
Thank-you letters, 191, 195
Third Sector Committee, 21*n*
"Three years and out," 263
Title page, 188
Track records, 150–151, 153
Trade magazines, 32
Tragedy of the commons, 263
Transcendental Meditation, 4
Treasury, Department of the, 23, 25, 113
Trusts, 102, 262
Tweaking, 17–18

Unexpended funds, 263
United Funds, 26
United Nations University, 241
United Way, 3, 89, 101, 102, 218, 247, 254, 263
Universities, 12–14, 151, 155–158, 226–228
University of California at Berkeley, 42–47
Unrestricted funds, 263
Unsolicited applications, 87, 263–264
Upward Bound, 44
Urban and rural development, funding for, 233–239

Vanity funding, 264
Veppel, Frederick P., 258
Vertical contacts, 139–140
Vesicle, Edward, 178
VISTA grants, 40
Vocational Rehabilitation system, 42

Washington University, 156
Wealth, reallocation of, 18, 19
Welfare, 18
White, Virginia P., 143
Wilson, Kirke, 89–95
Women's Bureau, 52
World Bank, 242
World Council of Churches, 241

Young, Andrew, 142

Zion Nonprofit Charitable Trust, 230
Zoom, 37